Art Treasures in the British Isles

0   50   100   150   200   M

0   100   200   300   K

D0470801

Maes Howe   ORKNEY ISLANDS

Pluscarden Abbey

ABERDEEN

Blair Castle

Dunkeld   Glamis

Fowlis Easter

Iona

NORTH SEA

ATLANTIC

Belfast

Monasterboice

New Grange

Galway   Clonmacnoise

IRISH SEA

Killaloe

DUBLIN

Holycross   Kilkenny

Cashel

Gallarus

Cork

Prehistoric Sites

Classical remains

Churches, Cathedrals and Monasteries

Castles, Houses, Palaces etc

Museums and Libraries

The museums and monuments
shown on this map are
listed on pages 164 – 172

ENGLISH CHANNEL

Art Treasures in the British Isles

Art Treasures in the British Isles

Monuments, Masterpieces, Commissions and Collections

Introduction by Sir Philip Hendy

Formerly Director of the National Gallery, London

McGraw-Hill Book Company

New York Toronto

General Editors
Bernard S. Myers
New York
Trewin Copplestone
London

half title illustration
Initial H from the Winchester Bible,
c. 1169–70; Cathedral Library,
Winchester
frontispiece
Equestrian portrait of King Charles I,
1636; Anthony van Dyck;
National Gallery, London
opposite
Bust of George III, 1767; John Nost;
Victoria and Albert Museum,
London

Library of Congress Catalog Card Number 76–76757
44227
Published jointly by
McGraw Hill Book Company, New York and Toronto
and The Hamlyn Publishing Group Limited, London and Sydney
Hamlyn House, The Centre, Feltham, Middlesex, England
Printed in Italy by Officine Grafiche Arnoldo Mondadori, Verona
Filmset by B.A.S. Printers Limited, Hampshire, England

Contents

EXHIBITION ROOM, SOMERSET HOUSE

1808–11
Thomas Rowlandson 1756–1827 and
Auguste-Charles Pugin 1762–1832
coloured lithograph
British Museum, London

In 1774 Somerset House was purchased by the crown, and part of the building was given to the Royal Academy, which had been founded in 1768. This view of the exhibition room is from *The Microcosm of London*, a work in three volumes showing scenes from London life published by Rudolf Ackermann in 1808–11. Ackermann, a fine-art publisher and bookseller, was largely responsible for establishing lithography as a fine art in England. In 1795 he set up a press, engaged some of the most eminent artists of the day to work for him, and made wide use of the process in many of his publications. His desire for perfection is well expressed in the introduction to *The Microcosm of London*: 'The great objection that men fond of the fine arts have hitherto made to engravings on architectural subjects, has been, that the buildings and figures have invariably been designed by the same artists. In consequence of this the figures have been generally neglected, or are of a very inferior cast, and totally unconnected with the other part of the print . . . The architectural part of the subjects that are contained in this work, will be delineated, with the utmost precision and care, by Mr Pugin, whose uncommon accuracy and elegant taste have been displayed in his former productions. With respect to the figures, they are from the pencil of Mr Rowlandson, with whose professional talents the public are already well acquainted. . . .'

Introduction

To these cool, remote islands culture came comparatively late, millennia after it had passed its zenith in the warm areas of the world, centuries after its climax round the Mediterranean Sea. In contrast with our great literary tradition, which began early and has been almost continuous, music and the visual arts in Britain have been by international standards outstanding only fitfully and at unevenly spaced intervals. It is tempting to explain the sporadic history of the visual arts in England simply by the nature of the people and the quality of the light: to say that the British do not use their eyes enough, and that what they see is not seen sharply and clearly. But then why J. M. W. Turner, why Henry Moore, why Christopher Wren – a painter, a sculptor and an architect – each great by the highest of international criteria? Plainly one must look also at social conditions. One form of society which was manifestly fertile soil for the arts was the city state. This gave to every articulate citizen a well rounded life, and this was plainly one of the reasons for the rich variety of Mediterranean culture. Its small scale was compensated, from the very dawn of modern art, by the Church, which provided both the *raison d'être* for the highest forms of art and a means by which culture became international.

The city state Britain never had. Art was either for the Church or for a more arbitrary patron, the Court, and just as the Italian Renaissance was gaining tardy recognition here, the nationalisation of the Church at the Reformation brought not only iconoclasm, which destroyed, mutilated, or at best covered over, much of the art of the past, but a puritanism which has worked against the very principle of art even into our own times.

So we may wonder not so much at the limitations of British art as at the constantly renewed will to have and to make it. I put the words in that order because there is no art without patronage. The oligarchs who ruled England from the beginning of the eighteenth century until past the middle of the nineteenth built palaces on their estates and imported collections of pictures and sculpture, and it was they who founded, out of their surplus energy, our national museums and galleries. They laid the foundations of a new tradition. British artists and craftsmen were quick to assimilate whatever was imported and to give it a British form and colour. English portraiture of the later eighteenth century was the best in Europe, and meanwhile a landscape tradition was developing which produced in Turner almost certainly the greatest painter of the first half of the nineteenth century.

Now, in the second half of the twentieth, the visual arts in England are once again riding high. A figure no less great than Turner and just as English, the sculptor Henry Moore, has established himself throughout the world. The younger generation of painters and sculptors it is early to judge, but one can state that in the great international exhibitions English artists have carried off more than their share of prizes. Recently, British government has lost a little of its traditional reluctance and has been patronising contemporary art through a characteristically British semi-official body, the Arts Council. It was fair enough perhaps that the collections of the great country houses should be largely dispersed to fill the new museums across the Atlantic; but recent governments have taken some steps towards the saving and display of what is left. Above all, they have given a new vigour to the national museums and galleries, which are now better supported than those of any other state. More art, more intelligently presented, is now accessible to the public in Great Britain than at any previous time.

Sir Philip Hendy

Representational art has a history of some thirty to forty thousand years, and all but the latest ten thousand years of it dates from the last ice age. In the middle and late parts of this age an ice sheet covered northern Britain, and man only lived in the country during relatively brief improvements in the climate. The two best examples of ice-age art, probably relics of such an occupation, both come from the Creswell Crags caves in Derbyshire. The first was discovered in the last century, in Robin Hood's cave, and is a fine engraving on a small piece of rib bone figuring a horse. The second is the human figure from Pin Hole cave, which is not far from the first site, and this is also on a piece of rib, possibly bison.

Sometime before 3000 B.C., when the climate had already become milder, the first peasant farmers began to settle in Britain. They must have come by boat or raft, and they brought with them domestic cows, sheep and pigs, and a knowledge of wheat cultivation. Locally they are called the Windmill Hill people, but their cultural affinities clearly lie with other western Neolithic (or farming) peoples. Their ceramics were simple, consisting of round-bottomed bowls with little decoration. This tradition was to continue for a long time, undergoing changes of fashion both in shape and decoration. The Windmill Hill stage gave way to the Peterborough series including flat-based pots, and then to a new ceramic series, the collared urn tradition, which survives until around 1000 B.C.

Some of the earliest Neolithic art seems to be linked with a fertility cult. In this respect Britain resembles western Asia and the eastern Mediterranean, where female idols abound amongst the early agricultural communities. The best-known English example is a crudely carved 2 chalk figurine left in the old flint mines of Grimes Graves in Norfolk.

During the third millennium B.C. the first traces of architecture appeared in Britain. There is one spectacularly well-preserved village of stone houses at Skara Brae in Orkney where benches, 'dressers' and tables of stone have been found intact after the covering of sand was removed.

The main tradition of building at this time was that of the Megalithic 11 tombs which are found widely in the British Isles. Some of the finest are at Carrowkeel in Ireland, Maes Howe in Orkney and in the Cotswolds. They usually have a stone-lined passage with chambers off it in which were buried several generations of adherents of the cult—sometimes many hundred. Some of the megaliths were carved with simple designs of concentric rings, inverted U forms and double spirals, which link up with those on continental megaliths. A kind of double-spiral motif is found on the Calderstones near Liverpool, together with footprints and other designs. The majority of megaliths and their art date from the late Neolithic period, but some were still in use when the Beaker people arrived around 1800 B.C.

A change in culture is noticeable at this time. The first metal objects—gold ornaments and copper daggers—seem to have arrived with the men who introduced the Beaker ceramics. The origins of these people are uncertain; they may have been a warrior aristocracy who imposed themselves on the existing peoples, and were subsequently absorbed into their society. With these Beaker people there are traces of the finery of a newly emerging wealthy class. Gold basket-shaped earrings are known from Radley in Oxfordshire and Orton in Scotland, and the Beaker ceramics are richly decorated, usually with lozenge and zigzag motifs. One must mention the 4 Rillaton Gold Cup in this connexion, since its shape is clearly derived from that of a beaker, even though its horizontal fluting is best paralleled on cups from the Mycenean world. The form of its handle closely resembles that on another art treasure of this period, the Hove Amber Cup.

Early Farmers, Celts and Romans

Prehistory to c. AD 400

I

RELIEF FROM A
TEMPLE PEDIMENT
possibly second or third century AD
Bath stone
diameter 78 in (198 cm)
Roman Baths Museum, Bath

The temple of the goddess Sulis-Minerva, who presided over the hot springs, stood next to the baths and formed part of the same complex of buildings. The pediment, together with a number of other sculptures which remain, testify to its onetime magnificence. The gorgon's head, which was believed to avert the power of evil and was closely connected with Minerva, occupies the centre of the pediment. It is a wild and compelling creation in which Roman art has been revitalised by the native traditions of Britain and Gaul. Instead of a conventional female face, the Celtic artist has depicted a water-god with almond-shaped eyes, a moustache, and hair in which the snakes are almost indistinguishable from the wavy locks.

2

STATUETTE OF A WOMAN

Neolithic c. 2000 BC
chalk
h. 4·75 in (12 cm)
British Museum, London

This crudely carved statuette was found in
the Grimes Graves caves in Norfolk, placed
on a shelf at the end of a short passage dug
to exploit the rich floorstone flint seam.
The digging had proved unexpectedly
sterile, and the placing of the statuette
suggests that the Neolithic miners believed
magic could control the fertility of even a
seam of flint.

3

CHALK DRUM FROM FOLKTON

Bronze Age c. 1600 BC
chalk
diameter 5·5 in (14 cm)
British Museum, London

This is one of three solid chalk cylinders
found in a child's grave near Folkton in
east Yorkshire. Their decorative motifs
include both Beaker and Megalithic
themes, notably the oculi designs. They
typify the fusion of British Bronze-Age
cultural influences.

A number of important objects are associated with the burials of the
Food Vessel people (probably local in origin) and contact with the
culture of the Beaker people is generally recognised. Perhaps the most
artistically important objects produced by these people are the carved
chalk drums from Folkton in Yorkshire, which combine typical Beaker
motifs with those of the Megalithic world. They are marvellous pieces,
skilfully carved in low relief in a hard but still friable chalk.

Jet was a favourite material of the Food Vessel people, and beads,
buttons and elaborate crescent-shaped necklaces are typical of this workmanship. The crescents or 'lunulae' were probably ceremonial wear, for
they were also made in gold. Several dozen such have been found in
Ireland, and others come from Cornwall, north Wales and Scotland.
Simple gold torques and armlets of twisted gold like that from Grunty
Fen in Cambridgeshire round off this list of astonishing treasures, whose
bullion value alone must be enormous.

These ornaments were made at a time when the Wessex culture was
emerging in the south of England, perhaps about 1600 B.C. The people
responsible for this culture have a unique importance in British prehistory,
for it was they who constructed Stonehenge in its latest and most impressive
phase. Such 'henge' monuments originate in an earlier period, and were
initially circular ditches with an outer bank. In Beaker times they were
elaborated with a ring of upright stones inside, as at Avebury, but only at
Stonehenge under the Wessex architects were lintels added to the outer
ring, while five gigantic 'trilithons' were set in a horseshoe shape.

The organisation necessary to build these monuments is impressive.
Hundreds of tribesmen must have been employed under the direction of
skilled architects to transport, shape and erect the great stones. Certainly
the chieftains of the Wessex culture were wealthy. In the barrows of
Manton and Bush many regal objects were found: a gold scabbard hook,
an ivory and shale sceptre, several axes and daggers, an amber pommel,
two gold-bound amber discs and collared urns.

The Wessex culture probably resulted from the arrival of a small
aristocracy who established themselves in some of the richer parts of
southern Britain. In spite of their wealth they do not seem to have had any
very permanent houses, let alone palaces. Judging by the 'Aldbourne'
cups they used, they stemmed from western France, where the ancestors
of such ceramics are known.

The kind of monumental works which we have been discussing became
rarer towards the end of the second millennium and then disappeared.
From the centuries immediately before and after 1000 B.C. some of the
commonest finds are weapons or bronzesmiths' hoards, and there are
numerous fine shields like that from Yetholm in Northumberland. We
should perhaps visualise more warfare and raiding, and social chaos may
have prohibited further feats like Stonehenge. The famous Heathery Burn
cave hoard included, beside fine cauldrons, some horse trappings, in-
dicating that horse riding and drawn vehicles were coming into fashion
at this time. Another piece of fine ornamentation, the gold 'peytrel' from
Mold in north Wales, may be put at about this time.

With the exception of some fine pieces of Celtic art scarcely earlier than
the time of Caesar's campaigns, the remainder of the prehistoric period in
England is largely devoid of art. In Ireland, however, fine objects continued to be made longer, and there is some spectacular goldwork such as the
gorget from Glenisheen. Gold pins and discs often have circular solar
motifs, reflecting the kind of sun cult known from Denmark at this time.

Desmond Collins

4 *right* THE RILLATON GOLD CUP

Bronze Age c. 1600 BC, h. 3·75 in (9 cm)
beaten from a single piece of gold with handle added
British Museum, London

This cup, named from the barrow in Cornwall in which it was
found, is a masterpiece of the art of the Bronze-Age goldsmiths.
The shape recalls the Bell Beaker ceramics, but both the ribbed
side and the technique by which the handle is attached (held by
gold rivets) are reminiscent of Mycenean gold cups.

5 *below* THE GRUNTY FEN TORQUE

middle or late second millennium BC, beaten gold
47·5 in (120 cm) overall length, University Museum of Archaeology
and Ethnology. Cambridge

Unlike most gold torques, the Grunty Fen find seems to have been
intended as an armlet. Together with three bronze axes, it was dug
out of the Fenland peat from near Wilburton in 1864.

6 *below* PREHISTORIC GOLD WORK FROM IRELAND

mainly middle Bronze Age c. 1400 BC
beaten gold
National Museum of Ireland, Dublin

Ireland's importance during the Bronze Age derived from the
discovery of gold and copper there and its large-scale exploitation.
The magnificent objects illustrated here testify to this wealth.
They are mostly adornments, such as collars and cloak fastenings.

7

THE GRAVE GOODS
FROM BUSH BARROW

Wessex Culture c. 1500–1400 BC
gold, copper and bronze
Devizes Museum, Wiltshire

These rich objects came from a bowl
barrow, the burial of a chieftain, near
Wilsford in Wiltshire. Besides the daggers,
one in copper and one in bronze, there is a
flanged axe, a polished stone macehead
with zigzag bone mounts for the same
mace, and three beaten gold objects, one of
which is probably a scabbard hook.

8 *top right*

GOLD ORNAMENT

late Bronze Age c. 1000 BC
width 22 in (55 cm)
British Museum, London

This curious object of beaten gold was
found in a tumulus near Mold in Flintshire
in 1833. Its purpose is rather uncertain; the
name 'peytrel', by which it is sometimes
known, indicates that it was part of a horse
trapping, but scholars have recently
interpreted it as a shoulder ornament,
possibly for a chieftain.

9 *centre right*

STONEHENGE

main phase middle Bronze Age c. 1500 BC
near Amesbury

From an initial phase when only a bank
and ditch and some pits existed, around
2000 BC, this monument has been elaborated in at least two stages by the
introduction of rings of sarsen stones
(sandstone boulders) and blue stones.
According to some scholars, it is a sky
temple so arranged that it can be used to
make a variety of astronomical predictions.

10

THE CAERGWRLE BOWL

late Bronze Age, c. 1200–800 BC
wood with gold leaf overlay
National Museum of Wales, Cardiff

This bowl is oval in shape and is believed to
represent a large prehistoric boat. If each of
the gold leaf pennants represents an oars-
man and his shield, there must have been
at least twenty-two men to each side.

11 *bottom right*

CARVED SLAB WITH
SPIRAL DECORATION

late Neolithic c. 2000–1800 BC
County Meath, Ireland

This slab is at the entrance to one of the
most famous chambered Megalithic tombs
in Ireland, New Grange. The dominant
designs are spirals in twos and threes, but
on this and other stones lozenges, zigzags
and multiple arcs appear. Many of these
motifs can be found on the Megalithic
monuments of Brittany.

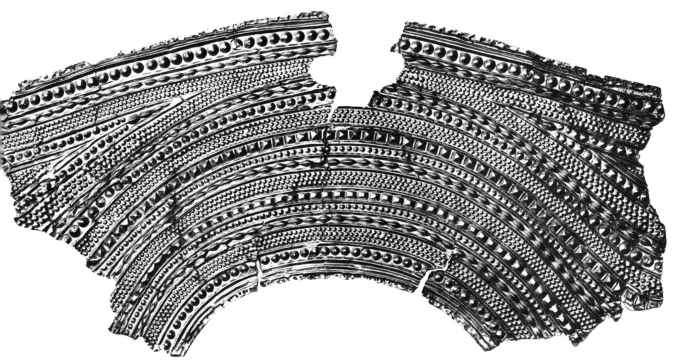

A first wave of Celtic invaders entered Britain from eastern Europe in about 600 B.C., bringing with them a sensitive appreciation of fine metalwork and a volatile temperament. Others followed in the fourth and second centuries, and here they created a settled society based on agriculture and developed their art to its finest pitch of attainment. In the course of time, through the agency of the Romans and of the Christian Church, they were to create a true civilisation of their own. Remarkable shields from the River Witham in Lincolnshire and from the Thames at Wandsworth are among the first manifestations of Celtic genius in the British Isles. They date from the third century B.C. and combine the techniques of continental smiths with the local metalworking traditions of Britain. The insular style rapidly developed its own characteristics, as the tribal rulers competed with one another in lavish display.

Masterpieces of Iron-Age art can be seen in jewellery, bronze mirrors, drinking tankards and cauldrons as well as in the decoration of spears, **24** shields and helmets. Although the British Isles were relatively isolated from the continent, they were far from being backward, and gradually assumed a position of paramount importance in the Celtic world. Here lay the centres of Druidic religion and, after Caesar's conquest of Gaul, of political influence. The great kings and aristocratic courtiers of such tribes as the Catuvellauni and the Atrebates were able to commission more expensive works than ever before. Sometimes their value lies in the extremely complex forms whereby the back of a mirror or a sword **25** scabbard is engraved with a balanced, abstract, symmetrical design, although many objects, for example the great golden neck-torques from Snettisham, Norfolk (British Museum and Castle Museum, Norwich) and Broughter (National Museum, Dublin), also have a high intrinsic worth.

Roman influence

Naturally, after Caesar's expeditions to Britain in 55 B.C. and again in 54 B.C., the British Isles were open to Roman traders whose wares circulated alongside the native products. The Marlborough Bucket in Devizes Museum and the Aylesford Bucket are decorated with animal and **12** human figures in a lively style partly derived from Roman art. Actual Roman silver cups and bronze vessels have been found in the tombs of warriors near Welwyn in Hertfordshire, and at a large number of sites pottery flagons and wine jars have been found alongside the elegant pedestal-based native wares.

The economy was transformed by the introduction of coinage – at first of gold, and in the first century A.D., of silver and bronze as well. Under Roman influence coinage came to replace barter as a means of trading. The types are as varied as Roman coins and, like them, reflect the propaganda and policies of the issuing authority. Where the Catuvellauni show an ear of corn, the Atrebates represent a vine leaf: native beer is contrasted with wine from the Roman empire. Similarly the Atrebates use a very Roman horseman on some of their coins, while the Catuvellauni counter with a fierce Celtic warrior waving a carnyx (or war trumpet).

Even before A.D. 43, the British Isles were within the Roman sphere of influence, and when the Catuvellauni drove Verica, King of the Atrebates, out of Britain he already had an ally in the emperor, Claudius. Almost a hundred years after Caesar had come to Britain, a Roman expeditionary force set out from Boulogne with the intention of subjugating the island. Fierce fighting took place at such great fortresses as Maiden Castle in Dorset and at Bredon Hill in Gloucestershire, but the cultural victory of Rome was already ensured. Rather than dwelling on the carnage that was

12
THE AYLESFORD BUCKET
before AD 43
wooden staves bound by three bands of
sheet bronze
h. 10 in (25 cm)
British Museum, London

Despite marked development of trade with the continent following Caesar's campaigns in Gaul, the British aristocracy continued to be as proud of their handsome pottery and metalwork as of the mass-produced articles from Gaul and Italy. This bucket, which contained a cremation, was found in a grave at Aylesford, Kent, together with imported bronze vessels and native pottery. The embossed bronze strip has a balanced composition of confronted animals and abstract devices. The two mask-like heads in cast bronze on the handles are clearly derived from Roman art, although in spirit they are far removed from classical naturalism.

the inevitable result of the invasion, we should marvel at the rapid growth of Verulamium (near St Albans), London and Chichester. In Colchester, which became the site of a colony or settlement of veteran soldiers, a great temple was erected in honour of the Emperor Claudius and as a focal point for provincial loyalties.

The Roman conquest intensified the contact between the two cultures, and the art of the Roman army replaced that of the Celtic aristocracy. Tombstones at Colchester, Wroxeter and Gloucester attempted to portray the deceased with lifelike honesty and even to summarise his philosophy of life. 'The gods will not allow you wine and water in the Underworld. Live honourably while your star gives you time for life.' This was the epitaph of Titus Flaminius, an Italian serving in the fourteenth legion.

The Roman army was much more than a mere fighting force designed to hold down subject peoples. It gave the natives peace and security in which to develop their own culture, and instructed the Britons in the new mysteries of building, administration and the customs of civilised life. The pace of Romanisation was, however, too rapid, as tribal customs could not be abolished overnight, especially amongst a people who, after their defeat, were only too willing to see the Romans as oppressors. In the minds of those opposed to Rome, misunderstandings and random acts of injustice coalesced into a sinister policy of oppression: some of the Roman colonists at Colchester seized land belonging to the tribe of the Trinovantes without offering compensation; the groves of the terrible Druidic religion were hacked down on Anglesey and elsewhere and the priesthood was suppressed. Finally when a native ruler of the Iceni tribe in East Anglia died, the Romans refused to confirm his wife Boudicca ('Boadicea') in the chieftainship. She retaliated with ferocity and speed, building on any accusation she could level against the Romans and on those who collaborated with them. The Romans opposed this dedicated nationalist and defeated her, and the whole Celtic system of patronage was thus destroyed.

Roman civilisation

Considering that the cities of Colchester, Verulamium and London had been sacked and 70,000 people killed, it was remarkable how quickly the province recovered. Theatres in Canterbury, Cirencester and Verulamium, bath buildings in Wroxeter, Leicester and Silchester and town squares in Verulamium and Wroxeter, together with the mosaics and wallpaintings in many private houses, illustrate Tacitus's description of the Romanisation of Britain. Writing about his father-in-law Agricola, the great governor of Britain, he mentions the private encouragement the latter gave to the construction of temples, town squares and private houses. Agricola also encouraged the spread of the Latin language, Roman dress and 'the amenities that make dissipation agreeable – arcaded streets, baths and sumptuous banquets'. This sense of security was not confined to the towns. The great palace of Fishbourne in Sussex is evidence of a prosperous countryside where the tribal aristocrat or Roman administrator who owned it could feel safe, and by the end of the first century little farms constructed in Roman style were being built throughout lowland Britain.

Civilisation was maintained in the north and west by a strong frontier garrison which could hold down the highland tribes. In the early second century the Emperor Hadrian built the great wall from the Tyne to the Solway which greatly facilitated the policing of northern Britain. This is still the most impressive relic of Roman rule in Britain. Sculpture from the wall area was sometimes the work of the Roman army, sometimes of Celtic craftsmen who blended representation with stylisation; only rarely is a completely foreign hand revealed, as in the tombstone of a

13
TOMBSTONE OF
MARCUS FAVONIUS FACILIS
AD 43–49
h. 72 in (183 cm)
Colchester and Essex Museum, Colchester

Marcus Favonius Facilis was an Italian serving as a centurion in the twentieth legion, which took part in the invasion of Britain. He died in Colchester during the short time that it remained a legionary fortress, and a tombstone was commissioned from a good sculptor (probably also an Italian) by his freed slaves Verecundius and Novicius. Although it employs local material there is nothing un-Roman about the tombstone; Facilis holds in his right hand his vine staff of office and in his left grasps his sword.

14 British lady married to a Syrian trader from Palmyra, which has been found at South Shields. The couple presumably lived in one of those little villages of traders and camp followers which clustered around Roman forts. As in southern Britain, archaeology has brought these people to life with their jewellery, tableware, figurines, clothing and tools. Although these possessions rarely achieve the status of art, they show how imported pottery and metal vessels, which in the Iron Age were owned only by rich chieftains, were now disseminated though all classes.

23 The religion of Roman Britain, like that of France, combined elements drawn from native and Roman traditions in which a deity frequently had two names. The great baths at Bath, fed by hot springs and attached to a magnificent temple, were dedicated to a local goddess, Sul (disguised as the 1 Roman Minerva), and the sculpture from the temple and the sacred precinct around it has a linear, Celtic quality. The native gods still ruled; indeed much of the artistic patronage of this time was directed to religious ends – a bronze statuette of the local equivalent of Mars from Lincolnshire was dedicated by two Britons at the cost of a hundred sesterces, and the statues which graced rich temples must have cost a great deal more.

The Golden Age

The long period of peace created great prosperity. Early in the third century, a Roman governor was able to send a gold brooch set with gems to a friend in Gaul – Britain was still a land where fine jewellery was made and appreciated. The third century also saw the beginning of those political upheavals which were to be a feature of life in the province for the following century and a half. Carausius, the commander of the channel fleet, set up his own 'empire' in Britain, which he ruled from A.D. 287 until 293. A beautiful and sophisticated coinage was struck by him and by his successor Allectus (293–96) with legends that included a catch-phrase from Virgil and references to a rebirth of the true Roman spirit. Naturally the government of the central empire did not look kindly at a breakaway movement in a wealthy province; indeed when it was recovered in 296, the Emperor Constantius Chlorus was hailed on a medallion struck at Trier in Germany as 'the Restorer of the Eternal Light'.

The 'reconquest' did not cause a ripple in the sea of rising wealth and self-confidence. Rich citizens of British towns and wealthy landowners were able to benefit from the urgent needs of the continent, and from the profits of the wool trade and trafficking in grain, metals and skins. They created great estates centering around villas like Chedworth and Wood-chester in Gloucestershire, Hinton St Mary in Dorset and Bignor in Sussex. These have floors paved in richly coloured mosaic which portray scenes taken from classical mythology. Sometimes the subjects are clearly allegorical: Orpheus taming the beasts at Woodchester represents the victory of good over evil forces. The mosaics at Lullingstone in Kent and at Hinton St Mary depict the hero Bellerophon slaying the mythical 15 Chimaera. At Hinton St Mary the head of Christ himself appears in the same scene, making the religious interpretation certain. All these mosaics were executed by guilds of travelling craftsmen based on neighbouring towns. An artist from the Cirencester firm responsible for the mosaic work at Woodchester and Chedworth later emigrated to Trier in Germany, which as an imperial capital offered better prospects for commissions.

The same bewildering variety of subject matter is found on silver vessels, of which many of the most important pieces from late antiquity 16 have been found in Britain. A silver flagon found at Traprain Law in Scotland is decorated with biblical scenes, while a magnificent silver dish

14

TOMBSTONE OF REGINA, WIFE TO BARATES

third century AD
h. 4 ft 1·5 in (1·25 m)
South Shields Museum

This tombstone is the work of a sculptor from the great desert city of Palmyra in Syria, who had settled in the north of Britain at the Roman fort of Arbeia (South Shields). It shows a woman seated in a basket chair wearing the long-sleeved tunic and heavy jewellery of a Palmyrene. According to the Latin inscription she was in fact a Briton of the Catuvellaunian tribe but she had married Barates, a maker of standards for the Roman army. When she died at the early age of thirty, Barates found one of his own countrymen to carve her tombstone, which has a short epitaph in Palmyrene below the main one.

15

HEAD OF CHRIST

fourth century AD
mosaic
diameter of roundel c. 3·3 in (84 cm)
British Museum, London

This mosaic was found in 1963 on the site of a Roman villa at Hinton St Mary, Dorset. It is divided into two sections. One of them, which shows Bellerophon slaying the Chimaera, represents the victory of good over evil, while the centrepiece of the other depicts the head of Christ with the sacred emblem, the Chi-Rho (the first two letters of his name in Greek). Side panels portray the Tree of Life, animals chasing each other in paradise and personifications of the four winds. No other floor mosaic in the entire Roman empire shows a Christian subject of this importance, indeed, even the placing of holy symbols upon a floor was strictly forbidden early in the fifth century. The owner of the mosaic was, however, a devout Christian and the room in which it was laid may have served as a chapel. The workshop responsible for laying the mosaic was probably based on nearby Dorchester.

16

FLASK WITH BIBLICAL SCENES

late fourth century AD
silver with gilded details
h. 8·5 in (21·5 cm)
National Museum of Antiquities of
Scotland, Edinburgh

The Traprain Law treasure was hidden in an abandoned hill-fort, almost certainly by pirates after they had conducted a successful raid on the coasts of Gaul or southern Britain. Many of the vessels it contained are fragmentary as they had been cut up for bullion, but fortunately it was possible to restore this fine example of church plate. The lower frieze depicts the Adoration of the Magi, the Betrayal of Christ, Adam and Eve tempted by the Serpent and Moses striking the Rock. Moses, as the most important figure in this scene, is shown on a larger scale than the Israelites, who hold out vessels to catch the running water.

from Corbridge celebrates the birth of the pagan god Apollo on the Greek island of Delos, and was probably made to celebrate the Emperor Julian's visit to his shrine in 363. The finest silver treasure was found in 1942 in a field near Mildenhall in Suffolk. It consists of dishes, plates, drinking goblets, bowls, ladles, and spoons all dating from the fourth century. It was presumably buried for reasons of safety; perhaps the owner was implicated in some political plot, or more likely there were barbarian raiders in the vicinity.

The great Oceanus dish shows the triumph of the wine-god Bacchus **28** over Hercules. The central roundel is enigmatic, with a mask of the sea-god Oceanus strangely reminiscent of the gorgon head on the Bath temple **1** pediment, although like the rest of the treasure, this dish was imported from Italy or even the eastern Mediterranean. There are also two fine flanged bowls decorated in repoussé with a frieze of animals and portrait roundels in their respective centres of Alexander the Great and his mother Olympias. Despite the pagan character of the larger pieces of plate three of the spoons have the Chi-Rho, the monogram of Christ, and the Greek letters alpha and omega, while the others have the kind of inscriptions often found on Christian objects: 'long life to Papittede' and 'long life to Pascentia'. In the end the family who owned the treasure became Christian, though it made no attempt to hide the traces of its pagan past.

Two features of fourth-century existence were felt by all classes: barbarian raids and the tension of religious and political conflict. Of these, the former is better known but less important. Most pirate raids were purely local in character, except the barbarian conspiracy of 367 when the Irish, Picts and Saxons combined to break through the frontier defences of the province. However, the strength of pagan religious feeling can be gauged by the building of a little native temple within the abandoned Iron Age hillfort at Maiden Castle and even more in the erection of a great sanctuary dedicated to a healing god, Nodens, at Lydney Park in Gloucestershire. At the same time Christian themes can be seen in crudely scratched graffiti at Chedworth Villa and on pewter vessels from East Anglia and Hampshire as well as on the silverware and mosaics of the aristocracy.

The decline of Roman Britain

Political discontent is a key factor in the history of the fourth century. The unsuccessful revolt of Magnentius in A.D. 350 was supported by Martinus, a governor of Britain. It was followed ten years afterwards by the successful bid for power by the pagan Emperor Julian backed by a new governor, Alypius. Julian's successors were not popular and in 367 there was a renewal of trouble – the Emperor Valentinian sent a special envoy, Count Theodosius, to Britain both to subdue incursions of the Irish, Picts and Saxons and to investigate the internal ills of the province. Finally the opposition found expression in the Pelagian heresy which emphasised man's free will both in personal life and in society, and encouraged the Britons to seize their independence and 'live under their own laws'.

A question mark hangs over the end of Roman Britain: it is hard to date much of the latest art and impossible to believe that the 'golden age' came to an end very quickly. The free Saxons in the east and the Irish in the west managed to secure a foothold, yet the Romanised Britons were able to maintain their independence under leaders like Arthur, and an imperial banner (the purple dragon of Wales) still protected the province. However, the army which now defended Britain against barbarians from outside the frontiers consisted of Saxon soldiers and wild hillmen from Wales and southern Scotland. Gradually the economic and cultural life

17

MALE HEAD

first century AD
British limestone with traces of red paint
h. 8 in (20 cm)
Gloucester City Museum

This may have been intended as an honor-
ific or funerary portrait of a provincial
aristocrat. A Celtic sculptor simplified the
plastic features of classical art and created
a mask with the same large eyes, long
sharp nose and thin mouth as the two
bronze heads on the Aylesford Bucket (**12**).
Here even the hair becomes a pattern of
overlapping locks, and the ears have the
curvilinear precision of metalwork.

18 *right*

HEAD OF THE GOD SERAPIS

late second century AD
possibly after the work of Bryaxis the Younger,
mid-fourth century BC
Italian marble
h. 17 in (43 cm)
Guildhall Museum, London

The Mithraic temple on the banks of the
Walbrook was one of the largest in western
Europe, and had a congregation wealthy
enough to own marble sculpture imported
from Italy. This fine head has a highly
polished face, and the hair and beard are
deeply cut in the manner of the late
Antonine period when sculptors were
becoming bolder in the use of the drill. In
the fourth century it was deliberately
concealed beneath the temple floor,
perhaps to protect it from destruction by a
Christian mob. Egypt was the granary of
the ancient world and it is not surprising
that this Egyptian deity wears a corn
measure (modius) on his head to distinguish him as a god of fertility. Serapis was
also Lord of the Underworld and thus
attracted veneration from religions such as
Mithraism which laid special emphasis on
the after-life.

of the towns and villas disappeared and the land reverted to its tribal state.

Although the Romans never subdued northern Scotland or Ireland,
Roman artistic motifs were taken to Scotland and inspired the Pictish
gravestones, while in Ireland the savage forms of native gods gave way
to the softer lines of Mediterranean art and the message of Christianity,
brought in part by a Roman-Briton, St Patrick. An Anglo-Saxon poem,
The Ruin, describes Bath as a ghost town from which 'the men have
departed', in which 'the work of the giants is crumbling'. Although the
British Isles have conserved neither Roman law nor a rich heritage of
Roman buildings, without Rome no early medieval Irish civilisation
would have been possible.

Martin Henig

CAPITAL FROM CIRENCESTER

third century AD
oolite from the Cotswolds, h. 41 in (104 cm)
Corinium Museum, Cirencester

The wild features of a Celtic god blowing
a horn and holding a stick emerge from
the acanthus foliage of this composite
capital. He is probably a fertility deity,
ancestor to the strange non–Christian
spirits found in the decoration of medieval
churches. It is likely that the capital is of
British workmanship and it may have
formed part of a column carrying a statue
of Jupiter, as it is too large and ornate to
have been incorporated into any known
building in Roman Cirencester erected at
this date.

20

THE COLCHESTER SPHINX

late first century AD, h. 33 in (84 cm)
Colchester and Essex Museum, Colchester

This tomb-sculpture was found in a cemetery outside the limits of the Roman Colonia, at Colchester. In ancient mythology the sphinx – a monster part woman and part lion with eagle's wings – was conceived as a fearful power of destruction, but classical tomb-sculpture frequently shows her in a less ferocious guise as the awesome guardian of the grave and a symbol of death. Here she is holding a portrait head of the deceased (probably a retired soldier settled in Roman Colchester) between her paws. The stone used is local, but the sculptor was certainly an immigrant from the continent.

21

A CHARIOTEER

second or third century AD, h. 7·5 in (19 cm)
private collection, Lincoln

Sensitive treatment of hair and drapery distinguish this fine study of a young charioteer urging his team on to win a race. It is almost certainly the work of a Celtic artist (perhaps a Gaul) who had fully mastered the technique of relief sculpture. The youth wears an ample cloak fastened by a brooch at his right shoulder, and a diadem around his head, suggesting that he came from a leading family in the town. Then, as now, racing was a favourite pursuit of British aristocracy. The purpose of the relief is unknown; it is likely that it formed part of a tombstone.

22

CASTOR WARE BEAKER

late second or early third century AD
decoration trailed en barbotine, h. 9 in (23 cm)
Verulamium Museum, St Albans

The potters of the Nene Valley in Northamptonshire produced one of the finest of all Roman wares. The manufacture of these attractive vessels began in response to a decline in the quality of Gaulish samian pottery and the subsequent closure of the factories where it was made. A market for the finer British substitute was at hand in both the forts of the north and, as here, in the towns to the south of the province. The form and the decoration of these vessels evolved in the north-western provinces of the empire and they reveal the linear precision of the best Celtic art.

23 *left*

THE GREAT BATH

first to second century AD
Bath

In Roman times, as in the eighteenth century, Bath was one of the most notable spas in western Europe. Here the sick could both seek help from the goddess Sulis-Minerva and take the life-giving hot waters which gush from the spring. The Great Bath stood in the centre of an open courtyard. Later it was roofed – the piers that supported the barrel vault can be seen on this photograph. Despite a misleading nineteenth-century colonnade the fine proportions of the bath are still apparent.

24

THE BATTERSEA SHIELD

late first century BC
gilt-bronze with red enamel insets
length 32 in (81 cm)
British Museum, London

By the first century BC Celtic ornament had become increasingly disciplined and symmetrical. British artists concentrated on line rather than on relief so that it is easy to distinguish their work from that produced in earlier times. The rich decoration of this shield and its fine state of preservation suggest that it was intended for display rather than for use in battle. It was almost certainly thrown into the Thames by its aristocratic owner as an offering to the river god. This custom was universal amongst the Celts, who had few formal temples.

25

THE DESBOROUGH MIRROR

early first century AD
bronze, length 13.75 in (35 cm)
British Museum, London

Ancient mirrors were usually made of highly polished plates of silver, bronze or white metal. The kidney-shaped back of this mirror (probably from a woman's grave at Desborough in Northamptonshire) is engraved with a delicate linear pattern that fills the entire field. The design has been arranged symmetrically around a central axis, and given greater emphasis by means of cross-hatching. Bronze mirrors of this type, which were made only in Britain, mark the apogee of pre-Christian Celtic artistic achievement.

26

THE DOLPHIN MOSAIC *detail*

mid-second century AD
17ft 2in × 17ft 5in (5·23 × 5·30m)
Roman palace at Fishbourne, Sussex

The north wing of the palace, constructed as the residence of an official in the first century AD, was converted into a luxurious private dwelling house at the beginning of the second century. This mosaic was laid by the new owners and is comparable with others of the same date from Romano-British towns, although it is much earlier than most mosaics from country villas. It is the work of at least two hands: the sea-horses and sea-panthers appear to have been executed by a master-craftsman, while an apprentice was clearly responsible for the central roundel. Although the mosaic itself gives no indication of the nationality of the artists they almost certainly came from Gaul.

27 *far right*
HEAD OF
THE EMPEROR HADRIAN

second century AD
hollow-cast bronze
h. 17in (43cm)
British Museum, London

This head originally formed part of a statue which may have been set up in a public building to commemorate the emperor's visit to Britain in AD 122. Hadrian took the duties of provincial administration very seriously, and the head reflects the genuine regard in which he was held throughout the empire, although it is almost certainly the work of a Gaulish craftsman. At some time, for reasons unknown – but perhaps connected with a Saxon raid – the head was hacked from the body, and thrown from London Bridge into the Thames.

28 *bottom*
THE OCEANUS DISH

fourth century AD
silver
diameter 24in (60·5cm)
British Museum, London

The decoration of the dish is arranged in three registers. The sea-god Oceanus presides at the centre, and around him swim nereids, sea-centaurs and various fanciful marine animals. The outmost frieze shows the triumph of the wine-god Bacchus. Here the artist has produced a brilliant rendering of the wild dance in which maenads and satyrs whirl in mystic ecstasy. The Oceanus Dish may have been made in Alexandria as a piece of temple plate, but ultimately it passed into the possession of a rich British landowner who added it to his private collection.

hGeneratio

The Roman legions left Britain during the first half of the fifth century. 'They gave energetic counsel to the timorous natives', wrote Gildas, the sixth-century historian of Dark-Age Britain, 'and left them patterns by which to manufacture arms . . . and then left the island never to return. No sooner were they gone than the Picts and the Scots, like serpents which in the heat of midday come forth from their holes, hastily landed again from their boats, . . . inspired with hunger for blood, and all of them more eager to shroud their villainous faces in bushy hair than to cover with decent clothing those parts of their bodies which required it.'

The end of Roman rule was, in fact, probably neither sudden nor unexpected nor particularly catastrophic, but it serves to mark formally the moment when Britain ceased to be part of the old civilisation of Europe. That civilisation itself, of course, was in process of breaking up under the repeated attacks of invaders from the east. Each generation was less literate than the one before it, more accustomed to violence, more limited in outlook and attitude.

In Gaul and Spain, as in Britain, classical art, absolutely dependent as it was on stability and a leisured, cultured class, ceased to exist. The material signs of Rome remained – the roads, aqueducts, temples and villas – but the expertise that produced them had gone. The population lived like squatters in the ruins of a world they could hardly remember, and when new people fought their way into the country from Denmark and northern Germany – the Angles, another wave of Saxons, and Jutes – Roman remains seemed to belong to an almost mythological age.

The revival, when it came, took its impetus from a part of the British Isles which had escaped both the benefits of Roman rule and the sense of desolation that followed its collapse – Ireland. Christianity, which had been established in Roman Britain but had completely disappeared after the fifth century (not to be restored until the arrival of St Augustine at the end of the sixth), took root sooner in Ireland. St Patrick landed there about 432, bringing with him a type of energetic monasticism which spread quickly to Scotland and then to England (as well as to many other parts of Europe, as far as Switzerland and north Italy). The monks submitted to discipline, but their community was less tightly knit than the Benedictine. In these Irish monasteries an art of manuscript illumination was born, and several of their names have become synonymous with the books that were made or preserved in them. The Book of Durrow 52 represents a style that stands at the opposite extreme from that of classical Rome, an art of flat, abstract pattern-making, fascinating in its intricate convolutions and resulting in a stylisation of animal and human shapes transformed into a strange, poetic geometry. Irish craftsmen continued to produce work of a high order into the next century and beyond. In 30 metalwork the most splendid example is the Ardagh Chalice, of gold and gilt-bronze with inlaid coloured enamel and glass. It seems to have been buried for safety soon after it was made, hence its perfect preservation.

St Augustine arrived at Canterbury in 597, and with him the classical tradition, represented in its Italian (or specifically Benedictine) form, re-entered the story of art in Britain. Pagan art, of course, had treasures of its own, the best collection being that found in 1939 at Sutton Hoo in Suffolk. This is a royal ship-burial dating from about 650 but containing 50 objects much older. The buckles, clasps and decorated weapons show no lack of sophistication, though alongside them were items of Byzantine origin, proving that even at this time there was traffic between England and the east. One large silver dish has a stamp showing that it dates from the reign of the Emperor Anastasius (491 – 518).

29
BOOK OF KELLS
760 – 820
13 × 9·5 in (33 × 24 cm)
Trinity College Library, Dublin
The Book of Kells (so called because it was once kept at the monastery of Kells in Ireland, though it was probably written at Iona) consists of the Four Gospels, with summaries, tables and a glossary. The illuminations range from portraits of the Evangelists and the Virgin and Child to decorative initials such as this, the opening of St Matthew's Gospel. The words *Christi autem generatio*, with the letters XPI, the Greek abbreviation for Christ, are woven into a fantastic pattern of abstract, vegetable, animal and human forms. It is full of intriguing details, for instance the cats at the bottom watching two mice eating a holy wafer.

Roman Christianity travelled north, through the kingdoms of Kent, Mercia and Northumbria, until inevitably came the clash with the Irish movement. The question of which monastic rule was to be followed was resolved at the Synod of Whitby (663) at which the Roman party was victorious, and henceforth, culturally as well as ecclesiastically, England was in communion with the Roman world. One of the late seventh-century archbishops of Canterbury came from Tarsus in Palestine. There was nothing unlikely in finding a Byzantine manuscript in a Kentish library.

29   The circles of classical inspiration spread outwards from this point of contact. They emerged weakly in the Book of Kells, produced in Ireland or Scotland between 760 and 820, which is still basically in the earlier Irish style. They washed with greater strength around the shores of the Northumbrian kingdom, which for about a century (670–770) assumed the cultural leadership of Britain. Two of its leading churchmen, Benedict Biscop, founder of the monastery of Monkwearmouth in 674, and Wilfrid, founder of Hexham and Ripon, visited Italy many times, bringing back with them, we are told: 'furniture, vestments, relics, pictures and a library of valuable books'. The most striking relic of this marriage of cultures is the Lindisfarne Gospels, made between 698 and 721, where pages in the tradition of Durrow lie next to others which owe everything to Italy.

A more unexpected result was the birth of the art of sculpture in Britain. It seems to have appeared *ex nihilo* in Northumbria in the last quarter of the seventh century, and took a form unknown anywhere else in Europe – tall, free-standing crosses covered in reliefs, which sometimes took the place of churches. Two crosses survive complete from this

38   period, those of Ruthwell and Bewcastle. Both continued the heroic tradition of Irish Christianity by portraying Christ and the saints as the champions of light against darkness. Both drew inspiration from Roman and Near-Eastern art in the simple dignity of their lines and the amazing confidence of their craftsmanship. On an entirely different scale and in a

31   different medium, the small ivory box known as the 'Franks Casket' displays the mixture of traditions yet more blatantly, showing scenes from Norse mythology, from the Gospels and from classical legend.

All over Europe there was a feeling that a dark age was lifting. Ancient manuscripts were recopied, classical buildings studied, imperial customs imitated. This movement – the Carolingian Renaissance – was common to all northern Europe, but its centre was Charlemagne's capital at Aachen, which, like a magnet, drew the best talents of other countries. Among these was the famous British scholar Alcuin of York.

Traces of an English Carolingian age are disappointingly small because of the new wave of Norse invaders that broke upon the country almost immediately after it. But the links were there. King Aethelwulf of Wessex (who reigned from 839 to 858), besides making two journeys to Rome, married one of Charlemagne's great-grand-daughters. Alfred, his successor, was himself an island Charlemagne. Having defeated the Danes and arranged for their settlement in the north (the Danelaw), he rejuvenated the literary life of the country, caused books that he particularly admired to be translated and distributed, strengthened the monasteries, opened schools, encouraged learning and made his court one of the most cultivated in Europe. He died in 899 but his achievement substantially endured, under members of his own dynasty, down to the beginning of the eleventh century.

The story of continental imports and influences during this period was still very much a matter of personalities. Grimbald, a monk from Rheims,

30

THE ARDAGH CHALICE
early eighth century
silver, with decoration in gold and enamel
National Museum of Ireland, Dublin

This is one of the finest pieces of Irish metalwork of the Early Christian period. It was made for giving the communion wine to the laity. Around the rim runs a belt of interlace pattern in gold thread, punctuated by circular studs of cloisonné enamel. Below the handles are similar studs, on the sides petal-shaped patterns of gold thread and enamel, and around the stem and base further zones of ornament, placed with exquisite precision on the chalice's curving surfaces.

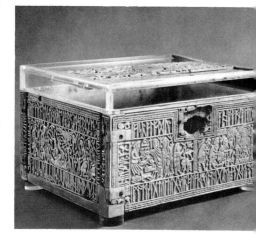

31

THE FRANKS CASKET
c. 700
whalebone
length 9 in (23 cm)
British Museum, London

This casket was carved, as the runic inscription tells us, from the bones of a whale washed up on the shores of Northumbria. The scenes on it are drawn from various sources and seem to have no particular meaning: on the left are Romulus and Remus being suckled by the wolf, who is lying upside down, while the front shows Weyland the Smith at his forge and the Adoration of the Magi. The casket was given to the museum by Sir A. W. Franks in 1867, hence its name.

had an important place at King Alfred's court. Dunstan, Abbot of Glastonbury, spent two years at Ghent, and his colleague Aethelwold had close connections with Fleury in Burgundy, where Oswald, Bishop of Winchester, also studied. The Emperor Otto, who married a sister of Aethelstan, presented him with a Carolingian gospel book. Soon there was a flood of manuscripts, reliquaries and jewellery from the continent to be eagerly examined and imitated by English artists.

Two of these native works are unique: the Alfred Jewel and the vestments of St Cuthbert. The first is a tiny portrait in cloisonné enamel of a royal figure; the second is an embroidered stole and maniple presented by King Aethelstan to the shrine of St Cuthbert at Chester-le-Street. The figures of saints on it, about six inches high, might have stepped out of a Carolingian manuscript, but the workmanship is English. Already in the early tenth century England was excelling in an art that would later be everywhere linked with her name – Opus Anglicanum.

Of all continental manuscripts, those which made the deepest impression were from the Carolingian school of Rheims. Its masterpiece is the famous Utrecht Psalter, a manuscript of the Psalms in which every image, almost every word, is illustrated in the most literal way, though the stylised treatment gives an effect more visionary than realistic. This book was in the library of Canterbury during the tenth century. It was meticulously copied, probably about the year 1000, and the copy reproduces the apparent spontaneity of the original in an amazing way. As evidence of the impact of Carolingian art, nothing could be more eloquent.

Although many of the greatest Anglo-Saxon manuscripts can be linked in this way with continental models, it would be wrong to suggest that they were entirely derivative. A flourishing native school was centred on Winchester, Alfred's capital. It is represented by numerous surviving manuscripts, for instance the gorgeous Benedictional of St Aethelwold, dating from about 975–80, a rich, glowing work, the scenes stately and monumental, the borders overflowing with silver and lush decoration.

Several interesting remains of buildings survive from this period. To the seventh century belong the gaunt, lonely church of Bradwell-juxta-Mara, the two Northumbrian churches of Escomb and Monkwearmouth, the crypts of Hexham and Ripon and – the most impressive – Brixworth Church near Northampton. This high, spacious building, its original arcade of four arches now filled in, is almost imperial in its ambition, though its Roman bricks are laid with a touchingly clumsy technique.

By the tenth century a growing accomplishment and contact with Carolingian models is evident. The cathedrals have all disappeared, but the modest parish churches of Deerhurst, Worth and Bradford-on-Avon, built between 900 and 1030, are good examples and contain such characteristic features as the triangular-headed windows and short baluster-columns. Several towers, such as Sompting, Barnack or Earls Barton, show a lavish display of ornament. One highly interesting adoption of a continental idea remains at Canterbury, where Abbot Wulfric, returning dazzled from St Bénigne at Dijon, the greatest abbey-church in France, began building his own small-scale version of the famous rotunda. He died before it was finished, but the foundations remain – a moving remnant of a bold and internationally-minded scheme.

Another usage taken over from continental precedent was the long alliance between sculpture and architecture destined to last to the end of the Middle Ages. High-relief figures of Christ at Castor and Barnack, a Crucifixion at Romney, flying angels at Bradford-on-Avon, 'hogback' coffins in Durham and Northumberland – all show real sculptural

32

THE ALFRED JEWEL

ninth to tenth century
cloisonné enamel in gold
Ashmolean Museum, Oxford

The portrait seems to represent a king and it bears the inscription 'Aelfred het me gewyrcan' ('Alfred caused me to be made'), so that the temptation to associate it with King Alfred is almost irresistible. The technique of cloisonné enamel, however, is continental rather than English, and it may have been imported and fitted into an English mount. The animal-head at the end recalls some of the Sutton Hoo treasures (**50**), and the stylised acanthus on the back has parallels in English manuscript illumination.

33

ALL SAINTS CHURCH

early eleventh century
Earls Barton

This tower is among the best-preserved examples of Saxon architecture in Britain. Its date is probably only shortly before 1066 and may even be post-Conquest, but it shows all the most characteristic features of Saxon work – the triangle-headed patterns and windows, the baluster shafts between the openings and the curious strips of stone decoration known as 'long and short work' which run up the sides almost at random and are thought to derive from timber constructions. The parapet at the top is, of course, much later.

imagination which is recognisably British. Greatest of all, perhaps, is the monumental Risen Christ at Bristol, one of the last works of pre-Norman English art.

Before the Conquest there was one more brief but intriguing interlude. The Norse settlers in Danelaw had from the seventh century onwards been producing carving in their own totally distinct Scandinavian style. In the early part of the eleventh century renewed Danish conquests put the dynasty of Sweyn and Knut on the English throne, and the style became dominant in the south too. It is an exciting art of interlacing animals, swirling lines and restless dynamic forms. Two superb examples are the slab later used as a tympanum in Southwell Minster, showing the Archangel Michael slaying the Dragon, and a tombstone found in London and now 37 in the Guildhall Museum, which has a fabulous stag enmeshed in conflict with a monster that has almost turned into a mass of spirals. Norse art was cut short by the Normans, but its echoes continued to sound in the centuries to come, especially in the far north of the British Isles, which lay near to the sea route between Norway and Iceland. On the Isle of Lewis 34 in the Hebrides some ivory chessmen were unearthed during the last century, which cast a new and unexpectedly homely light on these stern warriors. Whether the chessmen were manufactured in Scandinavia or Britain is not known. It is known, however, that the Norsemen were playing chess by the twelfth century, and such pieces as these were no doubt among the treasures of a royal or noble household.

The Normans in Britain

The Norman Conquest caused a revolution in architecture and changed the course of sculpture, particularly in the way it was used, but in painting its influence is barely noticeable. Such a pattern is to be expected. The ruling class dictated the nature of the large corporate undertakings such as abbeys and cathedrals, which immediately reflected the new tastes and conditions. However, in the more personal art of painting the earlier tradition could linger. The English craftsmen remained, and painting had always been of all the arts the most open to constant influence from abroad; no conquest was needed to bring foreign books into the country. Thus architecture is always the most characteristically national art and painting the most international and least affected by political changes.

The architectural revolution was not wholly unheralded; Edward the Confessor had already brought the Norman style to England when he began the new abbey church of Westminster between 1050 and 1065. It was still unfinished when his cousin William was crowned there. The style we call Norman is merely one local school of French Romanesque that blossomed in Normandy under the leadership of the eleventh-century dukes, and is to be seen in its early splendour at Caen, Jumièges and Mont-St-Michel. What distinguished it from other regional schools was its large scale, its fondness for the three-storey elevation (arcade, gallery, clerestory) often with alternating supports, its two-tower façades, its general lack of interest in vaulting and its preference for geometrical rather than figure sculpture in decoration. All these elements were transplanted onto English soil, and during the fifty years after 1066 nearly all the great abbeys and cathedrals were begun, usually on a scale far surpassing the most grandiose Saxon ambitions. Extreme length became almost an obsession with the Anglo-Norman builders. Winchester nave had eleven bays, Norwich fourteen, longer than any churches in Europe except the enormous third church at Cluny.

The great wave of Norman abbey and cathedral building belongs to political as much as to architectural history. Abbots and bishops were

34
CHESSMEN
twelfth century
walrus ivory
h. about 3 in (8 cm)
British Museum, London

In 1851 a collection of seventy-eight chessmen was discovered on the Isle of Lewis in the Hebrides. It is thought to have been the stock of a merchant. They are characteristic examples of Scandinavian Romanesque carving and were clearly produced in quantity by ordinary craftsmen. The pieces shown here are the king and a bishop. The backs of the seats are carved with snaky animal-style ornament.

35
ELY CATHEDRAL
twelfth to fourteenth century

Ely was unusual among Norman cathedrals in having a single big west tower instead of the more normal two towers. On each side of it a western transept spread beyond the width of the nave and aisles. Half of this transept, the north (left of the picture), collapsed at some unknown date and was never rebuilt. The Galilee Porch, projecting in front, in a pure Early English style with long lancet windows, was added in the thirteenth century, and the top storey of the tower about 1400. In the background can be seen the exterior of the octagon.

political nominees, and their function as lords spiritual was to impose Norman administration on the country as in their own way the lords temporal were doing.

Each church had its own mixture of the standard parts and its own proportions, and as the years have passed this individuality has been increased by all the additions and alterations in later styles. The most complete example of a Norman cathedral is Durham, though in one important respect Durham is an exception. It had high rib vaults from as early as 1077, possibly the first in Europe and for long unique in England. However, as a whole it may stand as representative of the best in English Romanesque architecture—strong and satisfying in its mass, perfect in the harmony of its proportions. 35, 41 49

The pride of the Normans was manifested more brutally in castle building. Here again they first imported and then developed new architectural techniques to serve urgent political needs. The typical motte-and-bailey (the motte being an artificial mound, the bailey a fortified enclosure round its base) was originally crowned with a wooden fort or keep. Later these keeps were rebuilt in stone. The castles were often large, and although the lords and barons would not normally expect to live in them, they were capable of providing fairly comfortable accommodation if necessary. The earliest is the Tower of London where, in spite of frequent restoration, some parts, for instance the chapel, still preserve their rugged simplicity. Others of similar design include Dover, Newcastle, Colchester, Rochester and Castle Hedingham. In some, complete Norman rooms with fireplaces remain practically intact. As time went on the design of keeps became more and more sophisticated, and the neatest of all is Conisborough in Yorkshire. 46

Castles and cathedrals shared a common vocabulary of decoration. The favourite Norman motifs—roll, billet, beak-head, cable and zigzag—appear equally often on both. Indeed, the most lavish of all is an internal doorway in Durham Castle, where the ornament almost dwarfs the opening. It was a vigorous but in the end stereotyped art, and in some ways it is a pity that it held the field so successfully throughout the twelfth century. There are no English equivalents of the great French Romanesque masterpieces such as Moissac, Autun and Vézelay; the nearest approach is the porch at Malmesbury. Italian as well as French influence is evident in the Prior's Door at Ely; here geometrical Norman ornament is entirely absent, and the door includes a figured tympanum, a rarity in England.

The most outstanding pieces of sculpture from the Norman period are either eccentric, problematical or imported. The charming group of works in Herefordshire villages around Kilpeck comes into the first category; it has been suggested that these were done by an English sculptor back from the pilgrimage to Compostela. Of the 'problems' there are three in particular. The first is the panels in Chichester Cathedral: the Raising of Lazarus and Christ's Entry into Bethany, which in dramatic power are comparable to anything in medieval art. They have some French features but also some Saxon ones; their date has been hotly disputed, but the late twelfth century seems now generally accepted. The second is the very fine relief of the Virgin and Child in the crypt of York Minster, which would certainly have been taken for a foreign importation were it not carved in Tadcaster stone. Here Byzantine influence is strong. The third is the famous Gloucester Candlestick. Although on a small scale (sixteen inches high) this has affinities with some giant candlesticks of which one survives intact at Milan, and which probably came from the 42 48

36 *far right*

EARDISLEY FONT

c. 1150
Church of St Mary Magdalen, Eardisley

The bowl-shaped font is carved with a
scene of two knights fighting, and on the
other side, the Harrowing of Hell. They
are separated by a haloed figure, seen here
on the right, wearing a robe whose doughy
parallel folds are, like the knights' surcoats,
characteristic of the Herefordshire school
of sculpture. The two heads, with their
stylised beards and big eyes, have a
Scandinavian look, comparable to the
Lewis chessmen (**34**) and the Franks
Casket (**31**).

38 *right*

THE RUTHWELL CROSS

last quarter of seventh century
Ruthwell

'On many estates of nobles and good men',
wrote St Willibald (who was born about
700), 'they are wont to have not a church
but the standard of the Holy Cross dedicated to Our Lord.' This panel shows
Christ being worshipped by the beasts of
the desert. The runic inscription is a
quotation from the Anglo-Saxon poem
The Dream of the Rood, in which Christ is
seen as an epic hero of light against the
powers of darkness. 'Then the young hero,
who was God, firm and unflinching, bared
his breast. He mounted on the high cross,
brave before all, to redeem mankind.'

40 *centre*

ILLUSTRATION FROM A PSALTER

c. 1000
British Museum, London

This is an almost exact copy, made at
Canterbury about 1000, of the Utrecht
Psalter, a Carolingian manuscript probably
written at Rheims in the early ninth century. This drawing illustrates Psalm VII:
'O Lord, my God, deliver me from all
those that persecute me, lest he tear my
soul like a lion. . . . If he turn not, he will
whet his sword; he hath bent his bow and
made it ready. He hath also prepared for
him instruments of death; He ordaineth
his arrows against the persecutors. . . . He
made a pit and digged it and is fallen into
the ditch which he made.'

41 *far right*

NAVE OF PETERBOROUGH CATHEDRAL

c. 1150–c. 1180

The long nave of Peterborough is typical of
major Norman churches. Arcade, gallery
and clerestory are equally emphasised, the
only vertical accent being the demi-shafts
that rise from floor to ceiling. Ornament is
practically confined to a little chevron at
gallery level. At the far end can be seen the
inside of the crossing tower and the later
windows of the chancel. The ceiling, which
is unique, is the original wooden one of
c. 1200, slightly canted, and painted with
diamond shapes containing figures of
kings, queens and saints.

37 *right*

TOMB-SLAB

c. 1030
oolite
width 24 in (61 cm)
Guildhall Museum, London

This tombstone commemorates a man
called Tobi, possibly the same as Tobiq, a
minister of King Canute. It was found in
the churchyard of St Paul's Cathedral.
The carving, which depicts a stag in com-
bat with a dragon, is clearly the work of a
Norse artist; it was originally coloured,
and is closely related to the Jellinge style
in Scandinavia. The stag is clearly recog-
nisable; the dragon has become almost
dissolved in a mass of spiralling lines.

39 *right*

CAPITAL IN THE CRYPT OF CANTERBURY CATHEDRAL

c. 1120

Much of the small-scale carving in medieval cathedrals and monasteries was secular
and even satirical in character. Animals
performing human actions were especially
popular and can often be related to fables
and stories like that of Reynard the Fox.
Here two goats play a violin and a pipe,
one of them riding on a dragon. The style
is close to contemporary illuminations in
manuscripts produced in the Canterbury
scriptorium. It was subjects such as these
which were soon to be denounced by St
Bernard as 'unclean apes, fierce lions, mon-
strous centaurs, half men'.

Meuse region of Flanders. The English example, however, with its
intricate all-over pattern and its tiny figures clambering through a jungle
of scrolls is so near to Saxon and Norse tradition that there is justification
for believing that it was made in the country. The only doubt is whether
anybody in twelfth-century England was capable of such a virtuoso feat
of casting.

Sculpture was imported widely, especially when it was small and easily
carried. In some cases, such as the outstanding small relief of the Adoration
of the Magi in walrus-ivory, it is virtually impossible to know whether the **43**
piece is local or imported. It is certainly the product of a 'Channel School'
active in the late eleventh century; the most recent opinion favours
southern England.

Of heavier imports the most interesting are the black marble fonts **44**
found in southern and eastern England, mostly carved with foliage or

abstract patterns but occasionally with figures. These all come from Tournai in Belgium; the same workshop also provided tombstones, including a fine one of a bishop at Ely.

To a great extent, however, the most pleasing examples of English Romanesque sculpture are small-scale works with no particular claim to greatness, done by artists in whom the Celtic and Norse traditions still lived. To study the sculptural details of Norman parish churches is to enter a world of luxuriant and barbaric imagination that goes back further than the faith it was meant to serve. On a tympanum at Stretton Sugwas a kilted Samson wrestles with a heraldic lion. On a font at Eardisley **36** soldiers with spear and sword fight amid the python-like folds of a vine, and in the crypt of Canterbury Cathedral a fascinating series of capitals **39** presents a zoo of fabulous creatures.

Art of this kind was not confined to non-monastic churches. It is clear from the protests of St Bernard that in France at least it was as popular in the cloister as anywhere else, and the manuscripts produced in the great monastic scriptoria will confirm this. Manuscript illumination, though more closely tied to its literary context, partakes of the same bizarre imagery.

Surviving evidence indicates that nearly all eleventh and twelfth-century painting was monastic. No doubt there were attractive secular manuscripts and wallpaintings, but hardly anything survives. Secular works were probably smaller in number and less outstanding in quality than those produced for the church. What we have today are nearly all illustrated bibles and psalters, lives of the saints, some theology and a few items of sacred verse, in particular an eleventh-century manuscript of Caedmon.

At Canterbury a manuscript style was evolved that showed some of the characteristics of the capitals in the crypt. It was a style that lent itself to pattern-making and ornament rather than to dramatic expression, and is particularly delightful in some of the illuminated initials.

The scriptorium of Winchester continued to extend its pre-Conquest expertise and produced as late as 1160–70 a book that has been called 'the giant of twelfth-century English manuscripts', the famous Winchester **51** Bible. The question of individual patronage is here definite and crucial, for the Bishop of Winchester from 1129 to 1171 was King Stephen's brother Henry of Blois, one of the most energetic statesmen of his time and a generous employer of artists, to the greater glory of both God and himself. He belonged to European culture as he was brought up at Cluny and spent some time in Rome. Most of the illuminations of the Winchester Bible are initials, all in the richly inventive style that characterises earlier work there, though they differ quite widely among themselves and six different artists have been distinguished. Henry also commissioned the great Winchester Psalter, which contains both miniatures in Byzantine style and others in the northern manner of the Bible initials.

Other centres, such as Hereford, Croyland and Bury St Edmunds, were now producing manuscripts of equal power. The schools of Hereford and Sherbourne excelled in compositions which in their economy, sureness and brilliance prefigure the century to come. The Shaftesbury Psalter contains **53** paintings that are among the masterpieces of Romanesque art.

Wallpaintings must surely have occupied talents as great, but there are **45** only a few survivals, and most are fragmentary in composition and spoiled in colour. At a few places, for instance Hardham in Sussex, enough remains to give some idea of what a Norman church originally looked like, but it needs sympathy and imagination.

Ian Richards

42 *below*

THE RAISING OF LAZARUS

early twelfth century, Purbeck stone
Chichester Cathedral

This, and another panel showing the Entry
of Christ into Bethany, were found built
into one of the crossing piers of Chichester
Cathedral and may have been part of the
old twelfth-century choir-screen. They
are certainly amongst the most powerful
pieces of Norman sculpture, though owing
much to the earlier Saxon-Carolingian
tradition. Christ towers over everyone,
his size – as usual in medieval art – being a
measure of importance. Two men hold
open the tomb, and Lazarus, a gaunt figure
wrapped in grave-clothes, rises stiffly, his
hands clasped in prayer.

43 *right*

ADORATION OF THE MAGI

early twelfth century
whalebone, h. 14 in (5 cm)
Victoria and Albert Museum, London

This carving has affinities with illuminated
manuscripts on both sides of the channel,
so it is impossible to say exactly where it
was made. There can be no doubt, however, of its quality. The Virgin, a sad,
hieratic figure, sits under an arched canopy
hung with curtains, their ends looped
round columns on either side. Above this
is an elaborate piece of architecture, from
which peer an owl and a man blowing a
horn. Beneath the Virgin's feet is a tangle
of fiercely struggling animals and a centaur
with bow and arrow.

44 *right*

FONT

late twelfth century
Tournai marble
3 ft 3 in long (99 cm)
Winchester Cathedral

There are seven of these Tournai fonts in
England; the one at Winchester is the most
interesting, since it is carved on all four
sides, two of which show narrative reliefs
of the life of St Nicholas. Here the saint is
shown giving a bag of gold to a man as
dowry for his three daughters (standing
next to him) who would otherwise be
forced into a life of shame. On the left is a
man with a hawk, possibly one of the
daughters' prospective husbands. On the
right is the view of a Norman church with
arcade, gallery and clerestory, and a
realistic door with hinges.

45 *bottom left*

ST PAUL AND THE VIPER

mid-twelfth century
wallpainting
69 × 66 in (175 × 167 cm)
St Anselm's Chapel, Canterbury Cathedral

'When Paul had gathered a number of sticks and laid them on the fire, a viper came out by reason of the heat and fastened on his hand. They said one to another, no doubt this man is a murderer, whom, though he hath escaped from the sea, yet Justice hath not suffered him to live. Howbeit, he shook off the beast into the fire and took no harm. . . . When they beheld that nothing came amiss to him, they changed their minds and said he was a god.' This incident, rarely represented in art, was painted on a wall that was covered up by a buttress in the Middle Ages, and so was excellently preserved.

46 *bottom right*

ST JOHN'S CHAPEL, TOWER OF LONDON

late eleventh century

William the Conqueror started building the White Tower as soon as he was safely in power, and it was finished by 1097. The chapel is still more or less as it was in his time, a room of some architectural refinement but still dark, grim and castle-like. It has an ambulatory, squat circular columns supporting a gallery (but no clerestory) and – a great rarity in England – a tunnel vault.

47

CHURCH OF ST LAURENCE

c. 700, late tenth and eleventh centuries
Bradford-on-Avon

This little church, seen here from the south, spans the whole history of Anglo-Saxon architecture. The lower parts of the nave and chancel walls remain from the early Benedictine church founded before 705. It had two *porticus* (side-chapels), but the south one is now ruined. In the late tenth century the upper parts were rebuilt, with unusually fine blank arcading inspired by continental models. The entire building, including the door shapes, reflects the Anglo-Saxon love of tall, narrow forms.

THE GLOUCESTER CANDLESTICK

1104–13
gilt-bronze
h. 16 in (40 cm)
Victoria and Albert Museum, London

Early medieval candlesticks sometimes reached enormous dimensions: one at Durham is reputed to have touched both sides of the transept. England can now only boast this very miniature example which was probably made for Gloucester Abbey at the instigation of Abbot Peter. The style seems to look back to pre-Conquest art, and the whole candlestick is full of movement; nine human figures and forty-two animals crawl and fight their way round it.

49 *far right*

NAVE OF DURHAM CATHEDRAL

late eleventh to early twelfth century

No English cathedral gives such an impression of massive strength as Durham, built by the Normans between 1093 and 1133. In the nave, circular piers ornamented with incised lozenge-shapes, zigzags and fluting alternate with others of more complex section reflecting the vaulting shafts and the mouldings of the arches they support. In the background can be seen the north aisle, with its decoration of blank interlaced arcading which was for a long time a favourite motif of English Romanesque.

50 *below*

SUTTON HOO TREASURE

early seventh century
gold with enamel and garnets
British Museum, London

The Sutton Hoo ship burial, discovered in Suffolk on the eve of war in 1939, is the most important single archaeological discovery in Britain. It consisted of a large ship, of which the timber had vanished, but much of the original equipment and offerings remained. There were no human bones, and it is surmised that it was the cenotaph of a king or chieftain who had been drowned. Among the treasures buried with it were this shoulder-clasp and purse-lid. The purse contained seventy gold coins. Ornamental motifs on the lid include the Man Between Beasts and the familiar interlace pattern.

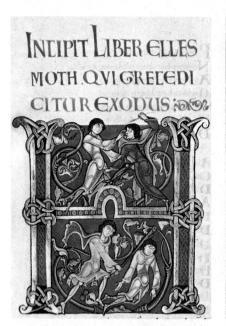

51 *top left*

THE WINCHESTER BIBLE

c. 1160–70, Master of the Leaping Figures
Cathedral Library, Winchester

This bible was one of the most ambitious works of medieval art.
It is nearly two feet tall and was originally bound in two volumes.
At least six artists worked on it, all of whom can be distinguished
by their personal styles. The artist who painted the letter H is
called the Master of the Leaping Figures because of his fondness for
violent gestures and swaying draperies. The scenes illustrate
Exodus, the Egyptian smiting the Hebrew and Moses slaying the
Egyptian.

52 *top*

THE BOOK OF DURROW

seventh century, Trinity College Library, Dublin

The Book of Durrow, a copy of the Gospels in Latin, is the
earliest British illuminated manuscript. It contains four painted
pages with symbols of the Evangelists and several others consisting only of ornament. The sources for these designs are varied
and have been much debated; this page, with its spirals enclosed in
circles, relates to the Sutton Hoo burial (**50**), where some of the
silverware has very similar motifs.

53

SHAFTESBURY OR LANSDOWNE PSALTER

mid-twelfth century, 9 × 5·5 in (23 × 14 cm)
British Museum, London

The Psalter was made for the Dorset nunnery of Shaftesbury. This
is the last illuminated page and represents the Last Judgment.
St Michael, here shown as a gentle and appealing figure, not the
stern judge of other such paintings, offers up a napkinful of souls to
Christ. The stylised yet strangely convincing lines of the limbs and
drapery make this a work of particular delicacy and charm.

54 *right*

BENEDICTIONAL OF ST AETHELWOLD

c. 975–80, 11·5 × 8·5 in (29 × 22 cm), British Museum, London

Aethelwold, Bishop of Winchester, was one of the most energetic
churchmen of the late eighth century. The Benedictional, probably made at Winchester on his instructions, embodies many
features of contemporary Carolingian painting, especially in the
lavish borders of flowery architecture. In this scene of the Death of
the Virgin the whole picture is set within a frame of arches and
columns whose capitals sprout multi-coloured acanthus leaves.
In the centre lies the dying Virgin; above her God's hand gives her
a heavenly crown; while at the bottom the Apostles mourn.

In the afternoon of September 5th 1174, a fire broke out in the town of Canterbury south of the cathedral. Sparks and cinders, carried up by the wind, settled on the roof of the church and by evening that too was in flames. A member of the monastery at that time, Gervase, has left a detailed account of what happened next. 'The people and monks assembled in haste, drew water, brandished their hatchets and ran up the stairs, full of eagerness to save the church—already, alas, beyond their help. But when they reached the roof and saw the black smoke and scorching flames they abandoned the attempt in despair and thinking only of their own safety made all haste to descend. The fire had loosened the beams from the pegs that fastened them together, and the half-burnt timbers fell into the choir below; the seats, consisting of a great mass of woodwork caught fire and thus the mischief grew worse and worse. ... In this manner the house of God, hitherto delightful as a paradise of pleasure, was made a despicable heap of ashes, reduced to a dreary wilderness and laid open to all the injuries of the weather.'

When they recovered from their shock and grief, the brethren consulted how to repair the damage. 'French and English artificers were therefore summoned ... amongst them a certain William of Sens, a man active and ready and as a workman most skilful both in wood and stone. To him and to the providence of God, was the execution of the work committed.'

William and his builders remained at Canterbury for three years and Gervase gives exact details of what was done during each season's work. In 1178 William fell from the vault and was seriously injured. He entrusted the building to a younger colleague, also called William, an Englishman, 'small in body, but in workmanship of many kinds acute and honest'. He continued the new choir and by 1180 it was sufficiently complete for the monks to start using it for services. The whole church was finished in 1184.

The east end of Canterbury marks the beginning of a new phase in English architecture, the Gothic style. The novelty was clear even at the time. Gervase, a perceptive critic, summarised the change thus: 'The pillars of the old and new work are alike in form and thickness, but different in height, for the new pillars are almost twelve feet higher. In the old capitals the work was plain, in the new ones exquisite in sculpture. No marble columns were there, but here are innumerable ones. There, in the circuit round the choir, the vaults were plain, but here they are ribbed. There, there was a ceiling of wood decorated with excellent paintings, but here there is a vault beautifully constructed of stone. The new work is higher than the old'.

The things that impressed Gervase—the height, the fine materials, the workmanship of the details—were all important aesthetic qualities that characterise the first stage of Gothic and distinguish it from Romanesque. Modern historians would emphasise two more crucial features: the use of the pointed instead of the semi-circular arch and the beginning of a system of buttressing the points of thrust (the points where the weight of the rib vaults rests) by means of masonry bridges across the aisles.

The Gothic style had been born and had come to maturity between 1145 and 1170 in the great cathedrals of the Ile-de-France such as Sens, the home-town of the Canterbury architect. But the style was not transferred intact and unchanged to England, which indeed was already showing definite Gothic preferences of her own—preferences that led almost at once to a completely self-contained vocabulary and caused nineteenth-century historians to christen the whole style 'Early English'.

As the work at Canterbury neared completion a new cathedral was begun at Wells in Somerset. It is clearly and confidently Gothic, but not

56, 63

68, 69

Church and Court in the Gothic Age
1174-1485

55
ST PETER
c. 1275
detail from the Westminster Retable
tempera on wood
whole retable 36 × 132 in (91 × 335 cm)
Westminster Abbey, London

These fine panels are among the few outstanding surviving examples of English thirteenth-century panel painting. Their original purpose is obscure: they probably formed the retable to an altar, but it has been suggested that they were part of the cover of Edward the Confessor's shrine. The central panel shows Christ in Judgment, and St Peter occupies the panel on the extreme left. The style, especially in the decorative backgrounds, has Italian features—another reason for connecting it with the Confessor's shrine.

in the least French. The proportions are long and low, there is no striving for effects of height, and the pier-section is thick and complex instead of slender and simple. In French Gothic the elevation divides naturally into bays separated by vertical shafts. At Wells the bays are given no separate demarcation; on the contrary, it was the long totality of the nave which the architect enjoyed and he articulated it by making the triforium one continuous series of arches.

The stage was now set for the evolution of English architecture until **57** about 1300. Lincoln, begun in 1192, took over Canterbury's use of dark Purbeck marble, developed the vaulting by adding subsidiary ribs and inaugurated the ridge-rib, a typically English feature that gives the whole space one strong horizontal accent. The east ends of Rochester and Chichester followed, even more clearly within the orbit of Canterbury. **73** Salisbury, begun in 1220, cool, spacious and restrained, eschewed sculptural decoration and relied solely on line, proportion and the gentle emphasis of Purbeck. All these cathedrals are marked by a certain looseness of plan which distinguishes them from their French counterparts.

The next milestone was Westminster Abbey. Work here was taken over by the crown, that is by Henry III, in 1245. It was the royal coronation church, the centre of religious and patriotic attention. Significantly, the king (like the monks of Canterbury) turned to a French architect – or so at least it is reasonably assumed – called Henry of Reyns (Rheims). Rheims was the coronation church of the king's cousin St Louis, and thus a natural **70** model to emulate. The result was French in its tall proportions, its chevet of chapels at the east end, and in one more very important feature – bar tracery. This had originated, apparently at Rheims itself, in the early thirteenth century. Henry of Reyns used it confidently, as well as the so-called 'spherical triangle' window, a motif introduced only a few years earlier at the Sainte Chapelle in Paris. In spite of the difficulties of appreciating it in its present crowded and noisy condition, Westminster Abbey, with its subtle contrast of dark Purbeck marble and creamy stone (originally brightly painted), is a building of serene and poetic majesty.

In the centre of the choir stood the new shrine of the abbey's founder, the saintly King Edward the Confessor. This was neither English nor French but Italian. The pavement, of porphyry, jasper and marble, was brought from Rome by Abbot Richard Ware in 1268, and apparently he also brought craftsmen to lay it, for it is signed 'Odericus'. The shrine itself, 'of purest gold and precious stones', according to Matthew Paris, was made in 1270 by Petrus Romanus, possibly the same man who worked on the tomb of Clement IV at Viterbo. It had twisted columns covered in coloured mosaic in the style known as 'Cosmati work' from the Italian family who were credited with inventing it. The lower part of the shrine has miraculously escaped the ravages of the Puritans and time.

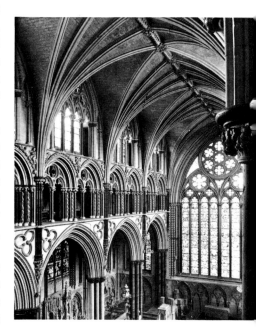

Imports from even further afield than Italy are known. The famous Islamic enamelled glass known as the 'Luck of Edenhall' was brought to England, perhaps by a crusader, soon after it was made in the thirteenth century, and must always have been prized as an exotic rarity. The Musgrave family of Edenhall in Cumberland, who owned it, regarded it with superstitious awe; if it were broken, disaster would follow. Its finely tooled leather case, made specially for it in the fourteenth century, seems to be French.

English achievement in sculpture at this time is meagre by comparison with the French. At Westminster French influence is evident in the censing angels high up in the interior of the north transept. At Wells the **68** sculptors of the west front, also aware of events in France and even more ambitious than those of Westminster, were unequal to their models. Wells remains, however, England's most complete thirteenth-century ensemble.

It would almost seem that English sculptors were intimidated by the challenge of the large, monumental, sacred figure. As in Romanesque times, their imagination ran more freely on a less exalted plane. Grotesques still leered out from buttresses and parapets, though there were fewer of them and they were less prominently placed. Tombstones called forth a degree of expertise equalling anything in Europe, for instance the stern and powerful effigy of King John at Worcester. And one small female **71** figure, nineteen inches high, at Winchester is an isolated masterpiece, so hard to fit into the story of English sculpture that an archaic Greek work, or a Roman copy, has been suggested as her model.

It was in foliage capitals that the English sculptor really came into his own. As the thirteenth century progressed the old French 'crocket' began to sprout into the so-called 'stiff leaf', which curled in graceful arabesques round its capital, and by 1260 or 1270 was swept by a gusty breeze bringing nature herself to life in the cold stone.

The possibilities of larger windows and the development of bar tracery gave a new impetus to the art of stained glass. Here again one must look across the channel. Craftsmen found it easy to cross from the Plantagenet provinces of France to the Plantagenet kingdom of England. It is impossible now to distinguish their hands in English glass. For the best one must go back to Canterbury. On the ground floor, still *in situ*, are complicated narrative panels showing the miracles of St Thomas. In the clerestory windows (now moved to the south transept) were larger figures of kings and prophets. Rich, deep and glowing in their colour, powerful in their **64** design, they must have given the choir of William of Sens a solemn spiritual authority such as can today only be experienced at Chartres.

These are Gothic figures. Their attitudes, their flowing drapery, their long sad faces and thoughtful expressions, belong to the new style as clearly as the buildings over which they watched. Reduced in scale and if anything intensified in feeling, they reappear in the pages of Gothic manuscripts, on wallpaintings (though these practically cease in the cathedrals and larger churches), on the wooden panels of altar paintings, of which the most famous today is the Westminster Retable, and on number- **55** less chasubles, copes and hangings, most of which have long fallen to dust. It was an age of mannered richness, of elegance straining against the bonds of discipline, of imagination held back by form and precedent. In the last years of the thirteenth century the bonds broke.

Early English had been a 'safe' style. Now, it was as if artists and patrons alike wanted more dramatic effects, startling ideas and original solutions to long-standing problems. Window tracery, for instance, evolved from the simple geometry of Westminster or Lincoln until in about 1260 it must have occurred to designers that at the top of the window they could simply fill the space with tracery of any shape, ignoring the logic of the lower lights altogether. The bars could curve up or down or across in any direction; they could emphasise the shape of the arch or they could contradict it; they could be like leaves, or snowflakes or flames. These English windows of about 1300–30, superb examples of the Decorated style, are arguably the most beautiful in the world. Three of the grandest and finest are the east window of Selby in Yorkshire, the south transept rose window of Lincoln and the west window of York Minster.

Vaulting shows exactly the same process. The early vaults had been four-part or six-part. Now several extra ribs were added, so that instead of

56
CHOIR OF
CANTERBURY CATHEDRAL
1175–84
The new choir of Canterbury, built after the disastrous fire of 1174, introduced the Gothic style to England. If this picture is compared to that of Durham (**49**) the differences are easy to see. Canterbury has a taller, more linear character, emphasised by the slender shafts of Purbeck marble and the ribs of the sexpartite vault. At the east end, behind the altar, stood the shrine of St Thomas à Becket, the most revered place of pilgrimage in England.

57
ANGEL CHOIR,
LINCOLN CATHEDRAL
1256–80
Most eleventh and twelfth-century cathedrals had to be enlarged during the thirteenth century by lengthening the choir, and this was also done at Lincoln. The Angel Choir represents the culmination of the Early English style to which the old choir and the nave had made such notable contributions. The east window consists of eight lights and a whole range of cusped circles in the head, while the tracery in the clerestory is doubled, giving a richer effect to the interior. The twenty-eight angels from which the choir takes its name are in the spandrels of the gallery.

a series of distinct compartments one is faced with a line of curving branches like palm trees, for instance in the nave of Exeter or the chapter house of Wells. Then to these 'tiercerons' were added shorter interconnecting ribs ('liernes') that had not even a pretence of structural function and could be arranged according to any caprice.

The effect was to introduce a play of interlocking surfaces, a sort of free dynamic movement, into what had hitherto been a logical expression of structure, whether Romanesque or Gothic; and this could be extended into the planning and articulation of a whole building. The lady chapel at Wells is made to interpenetrate the ambulatory of the choir, producing a complicated sequence of spaces that defies rational comprehension. The **58** choir aisles at Bristol are vaulted with ribs that rest on miniature bridges, so that one seems to look through the vault at the compartments beyond.
69 At Wells again, where the central tower showed signs of weakness, the crossing piers were strengthened by strainer arches, interlocking S-shapes with openings through which other spaces are dimly seen. At Ely the old **60** tower actually did collapse and was replaced by an octagon, admitting light diagonally into the crossing and crowned by another, wooden, octagon set cross-wise into the first (the corners of the first face the sides of the second, and vice-versa). The carpenter at Ely was William Hurley, the king's master-carpenter, and he probably designed the octagon. Half the credit, however, must surely go to his employer, the Prior Alan of Walsingham, who initiated not only this work but the new lady chapel and the repairs to the choir, all conceived with the same spirit and boldness.

Each of these instances is unique, an experiment never repeated. But they all reflect a common aesthetic sensibility, which seemed to unite all the arts. Architecture had become sculptural, sculpture responded by becoming architectural. Spanning these two worlds and partaking of both stands the ogee arch, the graceful though totally unfunctional double curve that so completely embodied the ideals of the early fourteenth-century builder. These arches occur on every scale from a few inches on tombs and chantry chapels to hundreds of feet over the east end of Gloucester Cathedral.

The first ogees in England had appeared on the Eleanor Crosses put up after 1290 by Edward I in memory of his queen. Within a few years the arches began to lean forward into a third dimension, or 'nod', and by the 1330s they were being knitted together into fantastic cages of stone. Two of the most successful feats of virtuosity are the Percy Tomb at Beverley and the Tomb of Edward II at Gloucester.

66 The actual effigy of Edward II is a superb feat of technical accomplishment. Almost hidden under its luxuriant canopy, it is made of alabaster, a relatively new material that had become popular in the last quarter of the previous century. Another newly fashionable material was bronze, which was expensive, largely confined to royal works and wholly dependent on foreign techniques. Several of the finest royal effigies in Westminster Abbey are of bronze. In 1291 Edward I commissioned those of his father, **65** Henry III, and his queen, Eleanor, from the sculptor William Torel, who may have been a Fleming. The technique was certainly Flemish, and the figure of Queen Eleanor was even gilded with the gold of Flemish florins.

Like every art-form when it reaches a peak of expressiveness, English sculpture of around 1300 combines an ever greater degree of artifice with ever greater fidelity to nature. As in previous periods, its merits are best appreciated in so-called minor works – bosses, capitals, corbels, mouldings and ornamental carving. A good example can be seen in the 'leaves of **59** Southwell', the capitals in the vestibule and chapter house of Southwell

58
BRISTOL CATHEDRAL, SOUTH CHOIR AISLE
1290–c.1330

The builders of Bristol Cathedral, which was then the Augustinian abbey church, were among the most original of the whole Middle Ages. The chancel, all that was completed, is unique among English churches in being a hall-church, that is, without gallery or clerestory, the aisles being as high as the centre. The weight of the central vault is taken by horizontal bridges across the aisles, supported on arches and themselves supporting the miniature aisle vaults. The whole design is made transparent by leaving open the spaces between bridge and arch and between the pairs of vaulting bays.

59
THE LEAVES OF SOUTHWELL
c.1300
chapter-house of Southwell Minster

The capitals of the vestibule and chapter-house of Southwell Minster contain the finest foliage carving of medieval England – or indeed of medieval Europe. The leaves lap over the mouldings in a way that is completely natural and completely controlled. This detail shows the right-hand side of the doorway into the chapter-house. The leaves on the left are vines; the three in the centre are buttercup, vine (with maple above, a headless dragon hiding in the leaves) and oak.

60
THE OCTAGON, ELY CATHEDRAL
1322–46
William Hurley, d. 1354

The octagon at Ely is one of the boldest conceptions in all medieval architecture. The old central tower of the cathedral collapsed in 1322. Instead of simply replacing it, the prior, Alan of Walsingham, decided to enlarge the central space by demolishing both the old crossing piers and the aisle bays adjacent to them, and to cover the whole space by a wooden roof supporting a lantern stage with windows. The whole structure rests on eight very large beams – roughly shaped tree-trunks sixty-four feet long – hidden above the vault.

Minster, carved between 1290 and 1295. Here, instead of the stylised foliage of earlier Gothic, are real plants and trees from the English countryside: oak, hawthorn, maple, buttercup, hop, bryony, ivy, rose and vine (which then still grew in England). The form of the capital is preserved, and it is still integrally an architectural member, yet in observation and in feeling is as full of natural delight as a poem by Wordsworth. The same spontaneity is apparent in the 'weepers' round tomb-chests and in the carved panels that occasionally enrich altars or sarcophagi. Even in larger figures the management of pose and drapery shows a sense of style and a confidence that owe nothing to continental models.

Artifice and naturalism: the same two qualities though in somewhat less easy conjunction also characterise the painting of this period. It was still, as far as surviving examples go, almost entirely manuscript painting. In the larger full or half-page compositions the elegant ogee line tends to dominate, so that often the whole design seems as if fabricated to fit the interplay of S-curves. There is a relaxation of intensity, an increase in decorative brilliance, a lightening of mood and of subject matter. The graceful and comforting figure of the Madonna dominates as she had never done a hundred years before.

At the same time the animal life of the margins shakes off every vestige of inhibition. Foxes, dogs, deer, rabbits, goats, pigs, squirrels and hedge- **75, 78** hogs, drawn with complete realism and evident affection, gambol and play oblivious of the sacred text beside them. Often humorous or traditional stories take over: a monkey goes hunting on a fox while an owl escapes on a rabbit. Or an imagination as bizarre as Brueghel's or Bosch's brings forth a lion's head walking on human legs, or a bearded harpy screeching from the body of a crow. Most famous of all such manuscripts is the Luttrell Psalter, made about 1340 for Sir John Luttrell, an East Anglian squire. Painting, in fact, was moving out of the monastic scriptoria and into the studios of professional artists, though for the most part the works illustrated were still devotional.

One other art-form for which Britain was celebrated, embroidery, was also becoming more professional. Though the only extant signed piece was made by a nun, great works like the Syon Cope were made generally **77** by men, in workshops, almost all in London. These vestments were exported all over Europe for ecclesiastical use; one great cope is still in Pienza Cathedral and another is in Toledo.

Painting remained without radical change until the second half of the fourteenth century, when influences from abroad, this time from Bohemia and Saxony, began to make themselves felt. In the meantime another revolution in architecture was transforming the whole face of England: the Perpendicular style.

Perpendicular was the last phase of English Gothic, the longest lived and the easiest to describe. Although it sprang from no outside influence, it was quite distinct from what had gone before, and its elements, once established, remained surprisingly constant for more than 200 years.

The reaction against the inventiveness and profusion of Decorated appears to have begun in London in the 1320s. Something less assertive, closer to a convention, seems to have been desired. The key monuments, St Stephen's Chapel, Westminster, and the chapter house of old St Paul's, are unhappily lost, and the earliest surviving examples of the new style are the south transept and choir of Gloucester, which were remodelled between 1330 and 1357. The old Norman piers remained, but in front of them a stone grid was erected of thin straight ribs, repeating the same rigid pattern almost from floor to ceiling. This indeed is the essence of

Perpendicular – straight lines and repetition. The tracery, instead of curving into intricate, wilful knots, was ironed out into flat panels, the window mullions going straight up into the top of the arch with undeviating rectitude. Mouldings became shallow but linear, arches depressed and often framed by rectangles. Windows became still larger, glass lighter, arcades and aisles wider, so that Perpendicular churches have a refreshing spaciousness and brilliance. They left, on the whole, little scope for individual genius and tend to a certain similarity, but they achieved grandeur by their sheer scale and by the lavishness of their decoration and furnishings.

The court of Richard II

After Gloucester there was a pause, corresponding to the period of the Black Death and subsequent shortage of labour. But during the last quarter of the fourteenth century, under Richard II, the most civilised king **81** to sit on the English throne, the arts blossomed into a new golden age.

Patronage was still much as before, with the king and the church accounting for all the major commissions. The monasteries were in decline and the only large monastic undertaking after the middle of the fourteenth century was the rebuilding of Bath Abbey. The cathedrals led the way, and **89** the bishops began to take in hand other projects, such as colleges and almshouses, that hitherto had been left to the monasteries. Royal patronage was also on the increase. Civic pride found expression in new parish churches whose real purpose was often more secular than religious, while the nobility (especially after the Wars of the Roses) could at last feel secure enough to build great country houses instead of fortresses.

Richard II, born at Bordeaux in 1367, succeeded to the throne at the age of ten, on the death of his grandfather Edward III. In 1382 he married Anne, the daughter of the King of Bohemia, became devoted to her, and was overcome with grief when she died suddenly in 1394. After a losing battle against his discontented and ambitious barons, he was deposed in 1399 and murdered in 1400.

During the last two decades of the century, however, Richard managed to create a court which in taste and talent was unequalled in Europe. Nervous and passionate by nature, he cultivated the pleasures of both the mind and the senses. He loved jewellery, beautiful clothes and perfumes. One of the most perfect survivals of these arts of gracious living is the so-called 'Studley Bowl', a silver-gilt bowl with lid, decorated with ornament **61** in the form of the letters of the alphabet. Richard also valued books, recognising the merits of Froissart, Gower and Chaucer, and he took the keenest interest in the royal building works which from this time occupied a vital position in the story of architecture.

The Perpendicular style was adopted by masons in the southern half of the country from about the middle of the fourteenth century. At Edington in Wiltshire, the collegiate church begun in 1351 by William of Edington, Bishop of Winchester, was built on a magnificent scale, with Perpendicular gradually replacing Decorated as the work progressed. Edington later decided to modernise the nave of his cathedral, which was still the crude early Norman of the eleventh century. He died before much had been done, but the project was taken up and brought to fulfilment by his successor, the great William of Wykeham, Bishop of Winchester from 1366 to 1404 and twice Lord Chancellor of England. As at Gloucester, the earlier structure was largely retained, but the arcade was heightened by knocking the gallery into it and the whole interior completely redesigned and given a new vault. The architect was William Wynford, who had worked on the west front of Wells, and went on to supervise William of

61

THE STUDLEY BOWL
late fourteenth century
silver-gilt
h. 5·5 in (14 cm); diameter 5·75 in (15 cm)
Victoria and Albert Museum, London

Both bowl and lid are very elegantly and ingeniously decorated with chased and engraved letters from the old black-letter alphabet. A, B and C are easily visible in the centre, and contractions used in manuscripts of the time are also included. The bowl stands on a circular base pierced with rings.

62

SKETCHBOOK

late fourteenth century
coloured drawing
9·75 × 7·75 in (25 × 19 cm)
Pepysian Library, Magdalene College,
Cambridge

This page comes from a sketchbook kept by many different artists, all probably belonging to the same workshop, and used by them as a pattern book for paintings, embroideries and even stained glass. It includes both religious and secular subjects, so there is no clue as to whether or not it was a monastic workshop. The studies of animals and birds are particularly delightful.

Wykeham's foundations of Winchester College and New College, Oxford.

Two of Wynford's associates at Winchester in the 1380s were Henry Yevele and Hugh Herland, both of whom graduated to the king's service. Yevele's chief works were the rebuilding of the naves of Canterbury Cathedral and Westminster Abbey. At Canterbury he produced a clear, lucid interior using standard Perpendicular motifs and mouldings. But at Westminster, for the sake of harmony with the older choir and transepts, he built a thirteenth-century pastiche, a fascinating early example of historicism in architecture.

Herland, the king's carpenter, was responsible for the new roof of Westminster Hall, among the first and certainly the grandest of that 74 English speciality the hammer-beam roof, a technique for roofing wide spans by constructing brackets (hammer-beams) which project from the wall and then resting the main roof on them. This allows sculptural enrichment by winged angels placed on the ends of the beams, and the filling of the spaces between the braces and the roof with tracery in wood. These roofs continued to be a feature of prosperous parish churches and palace halls until late in the sixteenth century.

Richard II's queen came from Bohemia, which at this time was among the leading European centres of painting. The fashionable style was that known as 'International Gothic', which was the end of the Gothic tradition when grandeur had given way to charm and intensity to prettiness. International Gothic pictures have dark backgrounds, rich jewel-like colours and attractive figures arranged in graceful, sophisticated compositions. Queen Anne certainly brought court artists with her from Prague and one of them may very possibly have painted the large portrait of her husband which now hangs in Westminster Abbey. They must also have influenced, though probably did not actually paint, the most famous of all the works of art of Richard's reign, the Wilton Diptych. Controversy still 81 rages over both these works. Some attribute both to French artists; others claim the Wilton Diptych as the work of a Frenchman or a Fleming (the name of Hubert van Eyck has even been suggested), and others again suggest an Englishman, perhaps the king's painter, Thomas Lytlington. All that can be said for certain is that with these works England was firmly within the International Gothic movement, which, true to its name, almost entirely conceals any national characteristics. The Lytlington Missal of 1383–84, now in the library of Westminster Abbey, illustrates the point. There is documentary evidence that several foreign painters were in England at this time. Hermann Scheere, who was either Flemish or German, was illuminating manuscripts; Herebrecht of Cologne painted an altarpiece for St Paul's Cathedral in 1398; while painters from north Germany were working on the chapter house of Westminster Abbey.

Among native schools, that of East Anglia absorbed these influences most readily, and a work such as the retable preserved in the south choir aisle of Norwich Cathedral has a distinctly German look. Even the English 79 fondness for naturalistically drawn animals and birds now found an echo in the late Gothic art of Europe: the sketchbook in the Pepysian Library 62 of Magdalene College, Cambridge, is distinctly reminiscent of Pisanello. A superb set of hunting tapestries, woven in the second quarter of the fifteenth century in the Netherlands or Burgundy, show the same style in another medium. They may have come to England when Henry VI married Margaret of Anjou in 1445, and were later acquired by the Duke of Devonshire.

When a medieval lord spent money on the arts, his greatest expense would almost certainly be on goldwork and jewellery, which roused an almost mystical rapture in the medieval mind. So much has been destroyed, re-worked and sold, that examples, especially of secular commissions, are rare. One gold cup inlaid with coloured scenes in enamel was made in 1380 for the Duke of Berry; he gave it to his nephew King Charles VI of France in 1391. In 1434 it came into the possession of the greatest of English collectors, the Duke of Bedford, Regent of France, who presented it to Henry V. By a happy chance the cup had left England by the time Cromwell seized the Crown Jewels, and by a yet luckier one it returned in the nineteenth century.

Churches, castles and country houses

Two more fruitful areas of artistic enterprise were the parish churches and the country houses of the nobility. Although in both the supreme achievements came later, under the Tudors, there was a period of exotic fertility from about 1400 to 1480. Chief among the causes of prosperity was the wool trade, which especially benefited the Cotswolds and East Anglia. A church such as Northleach in Gloucestershire bears witness to this prosperity both by its proud scale and by the host of brasses inside commemorating the merchants who paid for it.

The same piety and the same ambition are expressed in the great towers and spires that are so characteristic of Perpendicular architecture. Adorned with delicate tracery, pinnacles and toy-like battlements, they are compositions of pure aesthetic luxury, and still form the inevitable focus of almost every English village and small town. Out of many hundreds one may point to the west tower of St Cuthbert, Wells (1410–30), or the spire of Coventry–now all that remains of the old parish church (it became a cathedral in 1918). The west front of Beverley Minster, with its two sharply defined towers and high central gable, at last achieves in England a façade equalling the French cathedrals of the previous century.

Inside such churches, although the decoration tends to become stereotyped, such features as choir-stalls continued to reflect the inventive talents of ordinary craftsmen with undiminished vigour. Most entertaining of all are the misericords (the carved undersides of hinged tip-up seats) of which many hundreds still survive in all parts of the country. They show scenes from the Bible, popular proverbs, folk tales, and even anti-clerical satire, as well as providing a unique glimpse into the daily life of rural England during the Middle Ages.

Churches were now being filled with increasingly lavish tombs and chantry chapels–separate little rooms screened off from the main spaces by filigree walls and miniature vaults of their own. The most complete surviving example (actually an addition to the fabric of the church) is that of the earls of Warwick, the Beauchamp Chapel in St Mary's, Warwick. It is a combination of architecture, sculpture, stained glass and metalwork that is still practically unchanged since the mid-fifteenth century.

The earls themselves, of course, like most of the older nobility, still lived in their ancestral castles, surrounded by massive walls and a moat. But a new class of gentry was growing up who could afford comfort without needing protection, and around them a new architectural form was evolving: the great manor or country house. It can be traced back to the domestic quarters of castles, to certain sections of the monastic layout and to the large medieval farmhouse. Although it is a topic to be more fully pursued in the next chapter its origins can be briefly traced here.

In the thirteenth century, the Norman keep, within its defended area or bailey, gave way to a new system of fortification consisting of concentric rings of ramparts and towers, which was introduced from the Middle East by returning crusaders. In Britain the best examples are Edward I's

This view is taken from the spot where the shrine of St Thomas à Becket once stood. The chapel stands at the extreme east end of Canterbury Cathedral, on the site of the old Norman Trinity Chapel (hence the name) and represents the work of William the Englishman, carried out after William of Sens had returned to France. The coupled columns, however, are so clearly derived from Sens Cathedral that his influence must still have been decisive. In the background is the so-called 'Corona', a small almost circular chapel, its roof rising higher than the ambulatory vault. The stained glass, depicting stories of the Miracles of St Thomas, is original.

64

STAINED GLASS, CANTERBURY CATHEDRAL

late twelfth century

Canterbury Cathedral is the only place in England where early medieval glass of the highest quality can still be seen in something like its original setting. The windows made for the clerestory east end must date from soon after the reconstruction by William of Sens. They show ancestors of Christ and prophets, large monumental figures reminiscent of those at Chartres. The one illustrated here is Methuselah ('Matusale'). The windows have been moved from their original position and are now in the south transept.

65

EFFIGY OF QUEEN ELEANOR

1291
William Torel
Westminster Abbey, London

Queen Eleanor died in 1290 at Harby, Nottinghamshire, and the route of her funeral procession to Westminster is marked by the Eleanor Crosses erected by her husband Edward I. The gilt-bronze effigy on her tomb was made at the same time as that of Edward's father Henry III. The style is linear and graceful, the face appealing, though it was probably not intended as a portrait. Above her head a trefoil canopy projects with angels' heads and conventional foliage.

castles in Wales. Beaumaris on the Isle of Anglesey, though unfinished, is the clearest and best preserved.

The nucleus of the country house lay in the hall of the castle, which was normally within the inner ring of defences, often with small windows or none at all on the outer side, and larger ones toward the courtyard. Such a hall can be seen at Kenilworth Castle, Warwickshire, which formed part of the home of Richard II's uncle John of Gaunt. The high table would be at one end of the hall, raised on a dais and lit by a specially elaborate window, and the lord's own apartment would be reached by doors at this end. The public entrance would be at the other end, separated from the hall itself by a wooden screen. The kitchen was beyond the screen. This arrangement can be seen in innumerable early houses and still functions at Oxford and Cambridge colleges.

The first of the new-style country houses was Stokesay in Shropshire, dating in its present form from about 1290. It was still fortified with a walled courtyard and a strong tower, but was clearly not primarily a fortress. Old-style castles, on the other hand, continued to be built for another century. Among the last is Bodiam in Sussex, of about 1385, and one cannot help wondering how much of its sturdy towers and wide moat was seriously intended and how much was deliberate, picturesque nostalgia. Towers and battlements, superfluous militarily, became status symbols and enjoyed a prolonged posthumous existence. 'Licence to crenellate' was a valued sign of prestige and one that could be exhibited unmistakably to one's neighbours; witness Herstmonceaux in Sussex (1440) and Oxburgh Hall, Norfolk (1480). The tall gate-tower remained a popular feature well into the Tudor period. A similar tendency to romanticise the Middle Ages just as they are drawing to a close is seen in

66 *left*

EFFIGY OF EDWARD II

c. 1327
alabaster
Gloucester Cathedral

Edward II was brutally murdered at Berkeley Castle in September 1327. For three years the country was ruled by Queen Isabella and her lover Mortimer, and to accept the body of Edward for burial required a certain courage. John Thokey, Abbot of Gloucester, decided to take the risk, and was amply, though posthumously, rewarded. When Edward III seized the crown, the tomb of his murdered father became almost a national shrine. The canopy of the tomb is among the most elaborate ever made and the effigy, in alabaster, a masterpiece of sophisticated art.

67

STOKESAY CASTLE

c. 1270–1300

The hall of Stokesay Castle (the section with the three large windows on the right) was built soon after 1270 and is remarkable for having such an unfortified look. This side faces the courtyard, but there are equally large windows on the other side. To the left of the hall are the private apartments of the lord, and to the left of that a strong defensible tower built about 1291. In that year John de Verdun departed for the crusades and sold his house to Laurence de Ludlow.

the painted wooden shield of about 1480 now in the British Museum, in which a young man wearing Gothic armour pledges himself to die for his lady. In other respects the primary impression of these houses is one of good living, as rich and comfortable as could be managed, but without the pretentious display that became common later. Such was the English scene when Richard III, the last Plantagenet, was killed at Bosworth in 1485 and Henry Tudor, first of a new dynasty, assumed the crown.

Ian Richards

68, 69 *top right*

WELLS CATHEDRAL

c. 1230–60 and later

The west front of Wells is a gigantic screen for the display of sculpture, which here survives in greater quantity than anywhere else in England. Every canopied niche contained a statue, originally coloured. No one can be sure how the first architect intended to finish this façade. The gable belongs to the thirteenth-century fabric, but the two towers (from the base of the gable upwards) were added later; that on the right by William Wynford between 1365 and 1395; that on the left, an identical copy, about thirty years later. The nave illustrates the distinctively national style of Early English architecture, with its emphasis on horizontals and relative neglect of verticals. The strange strainer arch at the end, which has been likened to a gaping hell-mouth, is one of three inserted about 1340 to strengthen the crossing piers after the tower had been placed on them.

70

WESTMINSTER ABBEY

1245–c. 1270
Henry of Reynes

The tall, narrow proportions of Westminster Abbey immediately suggest the great cathedrals of the Ile-de-France, such as Amiens or Rheims; indeed the master-mason probably came from the latter city. As the coronation church of the English kings, it was given every luxury and refinement that the age could supply. Note the carved diaper patterns on the spandrels of the arcade and the doubling of the tracery in the triforium. Since the recent cleaning the contrast between the pale stone of the main fabric and the dark Purbeck marble of the shafts makes a particularly striking effect.

71 *far right*

TOMB OF KING JOHN

soon after 1216
Purbeck marble
life-size
Worcester Cathedral

'First', says the will dictated by King John before he died at Newark on October 18th, 1216, 'I desire that my body be buried in the church of the Blessed Virgin and St Wulfstan at Worcester'. He was buried, where he still lies, in the choir of the cathedral, between the shrines of St Oswald and St Dunstan, who are shown as tiny figures on each side of his head. This is the earliest royal effigy in England and, although probably not intended as a portrait, gives a strong impression of what we know of John's character.

72 *above*

MOSES

1200–10
Yorkshire Museum, York

This is one of several statues from the now
ruined abbey of St Mary, York. They are
not only of high quality in themselves but
are of unusual interest in being the only
known examples in England of true
figures-colonne, sculptured figures which
flank the portals of the great French twelfth
and thirteenth-century cathedrals. With
their heavy drapery, large heads and
stylised hair, they are closest to work at
Sens of about 1190–1200. Moses holds the
Tablet of the Law in one hand, the Brazen
Serpent in the other.

73 *top left*

SALISBURY CATHEDRAL
1220–60; tower and spire 1334–c. 1350

The cathedral is seen here from the north-
east, and the distinct articulation of each
part, characteristic of Early English, is well
illustrated. On the extreme left is the lady
chapel, with its aisle. Then rises the gable of
the choir and the two transepts, each with
their eastern aisle. On the right, the corner
of the west front is just visible. The famous
tower and spire, which now seem so inevitable, were in fact not intended by the
original builders, but were added nearly a
century later and rest on slender piers that
have needed constant strengthening ever
since.

74

WESTMINSTER HALL ROOF

1394–1402, Hugh Herland, London

The walls of Westminster Hall go back to the time of William Rufus; it was 240 feet long and nearly seventy feet wide, and the timber roof was supported on two rows of pillars. In 1394 Richard II decided to demolish the pillars and cover the whole space in one enormous span. His master-carpenter, Hugh Herland, utilised the hammer-beam system, then still in its experimental stage. Although the hammer-beams, ending in carved angels, are over twenty feet long and a yard thick, the whole roof achieves an effect of lightness by the delicate tracery between braces, trusses, hammer-beams and rafters.

75 *centre*

THE ADORATION OF THE MAGI

from the Queen Mary Psalter (MS Royal 2bVII fol. 112v.)
early fourteenth century, British Museum, London

The main picture is set within a sort of formalised church, with tiny figures of saints in niches at the sides. Underneath, the initial D of Dominus contains a small scene of God appearing to a king, while at the bottom is a purely gratuitous sketch of foxes. The psalter was probably painted in an East Anglian monastery, and was given its name because it was owned by Mary I.

76

BEAUMARIS CASTLE

1295–98, Anglesey

Beaumaris was the last of the great chain of fortresses built by Edward I to guard his recently conquered territory of North Wales. It is a perfect example of the concentrically planned castle, a type which became standard about this time throughout Europe, replacing the earlier motte-and-bailey. It has a moat, an outer rampart and an inner rampart with ten massive towers. Beaumaris was never finished and the only real fighting it saw was in 1403 when it was besieged by Owen Glendower.

SYON COPE

detail
early fourteenth century
embroidery of silk, silver and gold thread
whole cope 115 × 56 in (292 × 142 cm)
Victoria and Albert Museum, London

English needlework, known as Opus
Anglicanum, was famous throughout
Europe during the Middle Ages and was
eagerly sought after. Many of the most
splendid examples are in cathedral treas-
uries abroad (one is in Pienza and another
in Toledo), and the Syon Cope itself was
almost lost to the country when the Bri-
gittine convent of Syon, which owned it,
was suppressed by Henry VIII and the
nuns were forced to emigrate. Fortunately
they returned with it in the nineteenth
century. This detail shows St Michael
defeating a two-headed dragon.

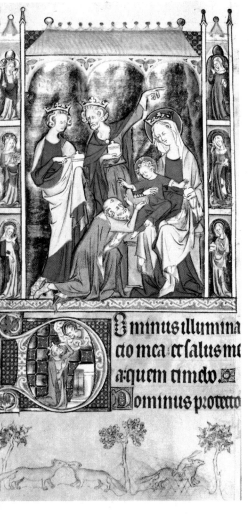

78 *right*

BOOK OF HOURS

c. 1308
Fitzwilliam Museum, Cambridge
(MS 292 f. 29 r.)

The illuminated initial D of Domine shows
Christ Blessing, but the most attractive
feature of this manuscript is the series of
animal scenes round the borders. They
have no relation to the text and were
clearly put there just for entertainment.
The squirrel on the left seems to be praying.

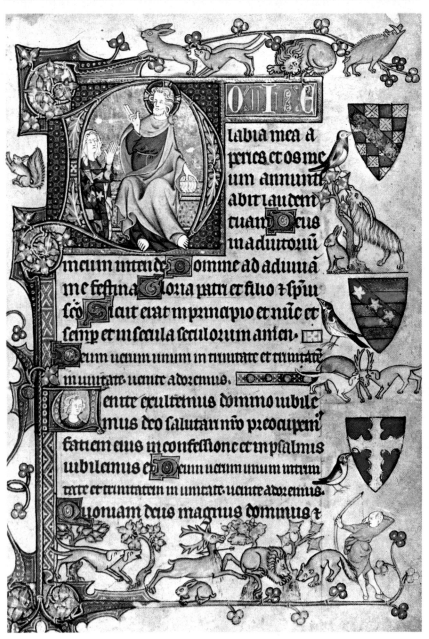

79 *left*

THE NORWICH RETABLE *detail*

c. 1380–90
tempera on wood, h. 34·5 (86 cm)
south choir aisle of Norwich Cathedral

The whole retable consists of five panels, and was probably made for the high altar of Norwich Cathedral. The style is close to that of the German Meister Bertram, the International Gothic artist from Hamburg, but is almost certainly by native East-Anglian painters. This panel shows the Resurrection. It still follows a fairly strict iconographic convention, without much attempt at naturalism. The pictures are full of interesting details, for example the two eagles at the top, who carry shields painted with the instruments of the Passion.

80
ROYAL GOLD CUP
c. 1380, gold and coloured enamel
British Museum, London

The cup illustrates the life of St Agnes, the daughter of a wealthy Roman of the time of Constantine, who vowed herself to God. In the first scene, at the bottom, she is being wooed by Procopius, who offers her a box of jewels, which she refuses. Procopius attempted to rape her and was strangled by a demon; Agnes stands by his prostrate body and miraculously restores him to life. In the next scene he kneels before her in repentance, but she was arrested and condemned for her faith. Finally she is shown being burnt at the stake while an executioner stabs her.

81 *below*
THE WILTON DIPTYCH
c. 1380
tempera on gesso, on oak panels
14·5 × 21 in (35 × 53 cm)
National Gallery, London

This was probably the altarpiece of a small chapel, but the circumstances of its commission are completely unknown. It shows Richard II as a young man kneeling with his patron saints, Edmund King and Martyr (killed by the Danes), Edward the Confessor and John the Baptist. The opposite side shows the Virgin and Child with a host of angels all wearing Richard's badge of the white hart. The painting is one of the masterpieces of the style known as International Gothic.

The accession of Henry VII is not an event in the history of art. There is, in fact, no Tudor style. It was a transitional age, when the momentum of the Middle Ages was dying down and genuine response to the Renaissance showed only fitfully. Yet Gothic – the Perpendicular style – still had a few splendid revelations in store. These appear especially in three buildings that are linked in patronage and background – the three royal chapels of King's College, Cambridge, of St George at Windsor and of Henry VII at Westminster.

Much of the dramatic effect of these three chapels is produced by that distinctively English fourteenth-century invention, the fan-vault. Many different forms of this were evolved, all of which made it possible to continue the all-over panelling of walls and windows on to the vault itself, and this is no doubt one reason why they appealed so strongly to the architects of the time.

The earliest known examples of fan-vaulting are the cloister at Gloucester, and in the chapter house at Hereford (now destroyed). Both date from around 1370 and both were on a fairly small scale. The idea was taken up more ambitiously a hundred years later at Sherborne Abbey in Dorset and the Divinity School at Oxford. By about 1500 the three royal chapels, as well as such works as the retrochoir of Peterborough Cathedral and

89 the choir of Bath Abbey, were under construction, all exploiting the device to the full.

King's College, Cambridge, has a complicated history. It was founded by Henry VI in 1440 to accommodate a provost, ten priests, six clerks, sixteen choristers and seventy scholars. The king at the same time founded Eton College, and it is clear that the whole scheme was in conscious emulation of William of Wykeham's foundations – Winchester College and New College, Oxford.

Some minor college buildings were built at Cambridge, but of the 'Great Court', which had been planned on a grand scale, only the chapel was ever begun. Work was frequently interrupted. The Lancastrians vacated the throne and the Yorkists took their place, to be succeeded by the Tudors. By then most of the walls were standing but it was roofless. In 1505 Henry VII ordered the work to be resumed under his own patronage, but he died four years later and it was completed under his son Henry VIII.

90 The architect of this final phase was John Wastell, who built the fan-vault (which had not been planned originally) and unified the whole design with admirable clarity. The chapel is a plain rectangle with turrets at the corners. There is a large window at each end and a succession of large windows with identical tracery down the sides. Inside, the effect is enriched by the stained glass, the very elaborate stalls and screen and the deeply undercut heraldic carving. Seldom has a single architectural idea been realised so lucidly.

83 St George's Chapel, Windsor, has a parallel history. It dated originally from the thirteenth century, and was the chapel of the Order of the Garter. The chivalrous-minded Yorkist king, Edward IV, decided to rebuild it on a lavish scale and perhaps to make it the new royal burial place, as the choir of Westminster Abbey was full, an idea which was taken up by Henry VII.

As at Cambridge, Henry VII continued work begun by his predecessors and his son Henry VIII presided over its completion. The two buildings share many of the same qualities, but at Windsor the economy of line is compromised by two embryo-transepts (hardly more than big bow-windows) which form a crossing intended originally to have been crowned by a tower. The only true fan-vault is under the crossing. Elsewhere there

The Growth of Secular Patronage

1485-1603

82

HENRY VIII

1542
Hans Holbein the Younger 1497–1543
oil and tempera on oak
36·5 × 26·5 in (92 × 67 cm)
Castle Howard, Yorkshire

This portrait, which was only positively identified as Holbein's in 1933 by the discovery of his initials and the date on the staff, forms a marked contrast with his early portrait of the king for Whitehall. In this one Henry is nearing the end of his life; the painter's art cannot disguise the puffiness of the face and the thick fingers. He wears a surcoat of red Venetian velvet, embroidered with pearls and gold, and carries a black staff. The picture has belonged to the Howard family since at least the early seventeenth century.

are variations of the Perpendicular all-over pattern, with much deep undercutting.

Undoubtedly the virtuoso piece of the three royal chapels is that at Westminster. It replaced a former lady chapel at the east end of the abbey, and was begun by Henry VII partly as his own chantry-chapel and partly as a shrine for King Henry VI, the saintly monarch who had been murdered by the Yorkists and whom Henry VII hoped might be canonised.

91 Everything that money and ingenuity could do was lavished on this chapel. It consists of a central 'nave' with aisles on either side and a chevet of chapels at the end. Every surface, both inside and out, is covered with the familiar Perpendicular grid pattern. The exterior is extravagant enough, but is surpassed by the interior. Over the main arcade is a close row of statues, each in a niche covered by an elaborate canopy. Above them rises the clerestory, and above that the amazing pendant vault. A whole team of sculptors worked on the chapel; many of them were from the Netherlands, and the sculpture is still exceptionally well preserved.

The centre of the chapel is taken up by the tomb of Henry VII. At first sight this also seems firmly in the Gothic tradition. It is surrounded by a bronze screen made by an English metalworker, Lawrence Imber. Effigies of King Henry and his queen lie gazing upwards with folded hands, very much like those of the other kings and queens nearby. It is only when one looks at the tomb-chest that one notices that it is pure Italian Renaissance.

The explanation is simple. The sculptor was Pietro Torrigiani, the Florentine, who came to England in about 1512, probably at Henry VIII's own invitation. He brought with him a style that had matured for nearly a hundred years in Italy, but which was completely new to Englishmen. In place of their ogees, trefoils and canopies, they saw classical pilasters, round arches and medallions; instead of angels and 'weepers' they saw healthy saints in Roman armour or classical drapery and smiling *putti*.

Torrigiani did several other works for Henry VIII and his court: the altar of the chapel, of which part remains, the tombs of Lady Margaret Beaufort and the Master of the Rolls, Dr Younge (now in the Public Record Office), and a portrait roundel of Sir Thomas Lovell. He left England for Spain in 1519, but others of his countrymen remained. One of them became Serjeant Painter to the king, and members of the same group must have been responsible for the screen and stalls of King's College Chapel, donated by Henry VIII in 1535.

Henry VIII is a man of considerable importance in the story of English art. In his early years he represented the best in the intellectual life of his time. He was talented in music and poetry, well read in classical literature, and jealous of the prestige of his young rival Francis I of France. One of his first acts on succeeding to the throne was to summon Erasmus: 'Come to England, and assure yourself a hearty welcome. You shall name your own terms; they shall be as liberal and honourable as you please. ... We shall regard your presence among us as the most precious possession that we have.'

Henry spent lavishly the money saved by his more prudent father. At the Field of the Cloth of Gold in 1520 he and Francis attempted to outshine each other and produced a magnificent spectacle which must certainly have been good for the pockets of the artists and craftsmen. When the French king began to build himself the great show-place of Chambord, Henry countered with Nonsuch Palace (now destroyed).

That was not until 1538. By then the 'antique' taste was well established. Cardinal Wolsey imported Italian workmen to enrich his palace of

83 *top*
ST GEORGE'S CHAPEL
WINDSOR *begun 1475*

The south side of St George's Chapel has a strangely un-Gothic symmetry, which is possibly a sign of readiness for Renaissance ideas. In the centre is the small transept, with polygonal sides and standard Perpendicular tracery. On each side of it are the nave and chancel, both seven bays long, and at each end a small polygonal chapel, that at the far end with two later storeys added to it. The buttresses all end in tall pinnacles crowned by carvings of the Queen's Beasts—modern restorations, but close copies of the original features.

84
CHURCH OF ST PETER
AND ST PAUL

c. 1495–1525
Lavenham

Lavenham church, built on slightly rising ground away from the town, is a perfect embodiment of the civic pride that inspired its builders, the rich Suffolk wool merchants. The tall tower and nave with its big windows of grid-like tracery are characteristic of Perpendicular churches all over the country, but the use of knapped flint for the tower marks it out as East Anglian. The chapel in the centre, with the three large windows, is that of the Springe family, the chief patrons of the church.

Hampton Court (relinquished to his master in 1525). The terra-cotta roundels of Roman emperors on the two gateways are by Giovanni da Maiano and his so-called 'closet' has an Italianate ceiling. Most interesting of all, and least known, is his own tomb which he commissioned from another Italian, Benedetto da Rovezzano. It is of black marble, an exercise in pure classicism. Wolsey, having no doubt enjoyed it in life, was denied it in death, and after his fall it lay unused for three centuries.

Henry's other palaces show the same combination of late Gothic structure with Renaissance ornament. They include the additions to Hampton Court (notably the Great Hall), Whitehall Palace (destroyed) and Nonsuch. The last was the most ambitious. It was demolished in 1687 and only a few doubtful fragments remain, but from documents and from the description left by John Evelyn it is certain that most of the decoration was carried out by foreigners – either Italian, Flemish or Dutch. An interesting item of royal furniture from one of these palaces still survives – a small table-desk covered with painted leather. Inside the lid are figures of **94** Mars and Venus copied from contemporary German woodcuts.

The idea of collecting works of art for their own sake had not yet occurred to anyone in England. Pictures were valued almost entirely for the subjects they represented – mainly, of course, portraits. Henry VIII did indeed own a Raphael (the only great Renaissance artist of that time known at first hand in England), but that had been presented to his father by Castiglione when he came over in 1560 on an embassy from the Duke of Urbino. Like everyone else Henry chiefly wanted portraits, but he also liked pictures with a political message. From Girolamo da Treviso he commissioned a series of anti-papal pictures, one of which showed the Evangelists beating the Pope with their Gospels.

By far the most outstanding visitor from abroad was Hans Holbein the **82, 98,** Younger. English painting had been killed by the Reformation, church **110** and monastic patronage dried up, and there was no one with any training in the new secular art that was coming into demand in Europe. Palaces had never been decorated with grand mural schemes (the English had always preferred wooden panelling and tapestries) and the only commissions left were portraits of the court and aristocracy, for which there was meagre native tradition. Holbein therefore had the field to himself.

He was born at Augsburg in 1497, migrated to Basel in 1519 and to England in 1532. His draughtsmanship inherits the clear-cut realism of Dürer, but his study of Italian painting had given him a technical range, humanist sympathies and a formal dignity that made him already a unique artist. His earlier works, especially the terrifying *Dead Christ* at Basel, show that probably his deepest vein was religious – a vein for which England gave little scope. But he belonged to the enlightened circle of Erasmus and More (both of whom he painted), and it is to him more than to anyone else that we owe our image of the Tudor monarchy. Henry **82** employed him widely, though not as widely as he deserved. His largest undertaking was a group portrait of the king with his parents and his current queen, Jane Seymour, painted in fresco in 1537 on the wall of the Privy Chamber at Whitehall. The fresco has long disappeared, but part of Holbein's cartoon survives. His other existing English works are all single portraits, except for the large, confident canvas *The Ambassadors* painted **110** in 1533. His drawings, of which there is a large collection at Windsor, are often masterpieces in their own right.

After the middle years of Henry VIII's reign royal patronage virtually ceased in England until the time of James I. Edward VI lived for too short a time to interest himself in the arts and Mary Tudor had other concerns.

85
THE VYVYAN SALT
1592–93
'W. H.'
silver-gilt
h. 13·5 in (34 cm)
Victoria and Albert Museum, London

The main body of the salt is set with panels of glass painted at the back with flowers so that the pattern shines through, in the technique of *verre églomisé*. These flower designs are based on an English emblem-book published six years earlier. The lid, which has medallions in the same technique showing heroes of antiquity (on this side, Cyrus) is supported on lacy filigree legs and surmounted by a figure of Justice holding scales and a sword. The salt originally belonged to the Vyvyan family of Trelowarren, Cornwall.

Elizabeth deliberately encouraged her subjects to spend large sums on building and entertainment to save herself the expense. There is therefore no 'court style' in England between Holbein and Inigo Jones and to follow the story of the arts one must look to the churches and to the country houses of the nobility.

Ecclesiastical architecture

The monasteries were by this time hopelessly in decline, but until the 1530s the cathedrals and parish churches were still a vital force artistically. Although no major projects were initiated in Tudor times, spectacular additions such as towers, chapels, screens and stalls could still be afforded. The central tower of Canterbury, 'Bell Harry', was built shortly before 1500 by John Wastell. Oxford Cathedral vault (c. 1480–1500) was a trial run for the Henry VII Chapel. Ripon gave itself a new nave between 1502 and 1522, at which point the work remained dramatically abandoned. The presbytery and lady chapel of Winchester were rebuilt at about the same time, and there are many other instances.

While the architecture of such churches remains wholly English, many of the men who worked on their decoration were foreigners. This applies particularly to the art of stained glass, in which the leading craftsmen were from Flanders. Two series of their windows survive almost complete, at Fairford in Gloucestershire (1495–1505) and at King's College Chapel, **93, 92** Cambridge (1515–31). In both, the Flemish characteristics are easy to see: the use of the window as a sort of transparent painting, the same scene often taking up several lights and ignoring the mullions; the fantastic architectural backgrounds deriving from northern Mannerism, and the interest in rich costumes, jewellery and heavy draperies.

In East Anglia, the Cotswolds and the West Country, magnificent **109** Perpendicular parish churches were still being built up to the very eve of the Reformation. A neat illustration of the new patronage and its relation to the class structure is provided by Lavenham, a rich wool town in Suffolk. Here a large new church was built between about 1486 and 1523. **84** As was traditional, the chancel was paid for by the lord of the manor, John de Vere, Earl of Oxford, and the nave and tower by the townsmen, chief among them a wool-merchant called Thomas Springe. The next few generations saw the merging of the two families, when Springe's great-grand-daughter married a great-grandson of the earl.

The effect of the Reformation

The Reformation is crucial to the story of art in England. The building of churches ceased, abbeys were despoiled of their treasures, many forms of religious art were rejected as 'popish', and the artists who created them had to look elsewhere for their patronage. Much of it was literally thrown into the melting-pot; the cartloads of church plate removed by Henry's officers were soon to reappear, new-minted, as the cups, bowls, and salt-cellars commissioned by the rich new class that was coming into existence. On the long communal tables of medieval and Tudor halls, the 'salt' was placed in the centre; distinguished guests sat nearest the host 'above the salt', humbler ones and retainers below it. Salts came in an intriguing variety of shapes. In some, human or animal figures support the bowl; others were composed of architectural elements; others took the form of hour-glasses. The Mostyn Salt (1586), though fairly sober in outline, has a wealth of gay decoration in relief, and the Vyvyan Salt, of a few years later, **85** with its lacy filigree legs and panels of painted glass, looks almost Rococo.

English silverware of the period shows the same eager acceptance of Renaissance ideas evident in other fields and often some precious or exotic object from abroad was used as the nucleus for a display of craftsmanship.

86 One of the best examples is the ivory and silver-gilt Howard Grace Cup.

The change from ecclesiastical to secular patronage might not in other circumstances have entailed a stylistic change, but at this particular time and place it did. The old patron had retained the religious values of the past, but the new patron was a humanist, or at least a man educated on the fringe of humanism. He knew what he ought to admire–the art of ancient Rome and its modern representatives the great Italian masters–but not always how to recognise it when he saw it. This was therefore the first great age of intellectual snobbery. The class which read Erasmus's *Adages* as a short-cut to classical literature formed an eager public for the pattern books and illustrated editions of Vitruvius which offered a short-cut to classical art. As one's Latin style had to be 'correct', so had one's classical detail.

It was the miniature architecture of tombs that offered the first field for innovation, and even here the appetite for change was limited. The tomb of Lord De La Warr at Boxgrove in Sussex shows Renaissance cupids alternating in the same band of panels with medieval angels. At Layer Marney in Essex, the first Lord Marney probably employed French craftsmen. They used a wealth of authentic Renaissance ornament in terra-cotta, modernising the details, though leaving the form of the tomb as a whole recognisably what it had been before. There are comparable tombs nearby at Norwich, Wymondham and Oxburgh, and the manor-house of Layer Marney itself has terra-cotta decoration of the same type round the windows, doubtless by the same team of artists.

This is characteristic of the way in which Renaissance ideas were even then being assimilated. They were regarded essentially as interesting details; Tudor builders were taking over the separate motifs without enquiring into the rules by which they were to be used. Even the development of domestic planning, which evolved in the direction of symmetry, compactness and proportion, was only distantly related to a similar evolution abroad, at least until the time of Robert Smythson.

During the first half of the sixteenth century there were two major types of country-house plan–one using the old 'castle' tradition of a courtyard or several courtyards; the other a single block with ends projecting at right-angles, which with the addition of a central porch became the 'E-plan'. Of the first type the finest example from Henry **101** VIII's reign is Hengrave Hall in Suffolk, whose gatehouse displays the same naive mixture of Gothic and Renaissance forms found in the tombs. It was built for a rich merchant, Sir Thomas Kytson, between 1530 and 1540. The E-plan, which goes back to the medieval manor-house, is first seen fully developed at Barrington Court in about 1530.

The square courtyard-plan normally comprised a gatehouse, hall, chapel, kitchen, living-rooms, guests' and servants' quarters and cellars. There were no special positions for any of these parts, except that the gate-house had to be in the centre of one of the sides. As the century progressed, there was a general tendency to tighten and formalise this loose conglomeration and to regularise the planning from a visual point of view. It was above all in the re-assessment and re-positioning of the hall that the most striking transformation took place. In eighty years it was to change from being the main meeting and eating place of the house to being a grand vestibule placed directly in the centre of the entrance front.

Henry VIII died in 1547. His son Edward VI was a minor, and the government was in the hands of the Lord Protector, Edward Seymour, Duke of Somerset, who fell from power in 1551, was charged with treason and felony and executed.

86

THE HOWARD GRACE CUP

c. 1525
ivory, silver-gilt, pearls and garnets
h. 12 in (30·5 cm)
Victoria and Albert Museum, London

The cup itself is ivory, mounted on a silver stand and covered by a silver lid. It is notable not only for the beauty of its materials and craftsmanship, but also for the way in which it mixes Gothic and Renaissance motifs. The band of lettering round the rim looks back to the fifteenth century, but the flowers, foliage and the figure on the top show a knowledge of contemporary Italian art. The whole inscription reads: 'VINVM TVVM BIBE CVM GAVDIO'–'Drink your wine joyfully.'

It was Somerset who presided over the second stage of the Reformation in England, and he set the stamp of his personality strongly on the intellectual life of his age. Old Somerset House, which he built between 1547 and his death, has been called 'unquestionably one of the most influential buildings of the English Renaissance'. Although it has entirely disappeared its appearance is known from drawings. The direct inspiration of the design was French rather than Italian, but it is safe to say that until the 1620s there was no other building that gave Englishmen such a convincing idea of Renaissance architecture.

They could learn a little more from books. In 1550 John Dudley, Duke of Northumberland, sent one of his household, John Shute, to Italy as a sort of research-assistant in classical architecture. The fruits of his visit were published in 1563 as *The First and Chief Grounds of Architecture*, the first treatise on the subject in English.

The circle of men which gathered round Protector Somerset during his brief period of power is of great interest. One member of it was Sir William Sharington, who bought the old nunnery of Lacock in Wiltshire in 1540 and proceeded to remodel it to his own sophisticated taste. A fireplace and part of an Ionic arcade survive, but the most impressive items are two octagonal stone tables made to go in the rooms of an octagonal tower; one is Italian in derivation, the other Flemish – both were unique in England at that time.

Another of Somerset's friends was Sir John Thynne, traveller, scholar 103 and dilettante, the builder of Longleat in Wiltshire. The history of this house is complicated. It was begun in 1554, but its present appearance seems to date from after 1568. Compared with Old Somerset House, Longleat is conservative and seems to look back towards Perpendicular.

87 At Kirby Hall in Northamptonshire, built about 1570, the inner courtyard is utilised on a grand scale and Renaissance motifs appear in a form that would have been up to date even in Italy. There is a definite desire for classical symmetry in the elevation, and the giant pilaster linking two storeys had been first used by Michelangelo only thirty years before.

The Elizabethan era

Queen Elizabeth came to the throne in 1558; a circumstance important for several reasons. Firstly, she provided a stable and continuous government and a focus for loyalty and patriotic feeling such as Englishmen had not known for a generation. There is in many fields of Elizabethan art – in music, in poetry, in the drama and in architecture (though not in sculpture and painting) – a freshness and an appetite for experiment that makes the parallel with Quattrocento Italy more than superficial. Secondly, Elizabeth's own contradictory personality – luxury-loving yet mean, vain yet shrewd, dependent yet independent – produced a situation in which the functions of a court art were transferred from monarch to subjects. Instead of the court dazzling the country (as at Rome, Paris and Madrid), it was the country that had to dazzle the court. The queen's public life was spent largely in ceremonial visits (progresses) to her nobility, and the houses where she stayed became palaces – grandiose, extravagant buildings so aptly christened by Sir John Summerson 'prodigy houses'.

England is rich in Elizabethan houses. Two of the grandest, but not for that reason the least typical, are Wollaton Hall, Nottinghamshire, and Hardwick Hall, Derbyshire.

88 Wollaton was built for Sir Francis Willoughby, Sheriff of Nottingham, between 1580 and 1585. The architect was Robert Smythson, who had worked for Thynne at Longleat. He devised an ingenious plan that abolished the courtyard altogether and made all four fronts symmetrical and

87 *top*
KIRBY HALL
1570–75

In the centre of the south side of the courtyard stands the three-storey porch leading to a 'screens passage' which in turn opens into the hall – the three large windows to the right. The two most remarkable features of Kirby are first, the advanced Renaissance detailing, especially the giant pilasters, and second, the way in which the wall on the other side of the porch has been disguised to look symmetrical with that of the hall. This side is in fact divided into two storeys by a floor cutting across the middle of the window. The first-floor window of the porch, with its broken segmental pediment, is an addition of 1638.

88

WOLLATON HALL

1580–88
Robert Smythson

Wollaton is one of the earliest examples of deliberate medievalism in architecture. The pilasters, obelisks and Flemish strapwork are completely up to date, but the turrets at the corners of the central block and its crudely traceried windows are intended to conjure up the age of chivalry. These windows belong to a great chamber built directly over the hall, which is lit by the smaller windows just visible above the balustrade.

almost identical, a unity of conception that places Wollaton immediately with Renaissance rather than medieval planning. The ornament, which is applied everywhere without stint, is also basically classical in origin, with demi-columns, pilasters and friezes, and at the top Flemish strapwork and miniature obelisks copied from the pattern books of Vredeman de Vries. In other respects, however, Smythson was conservatively English. The windows have the mullions and transoms of Perpendicular, and even in places a kind of debased tracery: the corners are marked by four square towers and the central section by tourelles, like a medieval castle. The hall, too, retains traditional features, with its dais at one end and screens passage at the other. It was in combining all these disparate elements that Smythson showed his talents, and the whole composition is both logical and bizarre in almost equal proportions.

The architect of Hardwick Hall (1590–97), who may well have been **102** Smythson too, rejected tradition altogether. Here for the first time the hall stands in the centre of the façade and is accepted frankly as a grand vestibule. It is from Hardwick that one must date the eventual separation of hall from dining-room.

Bess of Hardwick, for whom it was built, was a formidable character, and the house was very much her personal creation. Born in 1520, she was four times married (the first time at the age of twelve) and four times widowed. Every marriage left her richer than before, enabling her to indulge without inhibition her passion for building. Her last husband was the Earl of Shrewsbury, who died in 1590, only one month before Hardwick was begun. It was finished and occupied by 1596. Around the parapets of its four corner towers are carved the proud initials E.S. – Elizabeth of Shrewsbury – silhouetted against the sky.

The house lives up to the old tag about 'Hardwick Hall, more glass than wall'. This was certainly deliberate, since some of the windows are 'dummies' put in to give an effect of symmetry. The interior is well preserved and gives an excellent idea of Elizabethan furnishing and decoration. In the High Great Chamber is a fine set of Brussels tapestries, purchased in 1587, telling the story of Penelope, to whom Bess liked to compare herself. Two other parts of Hardwick may be noted as typical of the time and significant for the future. One is the development of the staircase as a monumental feature in its own right; the other is the 'long gallery' occupying the whole east front of the house, a feature of which Elizabethan patrons were particularly fond.

An alternative to Flemish tapestry was English embroidery, an aristocratic occupation. When Mary Queen of Scots was in the care of Bess of Hardwick (then Duchess of Devonshire) in 1570, they worked together on a set of four hangings, of which three complete sections are at Oxburgh Hall in Norfolk and one, cut up into small pieces, is in the Victoria and Albert Museum. The style is not of continental finesse, but like most English work of the period it has great vitality.

English sculpture during Elizabeth's reign was equally unsophisticated. Much ornamental carving – on the screens of halls, for example – is almost folk art. Practically all the serious work is on tombs, and the best is by foreigners. The medieval formula of a recumbent effigy was being enlivened by new poses from the continent. The dead person might be shown kneeling, or reclining propped up on one elbow, head on hand, 'as if they died of the toothache', as John Webster said. Classical details became the rule rather than the exception. The tomb of the brothers Philip and Thomas Hoby at Bisham in Berkshire is a good example of the **104** new tendencies, and may well be of French workmanship.

89 *right*

BATH ABBEY

1500 onwards

This building occupies the site of a much larger Benedictine abbey church, demolished about 1500. The new abbey was one of the last such enterprises to be begun before the Reformation. The choir, with its grandiose fan-vaulting, was finished by 1525, but the nave for a long time remained a carcass. It became a parish church in 1560, was completed with a plaster vault in 1616 and given its present stone vault in the nineteenth century.

90 *top right*

KING'S COLLEGE CHAPEL

1440–1515
Cambridge

King's College Chapel displays all the resources of the Perpendicular style at its best: the virtual elimination of the wall by a grid of windows filled with coloured glass, the fan-vaulting with its disciplined network of ornament, and the deeply-cut heraldic sculpture. The repetitive identical patterns achieve an effect of the utmost splendour combined with clarity. In the centre is the screen and organ case with angels, almost certainly made by Italian artists for Henry VIII.

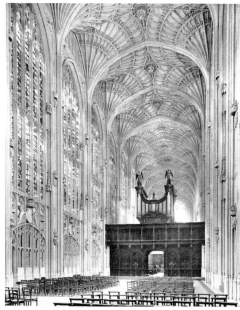

91

HENRY VII'S CHAPEL,

Westminster Abbey, London
1503–12

Outstanding as the chapel is for its sculpture and furnishings, it is the vault which first catches the attention. This is the end of the long story of Gothic architecture, after which no further development was possible. It has been called 'a superbly ingenious fantasy on the theme of fan-vaulting'. The stone pendants seem to hang in defiance of gravity like fruit from a tree. On the right is the bronze screen enclosing the tomb of Henry VII by Torrigiani. Here the Gothic and Renaissance styles meet.

92

EAST WINDOW, KING'S COLLEGE CHAPEL

c. 1526
Cambridge

The whole of the east window is devoted to one united scene telling the story of the Passion. It is divided into six sections of three lights, each containing one episode. Starting from the lower left-hand section, they show Ecce Homo, Pilate washing his hands and Christ carrying the Cross; then on the upper level, Christ being nailed to the Cross, the Crucifixion and the Deposition. It has been proved fairly definitely that the designer of this window was the Fleming Dirk Vellert from Antwerp, and that the actual painting was done by Galyon Hone, who also came from Holland or Flanders, and held the office of King's Glazier to Henry VIII.

93 *below*

STAINED GLASS

c. 1500
St Mary's Church, Fairford

Fairford parish church was completely rebuilt at the expense of a rich merchant, John Tame, who died in 1500. He provided not only the building, but also stained glass for its windows – twenty-eight in all, mostly consisting of four parts. The glaziers were almost certainly Flemish, though the glass was designed to fit the Fairford windows. This one shows Eve and the Serpent, Moses and the Burning Bush, Gideon and the Fleece and Solomon and the Queen of Sheba.

94 *top left*

HENRY VIII'S TABLE-DESK

c.1525
wood covered with painted and gilt leather
Victoria and Albert Museum, London

This is known to have been in one of
Henry VIII's palaces because it is listed in
an inventory made at his death. It is really
a box with drawers and compartments
inside for writing materials, which could
be closed and carried from place to place.
The painting on the lid is particularly
interesting: the royal coat-of-arms is held
by *putti*, and on either side are figures of
Mars and Venus. These are coloured
versions of woodcuts published about 1510
by the German artist Hans Burgkmair.
Burgkmair had been to Italy and his work
shows the mixture of styles so much
admired by the early Tudor court.

95 *top centre*

THE ARMADA JEWEL

c.1588
gold, diamonds and rubies, h. 2·75 in (7 cm)
Victoria and Albert Museum, London

This locket was given by Queen Elizabeth
to Sir Thomas Heneage, her treasurer
during the time of the Armada. It bears her
own portrait bust on the front and a miniature of her inside – possibly the work of
Nicholas Hilliard. On the back is a picture
of the Ark with the inscription 'Saevas
tranquilla per undas' ('peaceful amid the
fierce waves'). Around the edge are
diamonds and rubies in a setting of
enamelled gold.

96 *far left*

QUEEN MARY TUDOR

1554, Antonio Moro c. 1520 – c. 1575
oil on panel, 45 × 33 in (114 × 84 cm)
Castle Ashby

Moro was a Fleming – his real name was
Anthonis Mor – who made his reputation
in Spain and the Spanish Netherlands, and
visited England at about the same time as
his patron Philip II married Mary Tudor.
His portrait brings the sad queen vividly to
life, her unhappiness not making her in the
least more appealing. The formality of
Moro's style was an important influence on
Hans Eworth (**106**), but like Zuccaro (**107**)
he did not stay long enough in England to
give native painting much of his own high
quality.

97

THE ERMINE PORTRAIT

1585
oil on wood, 37·5 × 34 in (95 × 86 cm)
Hatfield House

This portrait illustrates both the exaggerated flattery that Elizabeth expected from
her courtiers and the typically Elizabethan
love of involved 'conceits'. The ermine
symbolised virginity because of its white
coat, and its fur was a traditional mark of
royalty. The jewels – diamonds, topazes
and pearls – also stood for purity. The
sword, of course, is the attribute of Justice.
How far the picture may be trusted as a
portrait is doubtful; the queen was fifty-
two when it was painted.

99 *right*
ALICE HILLIARD

1578
Nicholas Hilliard 1547–1619
oil, diameter 2·5 in (6 cm)
Victoria and Albert Museum, London

Hilliard's beautiful first wife was the daughter of a goldsmith, Robert Brandon, to whom he had been apprenticed when he first came to London in 1562. The wedding took place in 1576, when she was twenty. The miniature dates from two years later when the couple were living in France. She wears a flower-patterned dress, a lace ruff and black bonnet in the French fashion. On each side is the monogram N.H. The frame is later, but incorporates the coats-of-arms of Hilliard and Brandon.

98
ANNE OF CLEVES

1539
Hans Holbein the Younger 1497–1543
watercolour
diameter 1·75 in (4 cm)
Victoria and Albert Museum, London

After Jane Seymour's death in 1537, Henry VIII at once began looking for a new wife. Anne of Cleves was among a number of possibilities and Holbein was sent to Germany to paint her picture (he performed several other commissions of the same kind). The result was the large portrait now in the Louvre, of which the miniature shown here is a smaller version made by Holbein shortly afterwards. There is a persistent story that Henry agreed to marry Anne on the strength of this portrait, but when they actually met found that he 'liked the picture better than the original'. At any rate, he married her in January 1540 and divorced her in July of the same year.

100
RICHARD SACKVILLE, THIRD EARL OF DORSET

1616
Isaac Oliver d. 1617
watercolour
9·25 × 6 in (23 × 15 cm)
Victoria and Albert Museum, London

Oliver's feeling for the miniature was less subtle than Hilliard's, and many of his portraits look like reduced versions of pictures conceived on a larger scale. In this example the rich curtains behind the earl are draped in a way that recalls Venetian painting, which Oliver had known at first hand. But he fails to overcome the stiff formality that was the legacy of Tudor portraiture.

101

HENGRAVE HALL

1525–38

Hengrave was built as the country seat of a London merchant. Its showpiece is the porch. Several features are typically Perpendicular – the flanking turrets, the four-centred arch, even the trefoil-shaped bow window – but the sculpture, by a man recorded as John Sparke, shows clear knowledge of French or Italian models.

102 *centre*

HARDWICK HALL

1590–97
probably Robert Smythson c. 1536–1614

Hardwick has none of the rambling irregular charm that characterises medieval mansions, but it can reasonably be regarded as the end of the Gothic tradition as much as the beginning of the Renaissance. The windows especially, which take up practically all the wall space available, display the familiar grid-pattern of the Perpendicular style, and the only use of Italianate or Flemish detail is in the loggia and the ornament of scrolls at the top of the towers. In its planning, however, it was more revolutionary. Not only is everything subordinated to symmetry, but the hall (behind the projecting bay windows) has become the grand vestibule of the house rather than its social centre.

103

LONGLEAT HOUSE

c. 1567–72

Longleat was built for Sir John Thynne, a rich and powerful member of Edward VI's court, who had been deeply impressed by the developments in Italian architecture that he had seen on his travels. It is the first English house to show a classical and uniform treatment of the façade. The bay windows, while using Doric, Ionic and Corinthian pilasters, retain a certain spaciousness characteristic of the Perpendicular Gothic style. The doorway is an eighteenth-century addition.

During the later years of Elizabeth, families of craftsmen from the Netherlands dominated English sculpture. The Johnsons arrived from Amsterdam in 1567 and were soon producing elaborate painted tombs using all the familiar Flemish repertoire (columns, architraves, coffered vaults, niches, panels, obelisks and allegorical figures) at their workshop in Southwark for transport all over the country. One of the family, Gerrard, made the unendearing Shakespeare monument in the church at Stratford.

The Cures also probably came from Holland. Their most outstanding work is the tomb of Mary Queen of Scots in Westminster Abbey. Elizabeth's own tomb was by another Netherlander, Maximilian Colt. The face was based on a death mask and is a powerful piece of characterisation. **108** Colt's masterpiece is the tomb of Robert Cecil, 1st Earl of Salisbury, at Hatfield – a really original monument in which the bier is carried on the shoulders of four stalwart female Virtues.

In painting, the national genius was, if anything, even more backward. The only tolerable artists were foreigners (mostly Netherlanders) and almost all their pictures were formal portraits. Most notable among the short-term visitors were Antonio Moro and Federico Zuccaro. Moro came to London in 1554 and painted a portrait of Mary Tudor which brings the **96** sad queen vividly to life. Zuccaro's drawing of her sister Elizabeth, slight as it is, displays a delicacy and sureness beyond the reach of any **107** other artist in the kingdom at that time. Neither Moro nor Zuccaro stayed long enough to have a deep effect on English painters, though both were widely copied. Hans Eworth of Antwerp, who worked in London from 1549 to 1574, produced a great number of conscientious portraits but nothing that can be called exciting. One of his best works is a quiet double portrait of the unfortunate Lord Darnley and his brother – two **106** lonely black figures standing in a big empty room.

The pictorial medium *par excellence* of the Elizabethan age was the miniature – something new which could, without making undue demands, lead to pleasing originality. Two names stand out: Nicholas Hilliard and Isaac Oliver. Hilliard was born about 1547 and came from Devonshire. A large number of his miniatures survive, all of high technical quality and **99** many showing a poetry and wit that place his work alongside the best of the literature of the period. His book, *The Art of Limning* (painting), proves that he was not only intensely interested in people but also well versed in the latest Italian theories. His works have indeed an intellectual subtlety which may well be called Mannerist. Many are riddles – a youth amidst a background of flames, another surrounded by thorns and roses – and the meaning of some has been lost forever. Nothing, however, can diminish the sheer attractiveness of his jewelled and intimate style. Isaac Oliver, a Frenchman who came to London in 1568, has something of the same delicacy without the same imagination. But his miniatures are fine flattering likenesses and revel in the richness of jewellery, textiles, lace and **100** metalwork.

This delight in personal adornment was as typical of the queen as of her artists and courtiers; most of her portraits show her so smothered in jewellery that she almost has the appearance of an idol. A few of these jewels can be identified. In the *Ermine Portrait* at Hatfield she wears the **97** historic pendant of the House of Burgundy known as the Three Brothers. Another famous royal jewel which actually survives is the Armada Jewel, **95** an enamelled gold pendant set with diamonds and rubies, with a portrait of the queen on one side and a representation of Noah's Ark on the other.

During the 1580s and 90s one can see a change in the way works of art, especially paintings, were regarded. Most noblemen owned collections of

104

TOMB OF SIR PHILIP AND SIR THOMAS HOBY

c. 1566
alabaster and marble
Bisham

Sir Philip lies next to the wall, Sir Thomas further out into the chapel, and it is his effigy that we see here. He was a brilliant scholar (he translated Castiglione's *Courtier*), a traveller and a man of the world. The double tomb was erected by his widow, a sister-in-law of Lord Burleigh and an aunt of Francis Bacon. Her own talents lay in epitaph writing, and she composed a long Latin poem to go at the top of the tomb, and an equally long one in English for the bottom. The knights' feet rest on 'hobby-hawks', a pun on the name Hoby.

pictures (the Earl of Leicester, for instance, had over 200), though it remains true that the renown of the artist was only a minor consideration. Inventories always gave the subject of the painting, hardly ever the name of the artist. But some men do seem to have chosen or at least preserved works for their aesthetic value. John, 9th Lord Lumley, acquired the Holbein cartoon of Henry VIII and also Dürer's water-colour of Lord Morley, which the latter had commissioned when he was in Nuremberg in 1523. The great names–Raphael, Michelangelo, Leonardo, Titian, Tintoretto, Veronese–were certainly well known and are sometimes mentioned by men of letters. Sir Philip Sidney had his portrait painted by Veronese in Venice in 1574. By the end of the century Robert Cecil was writing of his desire for 'ancient masterpieces of painting', though he presumably meant antiques as well. Donne, some years later, owned a Titian (he left it to the Earl of Carlisle, who gave it to Charles I; Cromwell sold it to Mazarin and it is now in the Louvre). Indeed the age of the collector was about to dawn. Sir Henry Wotton, the first English connoisseur, had been born in 1568, and the Earl of Arundel, Inigo Jones's patron, was gathering his collection of classical sculpture, most of which is now in the Ashmolean Museum, Oxford. It was men like these who formed the taste of Charles I.

In the story of architecture, there is an epilogue to the Elizabethan age: the 'prodigy houses' of James I. Under James royal patronage expanded once more. The gentry continued to build ambitiously, with the king as an even more ambitious rival. The late Elizabethan style remained basically the same but became grander. Three of the biggest houses, Holland House, Theobalds and Wimbledon, have totally disappeared; a fourth, Audley End, built 1603–16, is a mere fragment. But there are many slightly

105

HATFIELD HOUSE
1608–12
Robert Lyminge, d. 1628

Hatfield came into the possession of the Cecil family when James I exchanged it with Robert Cecil, 1st Earl of Salisbury, for Theobalds, a vast Elizabethan house a few miles away. Cecil immediately rebuilt Hatfield, creating one of the grandest of Jacobean mansions. It has a conventional E-plan with wide arms three rooms thick, emphasised by angle tunnels. The loggia between them was originally open. In the centre rises the porch with superimposed Doric, Ionic and Corinthian orders.

105   smaller, such as Bolsover or Bramshill, which survive fairly intact, and one major house, Hatfield, remains practically unaltered and in possession of the same family, the Cecils, who built it in 1607. Like Hardwick, it gives up the courtyard but it goes back to the old-fashioned hall. The great staircase with its carved heraldic figures is clearly meant to strike the eye, and there is a long gallery in front of the hall range supported on an Italianate open arcade. Most of the detail, both here and in other Jacobean houses, is a free version of Flemish ornament. De Vries continued to be a model, together with a German engraver, Wendel Dietterlin. There were even Flemish architects; Audley End is by a Bernard Janssen. But the total result is decidedly English, its vigour more than compensating for its touches of vulgarity. The end of Jacobean under the influence of Inigo Jones marks the first real watershed of English taste since the Middle Ages.

Ian Richards

106 *right*

LORD DARNLEY AND HIS BROTHER

1563
Hans Eworth, working 1549–74
oil on wood
Royal Collection, Windsor Castle

Henry Stuart, Earl of Darnley, was seventeen when this portrait
was painted, his brother Charles only six. Eworth painted them in
a big panelled Tudor room furnished only with a table. Both are
dressed in black, but it is probably our knowledge of Darnley's
subsequent history that gives him such an air of pathos. Two years
later, in July 1565, he married his cousin Mary Queen of Scots; in
March of the following year he ordered the murder of her lover
David Rizzio at Holyrood House, and less than a year afterwards,
on February 10th 1567, was himself killed by an explosion at
Kirk O'Field – almost certainly the work of Mary's new lover,
Bothwell.

107 *above*

QUEEN ELIZABETH I

1574 or 1575
Federico Zuccaro c. 1543–1609
British Museum, London

The brothers Federico and Taddeo Zuccaro were among the
leaders of Italian Mannerist painting in the later sixteenth century.
Federico had worked on fresco cycles at the Vatican and the Villa
Farnese, Caprarola, before coming to London in 1574. He is known
to have painted full-length life-size portraits of the queen and the
Earl of Leicester, but both have disappeared, though a painting of
Elizabeth in the Siena Gallery has a claim to be his. The drawings,
however, have survived and show all his usual mastery and wit.

108 *right*

EFFIGY OF QUEEN ELIZABETH

1606
Maximilian Colt, working 1595–1645
white marble
Westminster Abbey, London

Colt's effigy of Queen Elizabeth is among the most striking portraits in English sculpture. The restraints imposed by the queen's
vanity had been removed, and the face, which was based on a
death mask, shows her as she was in old age – autocratic, intelligent and still strangely fascinating.

109 *top right*

PARISH CHURCH OF ST WENDREDA

first quarter of sixteenth century
March

Like many East-Anglian towns, March found itself growing rich
from the wool trade in the early sixteenth century, and sumptuous additions were made to the parish church. They included this
magnificent double hammer-beam roof, with seven rows of
angels – two along the corbels against the wall, four on the ends of
the hammer-beams and one in the centre of the roof.

110
THE AMBASSADORS

1533, Hans Holbein the Younger 1497–1543
oil on oak, 6 ft 9·5 in × 6 ft 10·5 in (207 × 209 m)
National Gallery, London

The men in the painting are the French ambassador, Jean de Dinteville, and his friend George de Selve, later Bishop of Lavour, who was paying him a visit in the spring of 1533. The shelves behind them are strewn with books and scientific and musical instruments, indications both of their wide humanist interests and of Holbein's love of symbolism – the mysteries of all the dates and times of day shown on the instruments have still not been fully solved. On the globe the only French towns named are Paris, Lyons, Bayonne and Polisy, the small village where Dinteville was born. The most extraordinary part of the picture is the skull at the bottom, painted in such grotesquely distorted foreshortening that it can only be recognised by squinting along the surface of the painting from the right hand side.

The tempo of life at Whitehall Palace quickened when in 1603 James Stuart came south from Scotland to claim the throne of England. He installed himself with ambitious ideas of transforming his court into a flourishing artistic and intellectual centre, comparable to the courts of the continental princes. Stuart patronage, especially that of Charles I, is a key factor in the development of seventeenth-century art in England. It reflects most subtly the social climate of that century, throwing into sharp relief the deep-rooted and usually opposing political and religious ideals of the Stuart monarchs and their subjects. The reigns of James I and Charles I are a tale of the dramatic struggle between the monarchy and Parliament, erupting in 1642 in the Civil War. It becomes apparent during the reigns of the later Stuarts, that as their wings were clipped and their power transferred to Parliament, the court was no longer the main centre of patronage.

Whitehall Palace must have burst into life overnight. The later years of the reign of Queen Elizabeth had been very dull at court, due to her age and her notorious parsimony. This situation was rapidly reversed by King James, a cultured, intelligent man, who desired congenial company and amusement. It was also fitting that a prince should have a suitable court, which would enhance his prestige. Thus King James and Queen Anne threw themselves into a round of lavish entertainments, the queen leading the courtiers on in the endless pursuit of pleasure. The lively court attracted many artists looking for commissions.

By a quirk of fate the Stuarts were served by two of the most outstanding English architects, Inigo Jones and Sir Christopher Wren. The most sought-after painters in Europe, Sir Peter Paul Rubens and Sir Anthony van Dyck, added a glorious lustre to the reign of Charles I. Men of this calibre lifted English art in the seventeenth century into the mainstream of European art, glorifying the Stuart dynasty, and reflecting England's fast emerging position in European affairs.

Inigo Jones rose rapidly in royal favour early in James I's reign through his successful designs for masque sets. The masque was an important feature of court life and was developed into a highly finished dramatic performance. At Queen Anne's command Ben Jonson wrote the *Queen's Masque of Blackness*, which was performed on Twelfth Night, 1605. Inigo Jones collaborated with Ben Jonson, and designed the most spectacular and ingenious sets that had ever been seen.

Jones's appointment as Surveyor to Prince Henry in 1611 is indicative of the position he had achieved at court. The Prince of Wales, in his contemporaries' eyes, fitted the Renaissance ideal of a 'universal man'. At the age of sixteen he had acquired a fine collection of paintings and medals. Among the young noblemen who gravitated around the prince was one of the most cultured men of his age, the Earl of Arundel. With Inigo Jones in his household, and surrounded by this learned company, Prince Henry might also have become a great Stuart patron if he had not died of typhoid in November 1612. Jones's prestige was so great at court that he did not suffer from his master's untimely death, and the following April was granted the Reversion of the Surveyorship of the King's Works. A month later he left England in the Earl of Arundel's retinue and spent seventeen months in Italy. In the library of Worcester College, Oxford, is his copy of Palladio's *I Quattro Libri dell'Architettura*, annotated with the observations he made on this visit.

When Jones took up his Surveyorship on his return from Italy, he was employed on improving and making additions to the royal residences at Whitehall, Newmarket and Greenwich. The Queen's House at Green-

2, 113

III
ENDYMION PORTER
c. 1643–45
William Dobson 1611–46
oil on canvas
59 × 50 in (150 × 127 cm)
Tate Gallery, London

This portrait of one of Charles I's most loyal servants was probably painted while both artist and sitter were at the royal court in Oxford. It is executed in a more robust and less elegant style than Van Dyck's portraits of courtiers in the previous decade. The bust of the poet and the relief are subtle allusions both to Porter's aspirations as a poet and his artistic activities. When Charles was forming his magnificent collection, Porter, who was a friend of Rubens's and a collector, often acted as the king's agent.

wich, built between 1616 and 1635, must have been studied with great curiosity as it was totally unlike anything seen in England before. It was as if an Italian villa had been planted on the green banks of the Thames. The **123** design was far more subtle than was immediately apparent. It was governed by the fact that the Deptford to Woolwich road ran through the grounds of Greenwich Palace, dividing the park and the gardens. Far from finding this a hindrance Jones took advantage of it and found an ingenious solution, building two blocks linked by a bridge over the road, which enabled the queen to have access to the park or garden without having to cross the road. Though Palladio's influence is discernible in the plan and the façades, the Queen's House bears Jones's highly personal stamp.

The heart of court life at Whitehall was the Banqueting Hall, which was burnt down in 1619. Within three months Jones had designed a new building, suitable for state banquets, reception of ambassadors, and the **114** presentation of masques. This building must have contrasted strangely with the Tudor palace and have startled the citizens of Westminster who passed it daily through the Holbein Gate. Like the Queen's House, it reflects Jones's study of the antique and Palladio. The interior is based on a Roman basilica, though he omitted the columns which would have blocked the view of some of the audience during the performance of a masque. The proportions were those of a double cube, which appear again at Wilton House later in the century. The two main external façades were **129** based on Palladian designs for town houses, with a rusticated basement, and superimposed orders. The final adornment was the painted ceiling by Rubens. This building marks Inigo Jones as the first Englishman who really understood the concepts of the Renaissance, and the achievement marks a new epoch in English architecture.

Charles I

Prince Charles not only inherited his brother's collections, but was also equally well endowed with artistic taste. Before he ascended the throne in 1626, he had amassed an extensive collection of paintings and objets d'art, and he became perhaps the greatest connoisseur and collector to reign in England. The Prince of Wales became the central figure in a select coterie of young aristocrats, known as the 'Whitehall group', all of whom were lavish collectors and patrons. The Earl of Arundel was perhaps the most erudite connoisseur, but the favourite Buckingham surpassed him in the speed with which he amassed his treasures.

A momentous experience in the prince's career was his abortive trip to Spain to seek the Spanish infanta's hand in marriage. There, for the only time in his life, he saw one of the great continental royal collections, that of the Hapsburgs, who had accumulated works representing the cream of the Italian and northern Renaissance. His appreciation and awareness of the value of art was stimulated and he particularly fell under the spell of Titian. There also, he sat for Velasquez who was to leave such poignant records in his portraits of the Spanish royal family.

One of his most fortunate purchases was the set of cartoons drawn by Raphael, from which tapestries were woven for the pope's private chapel **125** in Rome, the Sistine Chapel. Prince Charles bought them from a Genoese merchant in 1623, thus acquiring one of the finest examples of High Renaissance art. When Charles became king, treasures poured into the royal collection through purchases and gifts. Perhaps the greatest *coup* was the purchase of the fabulous collection of the dukes of Mantua, when the Gonzaga dynasty failed. Among these works were Raphael's *La Perla* and Andrea del Sarto's *Holy Family*, both sold during the Commonwealth. Rubens, who was instrumental in persuading his patron, the Duke of

112, 113

DESIGNS FOR MASQUES

1610

Inigo Jones 1573–1652

pen and wash

13 × 7 in (33 × 18 cm)

Devonshire collection, Chatsworth

The masque was a popular entertainment at court from the reign of Queen Elizabeth to that of Charles II, and Inigo Jones designed spectacular costumes and scenery for several masques performed during James I's reign. Sadly, these were made in highly perishable materials, but a fine series of drawings survives at Chatsworth, to give some idea of the lavish production of these displays. Those illustrated here are for the costume of Tethys in *Tethys Festival* or *The Queen's Wake* by Samuel David, and a set for *Oberon, the Faery Prince, A Masque of Prince Henries* by Ben Jonson.

Mantua, to buy the *Death of the Virgin* by Caravaggio, viewed it again in England. Among the works still in the royal collection is the *Triumph of Caesar* by Mantegna at Hampton Court, which illustrates the pre- **122** occupation of a Renaissance artist with the antique.

Diplomats brought back such prize pieces as Rembrandt's portrait of his mother, now at Windsor Castle and Dürer's *Self-portrait*, now in the Prado. Sir Dudley Carlton and Sir Henry Wotton kept the Whitehall group well posted about continental activities, acting as artistic agents in the course of their diplomatic duties in the Netherlands and Venice. Sir Dudley, himself a collector, exchanged his antique marbles with Rubens for tapestries and paintings by the master.

Tapestries were greatly valued, and Prince Charles probably bought the Raphael cartoons with the intention of having tapestries woven at the **126** newly established Mortlake Factory, which King James had founded in 1619 in emulation of Henry IV's establishment in France. Tapestry weaving was not an indigenous craft, and fifty Flemish weavers were brought over to establish the industry. Unfortunately the finances of the Mortlake Factory were never very secure; hard hit by the Civil War and changing tastes, the commissions for large tapestries petered out. In 1703 Queen Anne granted the land 'for other purposes than tapestry weaving'. In its heyday, Mortlake work was the finest in Europe, and was so highly prized that by his death Cardinal Mazarin had acquired eleven sets.

During the early years of King Charles's reign his court was momentarily brought into line with the continental courts, not only by his collecting activities, but by his continued efforts to secure the services of foreign artists. Lesser painters such as Honthorst and Gentileschi were already working for the king when Rubens visited England in 1629. Arundel had long tried to entice the courtier-painter to England, and Rubens was obviously interested in securing the commission to decorate the new Banqueting Hall, which he was granted in 1629. **121**

The *raison d'être* for Rubens's visit to England was to restore diplomatic relations between Spain and England. Though this visit was unofficial, no ambassador could have been more welcome to Charles I, with whom Rubens shared many enthusiasms. Both he and Van Dyck, who came to England in 1632, were cultured men of immense charm, and they achieved unprecedented status at court. During this visit Rubens painted the *Landscape with St George* (Buckingham Palace) and the allegory of *Peace and War*, in which there are subtle allusions to Charles's defence of England **133** and the benefits of the proposed peace with Spain. Above all, Rubens left England with the coveted commission for the decoration of the ceiling in the Banqueting Hall, the first great Baroque decorative scheme in England. **121**

The rising reputation of Anthony van Dyck, a former pupil of Rubens, had for some time attracted the attention of the English court. Van Dyck had visited England in 1620 under the protection of Arundel; he returned in 1632 and entered the king's service. His series of royal portraits made a tremendous impact on the Caroline court and had a lasting influence on subsequent English portraiture.

Van Dyck's sketchbooks at Chatsworth reveal that the greatest single influence on his work in England was his renewed study of Titian. The full-length portrait of Strafford at Wentworth Wodehouse recalls *Charles V with a Dog* by Titian, which King Charles had acquired on his portentous visit to Spain in 1623, and Titian's *Charles V at the Battle of Muhlberg* was the model for the *Equestrian portrait of Charles I* in the National Gallery. **frontis-** Such fluid brushwork and ravishing colour were at that time unknown in **piece** England. Van Dyck captured most eloquently the dazzling brilliance of **124** court life in his group portraits of the royal family and young nobles, such as the *Villiers Boys* (Windsor Castle) and the *Herbert Family* (Wilton).

In Van Dyck Charles found the equivalent to Velasquez, the court painter of Philip IV of Spain. The artist created an image of the king which embodied all the ideal attributes of a sovereign, and disguised the fact that the king was in fact a small, ineffectual man. In the equestrian portrait of *Charles I and M de St Antoine* at Buckingham Palace, the combination of Baroque illusionism and brilliant technique creates the impression of Charles riding majestically out of the picture. In December 1641 Van Dyck died, and significantly the days of the Caroline court were already numbered.

Civil War and the rise of the merchant classes

The outbreak of the Civil War in 1641 shattered the glittering life at Whitehall. The puritanical members of Parliament must have associated the lavish patronage with the king's tolerance of Romish practices and his distasteful foreign policy. The Catholic faction at court, centred on Queen Henrietta Maria, had cultivated the king's favour by giving him works of art. Among the gifts was a portrait bust of Charles by the great Italian sculptor Bernini, which was done from the triple portrait by Van Dyck at Windsor Castle. The king's patronage ceased and, tragically, the collections he had so assiduously amassed were broken up and dispersed over Europe. At the Restoration, an effort was made to restore some of his father's treasures to Charles II, but it proved impossible to retrieve many of the works.

The court had not been the only source of patronage. The seventeenth century was a period of rapid economic growth, which primarily benefited not the monarch or the aristocracy but the merchants and gentry. They built many houses, especially in the country, where they bought estates and established their families. Trading links with the Low Countries had been forged in medieval times, and Flemish influence can be seen in sixteenth-century English architecture. The new Italianate style of Inigo Jones made very little impact outside court circles. Swakeleys in Middlesex was built in 1638 for a city merchant and reflects his conservative taste. Built in red brick, with high gables, the design is based on Flemish traditions. A feeling for symmetry, which is found in architecture based on classical concepts, is found at Chevening in Kent, begun in the same year as Swakeleys for Lord Maltravers, the Earl of Arundel's son. This was a new type of house, which was developed in the seventeenth century. It consisted of a simple rectangular block, with windows arranged in a regular fashion, and crowned by a cornice. The roof and dormers rose up behind the cornice, without breaking it. The strong vertical and horizontal accents in the building give the characteristic feeling of order inherent in classical architecture. A drawing for Chevening by Inigo Jones survives at Worcester College, Oxford.

The fashion for collecting paintings was not restricted to the select Whitehall group and the aristocracy. The gentry also formed collections, decorating their homes with portraits of their families and friends. These collections reflected the strong preference for portraiture peculiar to England, which prevented artists from painting other subjects.

English artists, until the advent of Van Dyck, had looked to Holland for their lead, modifying the Elizabethan and Jacobean formula with Dutch realism. Their unsophisticated but vigorous school was eclipsed by Van Dyck. The portrait of Robert, 2nd Earl of Warwick, painted in 1632 by Daniel Mytens illustrates the point reached on Van Dyck's arrival in England. Cornelius Johnson also worked in this realistic style, but his

124

115

114 *top*

THE BANQUETING HOUSE, WHITEHALL

1619−22
Inigo Jones 1573−1652
London

This was Inigo Jones's first completed commission; building was begun on the 1st of June, 1619, and Nicholas Stone was appointed master mason. Jones's design is a personal expression of Palladio's ideas and his exposition of classical theory in *I Quattro Libri dell' Architettura*. The Banqueting House was the first building in England designed entirely in the classical idiom. It was originally built in three kinds of stone, but in the early nineteenth century the fabric was in such a poor condition that it was replaced entirely in Portland stone.

115
SWAKELEYS
1638

Swakeleys was built for a Cheshire merchant, Sir Edmund Wright, who became Lord Mayor of London in 1640. It is a brick and stucco house, several of which were built at about this time; the Dutch house at Kew is another example. The plan is traditional and asymmetrical; the outstanding feature is the fine show of 'Holborn' gables, an architectural device which first appeared in England on Lady Cooke's and Sir Fulke Greville's houses in Holborn about 1615.

patrons were not aristocratic. During the 1630s he stayed with a Dutch merchant, Sir Arnold Braems, in Kent, and painted portraits of the local gentry. Many artists followed this practice, moving from one area to another, going where there was a demand for portraits.

During the early years of the Civil War, when the court was based at Oxford, William Dobson emerged as the most talented native artist, and he portrayed many of the dashing cavaliers. His style was formed in the shadow of Van Dyck, but perhaps the greater influence was the collection of Titians at Whitehall. His feeling for warm Venetian tones is found in his impressive portrait of Endymion Porter in the Tate Gallery. Dobson, like **III** Inigo Jones, absorbed these continental influences and developed a highly personal style.

The field in which English artists still excelled was that of the portrait miniature. The art was indigenous, developing out of technical virtuosity acquired in manuscript illumination and an inherent interest in portraiture. The exquisite miniatures by Holbein, done when he visited Henry VIII's court, had quickened interest in this art. These small portraits, often set with precious stones or in fine enamel cases, were costly gifts of special significance. Cavaliers and their ladies exchanged them as personal presents, but both the Stuarts and the council of state during the Commonwealth sent them to foreign courts as diplomatic gifts. A miniature of Oliver Cromwell by Samuel Cooper was presented in 1656 to the Swedish ambassador. The quality of the portraits by Cooper was so high that he flourished whatever the political climate; almost immediately after the Restoration, the royal family and members of the Restoration court sat for him. His miniatures, such as the ravishing portrait at Windsor Castle of Charles II's queen, Catherine of Braganza, are memorable not **118** only for their beauty, but also for their understanding of character.

In 1647 a fire swept through the south wing of Wilton House, and several rooms had to be redecorated. The Civil War did not deter the renegade Earl of Pembroke from immediately commissioning Inigo Jones and his assistant Webb to begin the task. The idea of proportions based on a cube, used earlier in the Banqueting Hall, was taken up again at Wilton, and the Cube and Double Cube Rooms were designed as a setting for the portraits of the Herbert family by Van Dyck and his followers. The traditional type of panelling, conditioned by the width of an oak plank, was superseded by cream-coloured wainscotting relieved with gilded swags of fruit and flowers. Jones had developed this new type of interior decoration for the queen at Somerset House. This suite of rooms at Wilton, the only extant example of his decorative work, conveys some idea of the **129** rich decoration fashionable then, in contrast with the more restrained scheme used in the Long Gallery at Ham House.

Charles II and the Restoration

One of the results of the Civil War was that many royalist sympathisers went into voluntary exile on the continent. Men like John Evelyn and Roger Pratt returned to England well acquainted with continental artistic trends. Visits to the continent continued after the Restoration, and the foundations of the Grand Tour, which became part of every gentleman's education in the eighteenth century, were laid.

Roger Pratt was typical of a well-educated English gentleman deeply versed in the arts. On his return he became involved in the building of his cousin's house, Coleshill (destroyed by fire in 1952). Coleshill was very similar to Chevening, but longer and lower. Its design depended on the proportion of wall to roof, and on the arrangement of the windows. Kingston Lacy, Dorset, built for Sir Ralph Bankes, is the only house surviving of the buildings undertaken by Pratt before he inherited his estates in 1667. Pratt had a fine architectural library, and some of his notes, dated 1660, show his shrewd understanding of architectural problems. A change of emphasis is apparent in his work, which was directed not at the monarchy but at the gentry, then emerging as a powerful class.

The encounter with Dutch and French cultural developments during the prolonged exile of the court had immediate repercussions in England. The general character of French and Dutch art differed: the former was grand, while the latter had a more domestic nature. The Mauritshuis in The Hague was well known to many Englishmen, in particular the architect Hugh May. The outstanding features of the Mauritshuis were the giant stone pilasters and stone dressings on a brick ground, which May introduced at Eltham Lodge, built in 1664 for a rich vintner, Sir John Shaw. The mood of such houses is in a much lower key than the grand schemes influenced by French precedents instigated by Charles II at Windsor and Greenwich at much the same time.

Little furniture from the early years of the seventeenth century has survived. The Lumley Inventory of 1609 is contemporary evidence of the furnishings of a great house of which the predominant feature was rich fabrics, which are not very durable. The other noticeable feature is the narrow range of furniture, which was usually made out of oak and limited to chairs, tables, cupboards and chests.

However, in the relaxed atmosphere of Restoration England, demand grew for more luxurious furniture, reflecting the change in social habits and possibly stimulated by a greater knowledge of continental standards. Among the new types developed were the bureau and cabinet, the latter designed to hold the collections of china and porcelain that became so popular at the end of the century. Solid and veneered walnut were widely used, the fashion for inlaid and veneered furniture grew, and a variety of woods were used in elaborate inlaid patterns of acanthus arabesques. After the Revocation of the Edict of Nantes in 1685 many skilled Huguenot refugees settled in England, giving new impetus to the crafts, and by the early years of the eighteenth century English furniture was of high quality and distinctive character.

116   Among the most luxurious pieces are the silver tables and mirrors, now at Windsor Castle, which were presented to Charles II and William III and were undoubtedly inspired by the set of silver furniture made for Louis XIV at Versailles. The popularity of oriental lacquer grew rapidly. The East India Company had imported it since Elizabethan times, but as the fashion for chinoiserie became more widespread the demand increased 117, 128 and soon outstripped the supply, and English craftsmen developed an imitation, which is known as 'Japan' work.

Charles II did not inherit his father's passion for collecting paintings, but he was not an inconsiderable patron of the arts. No large official building schemes had been undertaken by the Council of State during the Interregnum, but King Charles embarked on lavish schemes at Greenwich Palace and Windsor Castle. The Tudor palace at Greenwich had fallen into disrepair and was no longer fit to accommodate the court and king. In 1663 the foundations of a new palace were laid, but only the King Charles block, which was built by John Webb, was completed. This block was only part of a complex building scheme on a continental scale, hitherto 138 unknown in England. It was later incorporated in Wren's plans for completing the palace as a naval hospital in 1694.

Recollections of the apartments in the Louvre of his cousin Louis XIV and knowledge of the latter's grand schemes for Versailles inspired Charles

116
SILVER TABLE
c. 1695
Andrew Moore of Bridewell
Royal Collection, Windsor Castle

This silver centre table together with a mirror were presented to William III by the Corporation of the City of London. It is known that Charles I possessed a 'silver table and frame' which were sold by the Council of State in 1650, and John Evelyn noted the tables of 'massy silver' during his visit to Italy in 1644. The fashion at the Restoration for silver furniture was inspired by Louis XIV's example at Versailles. The table is part of one of the few surviving sets; it was made by Andrew Moore of Bridewell and bears his monogram.

117
CENTRE TABLE
c. 1690
collection of the Duke of Buccleuch and
Queensberry, Boughton House

In 1688 John Stalker and George Parker published a *Treatise of Japanning and Varnishing*, setting down improved methods of imitating oriental lacquer. The popularity of Chinese lacquer was so great that the art of japanning flourished in the late seventeenth century. Both imported oriental lacquer and japan work were used in single pieces of furniture. The top of this table is made of oriental lacquer, while the frame is japanned with flower sprays and foliage in the Chinese taste.

II to create a similar setting for himself at Windsor. At the Restoration Windsor Castle was 'exceedingly ragged and ruinous'. Hugh May was appointed Comptroller of the Works at Windsor Castle, and during the next decade two new blocks replaced the old buildings on the east terrace.

The French artist Le Brun had gathered around him, while working at Vaux-le-Vicomte, a group of highly skilled decorative artists who later collaborated on the decorations at Versailles and the Louvre. Unlike Louis, Charles had no such task force at his disposal, as the lack of constant patronage in England had not facilitated the development of such a team. The king therefore looked outside England for a suitable decorative artist, and engaged the Italian Antonio Verrio to work alongside Hugh May. This was the first occasion in England that an architect and a painter, aided by a team of craftsmen, had closely collaborated to create a unified scheme. Unfortunately, during the early years of the nineteenth century, Hugh May's buildings were considerably altered by George III and George IV, but several rooms survive in the state apartments to show Verrio's treatment of May's rooms. The theme of glorification of the House of Stuart, which Rubens had used on the ceiling of the Banqueting Hall, was taken up again at Windsor, and Verrio opened up the coved ceilings with Baroque illusionist devices. In the queen's audience chamber, he depicted Catherine of Braganza journeying across the sky to the Temple of Virtue.

As a Catholic and a foreigner, Verrio enjoyed the special protection of both Charles II and James II. After working at Windsor he decorated the new Catholic chapel at Whitehall. His position was similar to that of Rubens and Van Dyck earlier in the century, whose work and presence had been a constant reminder of the Stuarts' Catholic sympathies. The new royal chapel at Whitehall was razed to the ground on December 22, 1688, and James II fled from England. Verrio, however, managed to weather the Glorious Revolution and eventually entered the service of William and Mary.

The foundation of the Royal Society in 1662 was a manifestation of the shift in intellectual emphasis in England. The Caroline court had been the centre of a belated Renaissance in England, where a study of Italian humanism and the antique had been cultivated. Closer contact with France and Holland had increased their influence in England. As the century progressed, greater intellectual energy and curiosity were focused on empirical and mathematical discoveries. The king was a keen supporter of the society, and among the most promising of the young founder members was Christopher Wren, referred to by John Evelyn as that 'miracle of youth', who dominated the English scene in the second half of the seventeenth century.

Wren, who was trained as a mathematician at Oxford, made use of his scientific knowledge in his first commission, the Sheldonian Theatre in Oxford. The plan was based on a Roman theatre, but the English climate demanded a roof. Employing a recent discovery, 'the geometrical flat floor', Wren constructed a roof, without supports, spanning seventy feet.

The City of London

The Great Fire of London in September 1666, following the ravages of plague, must have seemed catastrophic to the citizens of London. Nearly the whole of the city was in ruins, but like so many disasters, though much was lost, it proved to be a blessing in disguise. The slums were destroyed, and the devastation presented a unique opportunity for building a fine civic centre. The following year the Act for the rebuilding of the City of London was passed by Parliament, and the city as we know it today rapidly rose out of the ashes.

121

120

118
CATHERINE OF BRAGANZA
Samuel Cooper 1609–72
watercolour
5 × 4in (12 × 10cm)
Royal Library, Windsor Castle

Samuel Cooper was the outstanding miniature painter in England during the seventeenth century. He was working in the establishment of his uncle, John Hoskins, by 1625. Van Dyck's presence in England during his youth contributed to Cooper's mastery of design and draughtsmanship, and he developed a soft, sensitive handling of colour, qualities which are evident in this miniature of Catherine of Braganza, Charles II's consort. His work was so popular that the Civil War and Interregnum did not affect his career and he worked for both the Cromwell family and the royal family.

Several schemes were submitted, but Wren's plan, with St Paul's and the Royal Exchange as focal points, was accepted. The citizens of London rushed to rebuild their homes, often on exactly the same site, and it proved impossible to keep a strict control, though precautions were taken against another fire and the use of timber was prohibited. The burden of financing the rebuilding of private houses fell on the citizens, while the corporation and city companies were responsible for the civic buildings. An Act of Parliament was passed levying a tax on 'sea coal', which paid for the rebuilding of the churches and St Paul's Cathedral.

The city merchants were more conservative in their taste than the court, and preferred to employ their own craftsmen and architects rather than the more progressive court artists. The Royal Exchange, designed by Edward Jarman, the City Surveyor, was based on Flemish precedents

rather than on the example of Inigo Jones. The Exchange was burnt down in 1838, but the design is known to us from a contemporary engraving in the British Museum. The wealthier guilds rebuilt their guildhalls as soon as possible. The decoration of the state rooms in these buildings compensates for the traditional design of the exterior; the combination of carved wood and plaster work is very successful.

Wren was made Surveyor General in 1669, and his influence in the re-creation of the City of London is paramount. In the years between 1670 and 1686 he rebuilt fifty-one of the eighty churches destroyed. A record of Wren's sentiments on church design survives. A church should have 'a convenient auditory' in which 'everyone should hear the service and both see and hear the Preacher'. The sermon was regarded as the most important element in the service, and to meet this demand Wren developed a 'hall church' based on a Roman basilica plan.

119 *left*
ST PAUL'S CATHEDRAL
1675–1711
Christopher Wren 1632–1723
London

In 1687 many of the city churches were finished, and more money from the tax on sea coal was made available for completing St Paul's. In the following years the west front was built. A giant portico in keeping with the monumental scale of the building was envisaged, but the Portland quarries could not supply large enough blocks of stone, and Wren was forced to use a two-storeyed design. The towers and great dome were built between 1704 and 1708. The broken silhouettes of the Baroque towers complement the classical dome, for which Wren drew his inspiration from the great Renaissance architects, Bramante and Michelangelo. The dome is a masterpiece of engineering, as a mighty weight had to be supported. Wren overcame the problems ingeniously and created a beautiful architectural feature which dominated the City of London.

120 *above*

SIR CHRISTOPHER WREN
1673
Edward Pierce c. 1656–95
marble
h. 26 in (66 cm)
Ashmolean Museum, Oxford

This is one of the most sensitive works of Edward Pierce, who was a mason-sculptor. From 1671 he worked on the rebuilding of London, which left him little time for sculpture. The bust was done in 1673, possibly on the occasion of Wren's knighthood, and was given by the latter's son to the Ashmolean. This type of Baroque portrait bust was first established in Rome by Bernini in the early years of the seventeenth century. The direct presentation of the head and the restrained drapery contrast with Bernini's more theatrical busts in which a strong feeling of movement is conveyed through a play on diagonals in the drapery and a turn of the head.

121
CEILING OF THE BANQUETING HOUSE

1629–34, oil on canvas
Peter Paul Rubens 1588–1640, London

This ceiling was the first Baroque decorative scheme in England. The theme, expressed in allegorical terms, is the glorification of the House of Stuart and the benefits of the union of England and Scotland. As early as 1621 Rubens had expressed interest in the commission for decorating the ceiling in the new Banqueting House(**114**), and during his visit in 1629 he discussed it with Charles I. He painted the panels in Antwerp during the next five years, and they were put in place in 1635. The artist was paid £3,000. The coffered ceiling with canvas panels was inspired by the one in the church of San Sebastiano in Venice, painted by Veronese.

122
THE VASE BEARER

begun before 1478, completed after 1492
Andrea Mantegna c. 1431–1506
oil on canvas, 9 ft 5 in × 9 ft 5 in (2·75 × 2·75 m), Hampton Court

This painting is one of nine commissioned by Lodovico Gonzaga, Duke of Mantua, illustrating the Triumph of Caesar. The series was begun before the duke's death in 1478 and Mantegna was still working on the paintings in 1492. The artist drew on contemporary literary and pictorial sources, especially Valturio's *De Re Militari* published at Verona in 1472. Mantegna's extended visit to Rome from 1488 until 1490, during the execution of the paintings, deepened his knowledge of the antique, which finds expression in the careful treatment of classical detail. The paintings remained in the possession of the Gonzaga family until 1627, and two years later Charles I acquired them for his collection.

123 *left*
THE QUEEN'S HOUSE GREENWICH

1616–35
Inigo Jones 1573–1652
London

Work was begun on the Queen's House in 1616, but was stopped just before the death of Queen Anne three years later. In 1630 the house was granted to Queen Henrietta Maria, and it was completed in 1635, though the two blocks were not joined until 1661. Jones was inspired by Palladio's villas on the Veneto, and the house, with its Italianate appearance, was certainly quite unlike anything seen in England before.

124
QUEEN HENRIETTA MARIA
1632
Anthony van Dyck 1599–1641
oil on canvas
42·75 × 34 in (108 × 86 cm)
Windsor Castle

This was Charles I's favourite portrait of his
consort, Henrietta Maria, and it was hung in
his bedchamber at Whitehall. It was among
Van Dyck's first commissions in England,
dating from 1632 when it is mentioned in a
payment made to the artist as a portrait of
'our royall consort' dressed 'in a white
habbitt to the knees with two hands'. The
limited palette employed in this portrait is
characteristic of Van Dyck's English period.
The orange lacings on the queen's dress and
the flowers in her right hand complement
the silvery tones of the white silk dress, set
against the dark green draped curtain.

125 *far right*
MIRACULOUS DRAUGHT OF FISHES *detail*
second quarter of the seventeenth century
Mortlake tapestry
collection of the Duke of Buccleuch and
Queensberry
Victoria and Albert Museum, London

This tapestry from one of the cartoons by
Raphael (**126**) was woven at the Mortlake
Factory, which had been founded by James I
and was greatly patronised by Charles I.
It was commissioned by Charles I's
chamberlain, Phillip Earl of Pembroke
and Montgomery, whose arms are in the
upper border. The first tapestries were
woven in Brussels, where there were the
finest craftsmen and the most experienced
workshops. Enriched with gold and silver
thread, several were hung in the Sistine
Chapel for Christmas 1519. In England,
the cartoons were copied by Francis Cleyn,
who designed new framing borders, as the
original borders, full of Medici symbolism
referring to Pope Leo X, were not suitable
in Stuart England.

126
CHRIST'S CHARGE TO PETER
1515–16
Raphael 1483–1520
paper
11ft 3·25 in × 17ft 5·75 in (3·41 × 5·32 m)
Royal Collection, Victoria and Albert Museum,
London

Prince Charles commissioned Sir Francis
Crane, the manager of the Mortlake
Factory, to purchase seven of the set of ten
tapestry cartoons by Raphael depicting the
history of the early church. They cost
approximately £700. Raphael had exploited
the dramatic possibilities of each scene, and
the cartoons, known especially through
engravings, were studied for their range of
human expression. When they arrived in
England they were still cut in strips, but
during the reign of William II there was a
change in attitude towards the cartoons;
Wren was commissioned to build a special
gallery for them at Hampton Court, and
the pieces were stuck together. They were
now appreciated as works of art in their
own right, not just as a set of patterns for
tapestries (**125**).

127

POSSET POT

*1685, tin-glazed earthenware, h. 13·5 in
(34 cm)*
Fitzwilliam Museum, Cambridge

The manufacture of tin-glazed earthenware
was established in England in the previous
century; the method had been introduced
from the Spanish Netherlands and Italy.
During the seventeenth century several
factories flourished in London; this posset-
pot was made at the Lambeth pottery.
This type of earthenware was known as
'Delft-ware', which is misleading as Delft
only rose to fame as a centre for pottery
long after the method had been used in
England. The white glaze provided a
suitable surface for applying polychrome
decoration.

129

DOUBLE CUBE ROOM, WILTON

after 1647
Inigo Jones 1573–1652 and
John Webb 1611–72

The state apartments at Wilton were destroyed by fire in 1647 or 1648. The re-
decoration was inspired by the elderly
Inigo Jones, but carried out by his assistant,
John Webb. It is not surprising that French
influence is evident in this rich scheme:
Jean Barbet's *Livre d'Architecture*, which
was published in Paris in 1633 and again in
1641, had aroused considerable interest in
England. Also, the Francophile court of
Queen Henrietta Maria favoured this type
of decoration, which Jones had first developed at Somerset House.

128 *right*

JAPANNED CABINET

c. 1685
h. 65 in (166 cm)
The Vyne, Hampshire

The panels of japan work which make
up this cabinet are decorated with figures,
a flowering tree, and a pagoda. The composition, though attractive, lacks the
oriental flair for design. The cabinet rests
on a finely carved silver-gilt stand, and it
forms a pair with another, also at The
Vyne, which is made of oriental lacquer.

130 *right*

PANEL IN THE STALLS OF
ST PAUL'S CATHEDRAL
1690–1700
Grinling Gibbons 1648–1721, London

Grinling Gibbons was born in Rotterdam, but he was in England by 1671, at which date John Evelyn refers to him in his diary. His accomplished wood-carving soon attracted attention and under Hugh May he became involved in the decoration of Cassiobury Park and the apartments of Charles II at Windsor Castle. His naturalistic style is reminiscent of Dutch flower painting. Gibbons was one of the team of fine decorative artists employed on the furnishings of St Paul's (**119**) when it was nearing completion.

131
HUGH HARE
1685
Godfrey Kneller 1649–1723
oil on canvas
95 × 60 in (241 × 152 cm)
collection of the Earl of Radnor
Lancaster House, London

Hugh Hare, son of the 2nd Baron Coleraine, was a man of literary tastes and a well-known translator. He was a member of the aristocratic circles which patronised Kneller soon after his arrival in England in 1674. Kneller was trained in Amsterdam, and after visiting Italy he established himself in England. He was familiar with continental trends in portraiture and, though often dependent on Lely for patterns, he employed a more subdued palette. This portrait is one of the more impressive, capturing the serious mood of his subject both in pose and in the blue-grey tonality.

As the population of London increased and fewer churches were rebuilt, Wren solved the problem of accommodating the larger congregations by introducing galleries. Though the tax on sea coal provided the money to rebuild the churches, funds were by no means lavish. Brick and plaster, cheaper materials than stone, were used, but the austerity of the plain exteriors was relieved by the fine steeples, while wood carving in the pews and stalls, and white plaster work, enriched the interiors.

The task of providing designs for St Paul's Cathedral was fraught with difficulties. Wren not only had to please the civil commission, but also the Chapter of St Paul's Cathedral; thus he had to satisfy two patrons with different tastes and requirements. He put forward several designs, and his third scheme was approved by royal warrant in 1675. His first plans were for a centralised building with a magnificent dome which would dominate the skyline of the city, but the clergy wanted a more traditional plan

based on a Latin cross, with a nave which was better suited for services and processions. In the warrant design, Wren provided the nave, but also retained the magnificent crossing and dome. The visual effect of the great dome surrounded by the lesser spires of the city churches is one of Wren's **119** most exciting achievements.

During the building of the city churches Wren had collected round him a team of highly skilled craftsmen, among whom was Caius Cibber, the stonemason, and Grinling Gibbons, who carved the choir stalls. In the **130** early years of the eighteenth century, Sir James Thornhill, who was working on Wren's great hall at Greenwich Naval Hospital, decorated the **136** dome with scenes from the life of St Paul.

The Whig supremacy

The leading portrait painters in London in the second half of the seventeenth century were Sir Peter Lely and Sir Godfrey Kneller. After the Restoration Lely was overwhelmed with commissions for portraits. He **137** died in 1680 and Kneller succeeded him as the fashionable portrait painter. **131** Between 1702 and 1717 the latter painted the series of portraits of the members of the Kit Kat Club which is a record of the great Whig aristocrats who emerged at the Glorious Revolution as the most powerful class in the country. This faction was instrumental in offering the throne to William of Orange and Princess Mary.

Whig domination is reflected in the patronage of those times, and a new type of country house built on a grandiose scale became fashionable. William Talman built the magnificent south and east façades of Chatsworth for the Earl (later Duke) of Devonshire, between 1686 and 1696. The façades were built in stone, dominated by giant pilasters, and crowned by a balustrade, and the arrangement of the reception rooms, chapel and staircase was palatial. Teams of artists worked on the decoration of Chatsworth as they had done at Windsor.

Dominating the Yorkshire countryside outside York is Castle Howard, a
134 subtle massing of blocks rising to a climax in the dome. This building
replaced Henderskelfe Castle, which was burnt down in 1693. Sir John
Vanbrugh, assisted by Nicholas Hawksmoor, created for Charles Howard,
3rd Earl of Carlisle, a mansion befitting his mighty position as Acting Earl
Marshal of England, and his future office as First Lord of the Treasury. The
idea of incorporating a dome sprang from the plans for St Paul's and
Greenwich Palace, which had just been settled, but Castle Howard was the
first private house to be built with a dome. The great hall beneath the
dome was no less magnificent; a combination of stone and decorative
painting by Pellegrini was an exciting departure in decoration.

Mundane reasons often caused monarchs to embark on lavish building
schemes. William III was asthmatic, and he found the old Tudor palace at
Whitehall too damp and unhealthy. Hampton Court was chosen as the
site for a new palace, and Wren was commissioned to build it. His first
scheme involved the destruction of the whole of the Tudor palace, with
the exception of Henry VIII's hall. An impressive approach was planned
through an avenue and courts, but probably due to expense this scheme
139 was abandoned, and building on a smaller scale began in April 1689. There
is a great contrast at Hampton Court between the impressive garden and
park façades and the relatively small cosy rooms in the queen's apartments,
reflecting French and Dutch influence.

To complement her husband's military foundation at Woolwich,
Queen Mary decided to establish a naval hospital. Greenwich Palace,
which had fallen from favour, was granted for this purpose. This is the
most complete of Wren's designs for civil architecture, but even here his
original plan was rejected by the queen before her death in December
1694. Wren planned two courts, rising impressively from the river bank,
and terminated by a block containing a hall and a chapel, linked by a
domed vestibule. The domed block would undoubtedly have excluded
the view from the Queen's House, which she insisted was preserved. Thus,
the large-scale Baroque scheme was abandoned, and Wren drew up a
138 compromise plan retaining the view and separating the hall and chapel,
which were moved forward to the end of the first court. The building of
Greenwich continued well into the eighteenth century, but Wren was
responsible for its character.

The magnificent pile, Blenheim Palace, was Queen Anne's gift to the
Duke of Marlborough for his services rendered to her and to England on
the battlefield of Blenheim. The queen not only wanted a 'private
habitation' but also a 'royal and national monument'. It was to represent,
as well as the duke's private success, the triumph of English foreign policy,
and the supremacy of her military prowess. Vanbrugh, as Comptroller of
the Works, was given the commission in 1705, and Hawksmoor
collaborated with him. Sarah, Duchess of Marlborough, was as contrary as
usual, and wanted a small, private house; but Vanbrugh, in accordance
with his royal mistress's wishes and his own inclination, built a grand
140 Baroque palace. The plan is similar to Vanbrugh's first commission,
Castle Howard, but Blenheim has a more austere, monumental aspect.

Blenheim represents the sum of England's achievement in the seventeenth century, and the nation's new power is reflected in the artistic
patronage which had brought English art into the mainstream of European
artistic developments. Closer contact with the continent had quickened
the appreciation of the arts by the gentry and aristocracy, and so the stage
was set for the development of eighteenth-century patronage.

Janet Holt

132 *left*

THOMAS, EARL OF ARUNDEL

c. 1622
Daniel Mytens c. 1590 – before 1648
oil on canvas, 81·5 × 50 in (203 × 127 cm)
collection of the Duke of Norfolk,
Arundel Castle

Born in Holland, Daniel Mytens was trained in The Hague and became a member of the Guild of St Luke in 1610. His style was inspired by the simple, realistic approach of the school of portrait painters at The Hague. In 1618 he came to England and entered the service of Thomas Howard, Earl of Arundel. The latter, who was known as the 'father of Vertu in England' is portrayed here in a setting which indicates his learned interests. He was among the first Englishmen to appreciate the Italian Renaissance and study the antique civilisation. Mytens has shown him seated at the entrance of the gallery where his collection of classical sculpture was housed.

133 *bottom*

PEACE AND WAR

1628 – 29
Peter Paul Rubens, 1577 – 1640
oil on canvas
78 × 116 in (198 × 294 cm)
National Gallery, London

This picture is a valuable contemporary document on the condition of Europe. During his visit to England in 1629, Rubens was impressed by the peace and prosperity of this small island compared to the misery raging on the continent. He recorded these impressions, illustrating the benefits of peace and horror of war, and presented the painting to Charles I as a compliment on his wise rule. It is full of classical symbolism, and is typical of allegorical painting in the seventeenth century. Minerva protects Peace from the god of war, Mars, and in the foreground are the horn of plenty, Pan, and Happiness striking a tambourine, symbolising the benefits of Peace.

134 *centre*

CASTLE HOWARD

begun 1701
Sir John Vanbrugh 1644 – 1726

Charles Howard, 3rd Earl of Carlisle, commissioned Sir John Vanbrugh to rebuild Castle Howard in 1699. This was Vanbrugh's first commission as an architect, which he probably received through his friendship with the Whig nobility. He was assisted by Hawksmoor, and building began in 1701, but due to a shortage of money the house was never completed. This engraving shows the proposed designs for the north façade. It was published in Colen Campbell's *Vitruvius Britannicus*, and is a valuable record of Vanbrugh's original intentions. The west wing was built during the 1750s in the Palladian style by Sir Thomas Robinson, a follower of Lord Burlington, thus altering the original character of the building.

135 *above*

CHIMNEYPIECE

c. 1610
Maximilian Colt, working 1596 – 1641
The Van Dyck Room, Hatfield House

Maximilian Colt was a refugee from Arras and one of the many Flemish sculptors to settle in England at the end of the sixteenth century. Under the patronage of the Earl of Salisbury, whose tomb he carved in 1612, he made several chimneypieces for Hatfield House. It was through these emigré sculptors that Flemish influences entered this country during James I's reign. This chimneypiece, carved out of different marbles, is a mixture of classical elements and Flemish strapwork. The caryatids and figures in relief all bear classical symbols such as the cornucopia. Although Colt is still known of in 1641, his work was not popular with the more sophisticated court of Charles I.

136

PAINTED HALL, ROYAL NAVAL COLLEGE

1708 – 14, James Thornhill 1675/6 – 1734, Greenwich

The commission to decorate the Lower Hall at Greenwich Naval Hospital was given to Sir James Thornhill in 1707, and the work was completed eight years later. The theme is the Triumph of Peace and Liberty, referring to King William III's and England's defeat of Louis XIV, symbolising Arbitrary Power. The painted oval frame within a rectangle was probably inspired by the ornately carved framework around the central panel of Rubens's Whitehall ceiling (**121**). Thornhill was the first English artist who was capable of such a complex Baroque decorative scheme.

137 *far right*

ROBERT, SECOND EARL OF SUNDERLAND

c. 1658, Peter Lely 1618 – 80
oil on canvas, 48·5 × 39·25 in (123 × 100 cm), Knole

Sir Peter Lely was born in Westphalia, the son of a Dutch soldier, and he was trained in Haarlem. He was in England by 1647, and soon secured the patronage of the liberal Earl of Northumberland. Lely's reputation has suffered because a great number of mediocre portraits actually by his workshop have been attributed to him. This portrait shows him at his best; he absorbed Van Dyck's ease of style and the earl is depicted in a very relaxed attitude, seated at the base of a column. The artist's handling of the cloak indicates his gift for painting material and his fine sense of colour.

138 *below*

GREENWICH PALACE

This eighteenth-century engraving, a bird's-eye view of Greenwich Palace, gives a clear idea of the magnificent layout of Greenwich Hospital, which was a compromise on the part of Wren. It clearly shows how his original plan for a domed block terminating the upper court would have blocked the view from the Queen's House. The two domes over the vestibules of the chapel (completed 1745) and the Painted Hall (completed externally 1704) are the commanding features. The elderly Wren was assisted by Vanbrugh and Hawksmoor; two of the most brilliant exponents of the Baroque style in England.

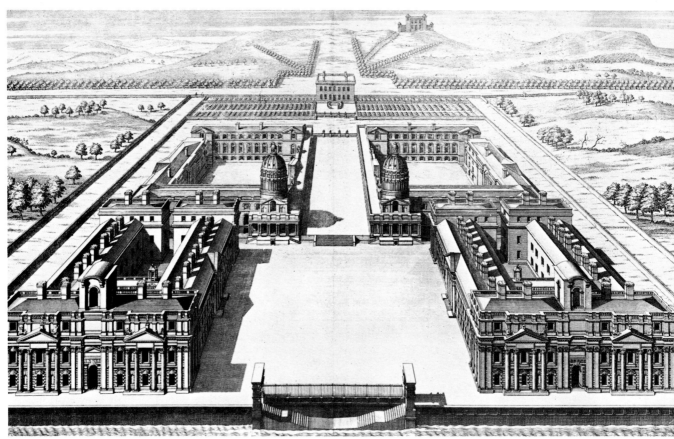

Lord Sunderla

139
HAMPTON COURT

alterations begun April 1689
Christopher Wren 1632–1723

Early in the new reign, grandiose plans
were made for rebuilding Hampton Court
entirely, only retaining Henry VIII's hall,
but in April 1689 a more limited scheme
was begun and the Tudor palace was
preserved. Building halted in 1694 when
Queen Mary died, but work was resumed
after the disastrous fire at Whitehall in
1699, when fresh accommodation was
speedily required. The Queen's apartments, which are in this block, were
decorated by Queen Anne. Wren's simple
bay design is repeated monotonously,
only relieved by the centre pavilion. It is
built in fine brick and stone, the latter
emphasising the horizontal and vertical
elements which give Hampton Court its
monumental character.

140 *below*

SOUTH FRONT OF BLENHEIM PALACE

begun 1705
John Vanbrugh 1664–1726

Vanbrugh's plans were conceived on a grand scale, in keeping with Queen Anne's expressed desire that the building should be a national monument as well as a home for the Duke of Marlborough, for whom it was built at her command. Vanbrugh soon outran the original grant of £100,000 and the house eventually cost £300,000, to which sum the duke himself contributed one fifth. In 1716 the architect was dismissed by Sarah, the ever-contrary duchess, and the work was continued by Nicholas Hawksmoor. Vanbrugh achieved the maximum grandeur by placing four monumental towers at the corners of the main block. Unlike Castle Howard, his first commission, Blenheim appears stern and magnificent, especially in this view, denuded by Capability Brown of the original formal gardens.

In the eighteenth century a strong aristocracy and middle class contrasted with a monarchy that was, by European standards of the time, comparatively weak. The revolutions of the previous century had succeeded in limiting the political and economic power of the crown, and patronage reflected this situation. Between 1720 and 1830 there was little court patronage of any significance compared with the royal patronage in France. Also there was hardly any from the established Anglican Church, which, in the age of Locke and Voltaire, was becoming increasingly liberal, tolerant and sceptical, but still, of course, Protestant and thus basically anti-art. The aristocracy and the middle classes played the major part and were responsible for most of the commissions.

How far were these secular patrons responsible for changes in style and content in art? Did they lead, follow, or oppose artistic endeavour? They were often in the vanguard. The Earl of Burlington, both patron and architect, helped to inspire a new movement in architecture; Sir William Hamilton collected Greek vases and thus gave impetus to the Neoclassical movement; Captain Coram encouraged painters by filling his Foundling Hospital with 'history' paintings; Horace Walpole triggered off a new style by turning his cottage at Twickenham into a 'Gothic' castle. Patrons were often eager to take up new styles in architecture and the decorative arts as soon as they were evolved. The 'Gothic' and the 'Greek' followed on the heels of Palladianism, whilst Wedgwood's 'Etruscan' ware was adopted as soon as the gaiety of Rococo shepherdesses had begun to pall.

Nevertheless, underlying conservatism ensured the existence of a struggle between patrons and some progressive artists, especially in painting. Gainsborough wanted to paint landscapes, but was forced to paint portraits in order to make a living. Hogarth and Reynolds wanted to paint 'history' subjects, but could receive hardly any commissions for them. Although there was more willingness to accept new styles than in our own day, these new styles were only accepted as long as they did not challenge established attitudes of mind – attitudes which laid down what a picture should look like and what should be its subject, what a building should be for and how it should be constructed. Most patrons could not appreciate Turner's later and more abstract landscapes. Neither could they accept Constable's claim that green grass should be painted green, such was their reverence for discoloured old masters. In a century which is generally thought of as a period of calm and stability, the overall scene was complex. Some patrons led, more followed, but many opposed change and development.

The Palladian Phase

In 1712 the 3rd Earl of Shaftesbury published a *Letter concerning the Art or Science of Design*. In it he condemned Wren as a 'Court' architect, criticised the style of architecture which has become known as the English Baroque, and argued for a more dignified and sober school of design. By 1720 the Palladian style had been established and had been eagerly adopted by the new Whig oligarchy. Classical restraint, sobriety and a static dignity were its chief characteristics, and it was ideally suited to the needs of a new aristocracy and middle class determined to demonstrate their prosperity and independence by building villas and country houses on their estates. Palladian architecture had been launched by Colen Campbell's *Vitruvius Britannicus*, the first volume of which had appeared in 1715, and was subscribed to by twenty-two dukes and most of the main officers of state in the new government.

The most ardent disciple and disseminator of the new style was Richard Boyle, Earl of Burlington, who had visited Italy in 1719 and returned with

141

THE MORNING WALK

1785
Thomas Gainsborough 1727–88
oil on canvas
93 × 70 in (236 × 178 cm)
National Gallery, London

This painting is one of Gainsborough's finest late portraits. The two figures are William Hallett and his wife Elizabeth, and the picture is evidently a marriage portrait. Gainsborough had by this time stopped sending paintings to the Royal Academy exhibitions because of a dispute over hanging. He considered that his paintings were hung too high on the walls, and when the Academy did not comply with his wishes, he refused to exhibit there again.

261

the English artist, later to turn architect, William Kent and many original drawings by Palladio. Burlington's active patronage and his own architectural designing finally established the style. He built Chiswick House between 1724 and 1729 and it became the visible and material apologia of Palladian doctrine. Another important early patron of the Palladian style was Lord Herbert, who commissioned Roger Morris to build a villa for him at Marble Hill, Twickenham. The new Whigs, and to a lesser extent the Tories, with their vested interest in the maintenance of the new Hanoverian dynasty, took up the building style eagerly. It was not only the aristocrats who were, in Vanbrugh's words, 'running mad after building'. In 120 documented cases, between 1710 and 1740 twenty-seven builders of new houses were peers, but ninety-three were commoners. Many of the latter were at one time or another members of Parliament, and in the period from 1710 to 1725, seventy per cent of the commoners were members of Parliament. These figures show that, while the transfer of patronage from crown to subject started after the 1688 Revolution with the first-generation Whigs, it was the large body of second-generation Whigs who completed this change with their desire to establish their own independent positions as powerful local magnates free from any control from the king or the court. In the eighteenth century, unlike the seventeenth, there were no grandiose court projects for palaces for the monarch. Later in the century, Buckingham House was bought by the king from a subject, and Nash's subsequent rebuilding of it was not on the magnificent scale of the architectural projects of Charles I. Power, economic, political and social, had moved from the king to the subject.

The devotees of the Palladian school eagerly adopted a style of interior decoration that was gay and uninhibited compared to the dignity of the exteriors. This was reflected, too, in the furniture. The Rococo William Kent style, so called because of Kent's own schemes of interior decoration, produced chairs and tables that exhibited flowing curves and scroll work and a profusion of gilt wood.

The aspiring middle classes, not content with new houses, also wanted paintings. As well as portraits, the 'conversation piece' appealed to these new patrons, and small, informal pictures, ideally suited to line the walls of the smaller houses and villas of the Palladian style, became popular. The paintings usually showed groups of people, often families, joined together in the informal atmosphere of a music party or taking tea. The style, though essentially English, had its roots in France with Watteau, and was probably transmitted by Philippe Mercier, an artist who had come to England sometime after 1726, possibly at the command of Frederick, Prince of Wales. It was first practised by such English artists as Hogarth and Hayman in the 1730s and later achieved a high-water mark in the hands of Arthur Devis, who, with his doll-like figures and attractive backgrounds, expressed perfectly the striving for respectability which characterised the middle classes in the middle of the century.

Patronage and landscape
Many hospitals and schools were built in the eighteenth century, which in some ways saw the beginning of philanthropic social services. In 1739, Captain Thomas Coram, a middle-class merchant adventurer, started the Foundling Hospital for orphans. Its interest from the point of view of patronage is that a number of contemporary English artists contributed paintings to hang on the walls. Hayman and Highmore adorned the new institution with history paintings, a kind of picture which, although regarded by theorists as the highest genre in painting, was not normally

143
THE HARLOT'S PROGRESS
1732
William Hogarth 1697–1764
engraving
British Museum, London

96

CHISWICK HOUSE

1724–29
Richard Boyle, Earl of Burlington 1694–1753
Chiswick, London

Lord Burlington's villa is a variation on the theme of Palladio's Villa Rotonda which Colen Campbell had imitated more closely at Mereworth in 1723. A lesson in architecture, rather than a house to be lived in, Chiswick House was one of the most important buildings of the Palladian movement and, together with Campbell's Wanstead in Essex, confirmed a new style in country house architecture–precise, sober, dignified and classical.

This is the first scene of the *Harlot's Progress* series which Hogarth engraved and published in 1732. The original paintings were sold to Alderman Beckford in 1745 and are believed to have perished in the Fonthill fire of 1755. Hogarth made far more money out of the engravings than from the original pictures, and it was largely through his efforts that the Copyright Act of 1735, or 'Hogarth's Act', was passed by Parliament, safeguarding the interests of the original artists against the pirates who used their designs and sold the engravings at a cheaper price.

commissioned. Landscapes were also painted for the hospital by Gainsborough and the young Richard Wilson. Hogarth throughout his life had ambitions to be a 'history' painter, that is, to paint grand epic pictures with subjects taken from the Bible or classical history and mythology, but he could not obtain commissions for them, although he did paint *The Pool of Bethesda* for St Bartholomew's Hospital in 1735–36. Most English patrons believed that English artists should only be portrait painters, and they turned to Italian old masters as the only artists capable of history painting. Thus the importance of such patrons as Coram was that artists were enabled to paint whatever kind of picture they wanted. Hogarth objected to what he considered to be an absurdly exaggerated veneration for old masters and attacked the flourishing trade in old master paintings, which was susceptible to the danger of faking and forgery and to the unscrupulousness of profiteering art dealers.

Another enlightened patron was Jonathan Tyers, who opened the Vauxhall Pleasure Gardens in 1732 and commissioned artists to paint pictures for the pavilions and boxes where people danced and dined. Hogarth, Hayman, Marcellus Laroon and others painted for Tyers, and their work for Vauxhall varied from light-hearted history painting to illustrations of Shakespeare, fancy pictures and scenes from contemporary life. Tyers also commissioned Roubiliac's statue of Handel for his pleasure gardens and was one of the most progressive patrons of native artists in the first half of the century.

William Hogarth's wealth was made from engravings, not paintings. The originality of his engraved series, *The Harlot's Progress* (1732), *The Rake's Progress* (1735) and *Marriage à la Mode* (1745), moral satires on contemporary life, reached a wide public through the medium of engraving, and as most people could afford a few shillings, his series were bought by the poorer classes as well as the rich. The topicality, humour and contemporary subject matter of Hogarth's engravings ensured their popularity and they could be appreciated on many levels, from the intellectual to the bawdy. The importance of the sale of these engravings cannot be over stressed, for it initiated a new phase in the patronage of art. The work of artists became available to all classes and was no longer the province of the rich alone. **143**

One of the most important factors in forming the taste of patrons was the Grand Tour. By the middle of the century it had become fashionable for a young aristocrat or man of wealth to travel to Italy through France and Switzerland, and spend a number of weeks or months in Rome, Florence, Naples, and to a lesser extent Venice. The Tour was conceived of as the completion of his education.

One of the most popular artists to be collected by the English was Claude, whose calm classical landscapes, with their idealisation of nature, became the yardstick by which all landscape painting was judged in England. Many of his paintings found their way into English collections, and the wealthy dilettante Richard Payne Knight made a large collection of his drawings which he bequeathed to the British Museum. Indeed, early in the century, English artists aspiring to be landscape painters had to imitate the style of Claude in order to sell their work. Gaspard Poussin **160** was another seventeenth-century landscape painter much admired, as was Salvator Rosa, with his sublime depictions of wild untamed nature, and Nicolas Poussin, with his classical and intellectual interpretation of landscape. **166**

These four artists had all worked in Italy, though the two Poussins and Claude were French, only Salvator being Italian. Undoubtedly the

142

Grand Tour strengthened the Englishman's belief that Italy had produced the greatest painters, and their collections reflected this preference. The great names like Raphael were difficult to come by, but eighteenth-century British houses were full of paintings by, or believed at the time to be by, **168** such artists as Guido Reni, Carlo Maratta, Domenichino and the Carracci family. In this atmosphere it is hardly surprising that Canaletto, the **146** Venetian view painter, was so successful when he came to England. In fact he found that he attracted more patrons in England than in his native Venice, and he stayed in this country from 1746 with only a short break until 1755. There is, today, hardly a Canaletto of any importance in any of the public collections of Italy.

Towards the middle of the century collectors began to turn to the Dutch seventeenth-century naturalistic landscape painters. Claude was still venerated, but the more intimate and humble aspects of nature were beginning to be appreciated. Between 1748 and 1750 no less than a hundred paintings by Jacob Ruysdael were auctioned in London, and after 1750 there was a considerable rise in the sale of paintings by such artists as **147** Hobbema, Wynants and Wouvermans in Britain. This change in taste was all the more surprising because academic theorists still regarded the Dutch artists as practitioners of one of the lowest genres. The appreciation of Dutch landscape nonetheless increased, and affected and **148, 149,** influenced English artists such as Gainsborough and Morland with their **164** 'picturesque' interpretation of English landscape.

Despite this interest in landscape on the part of dealers and collectors, English artists still found it difficult to sell this kind of picture. Gainsborough claimed that he preferred painting 'landskips', but he was forced through financial necessity to make his living by painting portraits. **149** His *Watering Place*, painted in 1777, and said by Horace Walpole to be 'in the style of Rubens, and by far the finest landscape ever painted in England, and equal to the Great Masters', was not sold until 1797, and then only for ninety-seven guineas. In contrast to this, in 1787 he was charging as much as 160 guineas for a full-length portrait. English landscapists did find some patrons, but it was the exception rather than the rule. One such was Lord Shelburne, later the Marquess of Lansdowne, who commissioned landscapes from Barret, Deane, Gainsborough and Wilson in the 1760s to decorate the drawing room at Bowood.

The career of Richard Wilson provides an interesting reflection on the way English landscapists were treated by patrons. Ruskin, in the middle of the nineteenth century, praised him and wrote that 'with Richard Wilson the history of sincere landscape art founded on a meditative love of nature begins in England'. He was also valued and esteemed by Constable, Turner and Crome, but his life was one of increasing gloom and poverty. At the beginning of his career he had some success, and during his stay in Italy (1750–58) and for a short time after he was patronised by a number of aristocrats, notably the Earl of Dartmouth, the Earl of Leicester and Lord Pembroke. The latter commissioned four views of his estate at Wilton after his return from Italy. This was, as it turned out, an enlightened piece of patronage, for the pictures are among the finest of Wilson's landscapes, but it also demonstrates that English artists were still thought of as topographers rather than as landscapists who could paint whatever natural scenery they wanted. George III himself preferred the lighter and more artificial style of Zuccarelli, a Venetian painter who worked in London between 1751 and 1762 and again from 1765 to 1771. From 1770 to 1775 Wilson declined from relative prosperity to poverty and received few commissions. In 1775 he accepted the post of Librarian

144
CAPTAIN CORAM
1740
William Hogarth 1697–1764
oil on canvas
92 × 55·5 in (233 × 141 cm)
Thomas Coram Foundation, London

Captain Thomas Coram, a retired merchant, started the Foundling Hospital for orphans in 1739. In 1740 Hogarth presented this portrait to the hospital, which was filled, largely on his instigation, with paintings by contemporary native artists. As the public had some access to the building this was one of the first steps towards the idea of an academy or gallery where works by British painters could be seen by everyone. It was significant that the middle-class sitter was given the grand style treatment, formerly reserved only for kings or aristocrats.

145 *above*

MARRIAGE A LA MODE:
THE COUNTESS'S
MORNING LEVEE *detail*

completed by 1745
William Hogarth 1697–1764
oil on canvas
27·75 × 35·75 in (70·5 × 91 cm)
National Gallery, London

The series shows the collapse of a marriage
entered upon for reasons of financial gain,
vanity and snobbery. In this fourth picture
of the series, the countess is arranging an
assignation with the lawyer, Silvertongue.
The pictures on the walls are a good indication of the taste of the time as well as
being subtle comments on the story. On
the wall on the right (not visible here) is a
copy after Correggio's *Jupiter and Io*, and a
picture attributed to Caravaggio, *Lot and
his Daughters*. On the left, under the portrait of Silvertongue, is a copy after Michelangelo's *Ganymede and the Eagle*.

THE THAMES FROM RICHMOND HOUSE

1746
Antonio Canale (Canaletto) 1697–1768
oil on canvas
43 × 47 in (109 × 119 cm)
collection of the Duke of Richmond and Gordon, Goodwood House

This was one of the first pictures painted by Canaletto after his
arrival in England. His early London views are the best of his
English paintings; the quality of his work tended to decline in the
later years of his stay. Canaletto was lured to England by the
prospect of numerous commissions and he prospered while he was
in this country. As an Italian he enjoyed great favour, along with
the painter Zuccarelli and the many Italian opera singers who
worked in England at the same time.

147 *below*

WOODY LANDSCAPE WITH WATERMILL

Meindert Hobbema 1638–1709
oil on canvas
24·5 × 33·5 in (62 × 85 cm)
Dulwich College Picture Gallery, London

The naturalistic and unidealised landscapes of seventeenth-century
Dutch artists such as Hobbema became popular after about 1750,
influencing many English painters from Gainsborough to Crome.
This picture was, like Guido Reni (**168**), given to the Dulwich
Gallery by Sir Francis Bourgeois. During the early years of the
nineteenth century Dulwich was the major English picture gallery
and remained so until the National Gallery on its present site was
declared open by Queen Victoria in April 1838.

148 GAINSBOROUGH'S FOREST

detail, oil on canvas,
48 × 61 in (122 × 155 cm)
Thomas Gainsborough 1727–88
National Gallery, London

The picture is undated, but it was almost certainly finished by the end of 1748, when Gainsborough was at Sudbury, Suffolk, seeing to his deceased father's estate. It is an excellent example of his early landscape style: it seems to be the very breath of the English countryside, but in fact the composition is planned and artificial, as in the Dutch paintings which inspired it. Gainsborough himself described these paintings as his 'imitations of little Dutch landscapes'.

149 *below* THE WATERING PLACE

c. 1785, Thomas Gainsborough 1727–88
oil on canvas, 58 × 71 in (147 × 180 cm)
National Gallery, London

Gainsborough found it difficult to sell straightforward landscapes such as this one, though he was immensely successful as a portrait painter. Since the early 1760s he had been inspired by the landscapes of Rubens. The handling and style of this painting is reminiscent of Rubens's picture of the same subject belonging to the Duke of Montague, which Gainsborough saw many years before.

150

THE APOTHEOSIS OF HOMER

John Flaxman 1755–1826
Wedgwood vase
Wedgwood Museum, Barlaston

The original design on this vase was produced by Flaxman in 1788 for Josiah Wedgwood, and it was used on a number of Wedgwood's products, including a jasper-ware plaque which is now in the British Museum. The composition is directly derived from a relief then in the Colonna Palace, which Flaxman could have known either from a cast or from an engraving. Wedgwood's patronage of Flaxman, as of the other artists he employed, was on a strictly businesslike basis and he rejected or altered any designs which he considered to be unsatisfactory.

151

RED-FIGURED HYDRIA

c. 410 BC
Meidias painter
h. 52 in (205 cm)
British Museum, London

This is one of the vases collected by Sir William Hamilton which was acquired by the British Museum in 1772. These vases were generally believed at the time to be Etruscan. Thus Adam's room at Osterley was called the Etruscan room, when in fact it was inspired by Greek vase painting. Hamilton's collection also influenced Flaxman's designs for Wedgwood (**150**), and Wedgwood's own factory was called Etruria. The upper register shows the Rape of the Daughters of Leucippus; the lower register, Hercules in the Garden of the Hesperides.

152

BATTLE OF
LAPITHS AND CENTAURS

sculpture from one of the metopes on the Parthenon
mid-fifth century BC
marble
British Museum, London

The Earl of Elgin was appointed British Ambassador in Constantinople in 1799. His first intention was merely to survey and make measured drawings of the Parthenon and its sculpture, but when he saw the decay into which it was falling and how the sculpture itself was being sold off to anyone who wanted to buy, he obtained the permission of the Turkish authorities to ship it to England, where it was bought for the British Museum in 1816.

to the Royal Academy at £50 a year, but he painted little after 1774. He died in 1782, a bitter and impoverished man.

Neoclassicism

Neoclassicism was the most important movement in art to affect English taste in the eighteenth century. Its importance in the sphere of patronage lies largely in the fact that the style embraced all the arts, from painting, sculpture and architecture to interior decoration, pottery and silver. The aim of these artists and critics was to bring a new seriousness to the arts in reaction to the 'frivolous' and 'decadent' style of the Rococo. Stylistically and formally, the sculpture, architecture and painting of the Greeks and Romans was the model to be imitated and revered. The most serious practitioners of the style produced works that were severe, rigorous and even cold in conception, but in England at least Neoclassicism signalled the birth of a pleasing and elegant decorative style that can be found in the architecture of Adam, the sculpture of Flaxman and the pottery of Wedgwood.

English, French and German enthusiasts initiated the movement in the late 1750s and early 1760s, but it was Italy which provided the inspiration for the style. The recent excavations at Pompeii and Herculaneum, the discovery of Greek temples such as those at Paestum, and the new surge of archaeological enthusiasm provided the sources. Englishmen on the Grand Tour eagerly purchased Greek, or what they believed to be Greek, statues, coins and medals and dealers in Rome pursued their trade with vigour, if not with complete honesty. In 1734 the Society of Dilettanti was formed in London. Originally devoted to discussion by travellers returning from the Mediterranean, it soon acquired a serious interest in archaeology and supported several expeditions to Greece and Asia Minor. Stuart and Revett travelled to Greece between 1751 and 1755 in order to make drawings of ancient Greek buildings and on their return were elected members of the society. This assisted them in the publication of *The Antiquities of Athens*, the first volume of which came out in 1762. English country houses soon began to exhibit Greek ornaments and architectural motifs, and parks were dotted with accurate imitations of Greek temples. The first of these was built at Hagley in 1758.

Gavin Hamilton (1723–98), painter, dealer and archaeologist, was one of the most important disseminators of the 'new style'. He spent much of his life in Italy and bought many statues which found their way into British collections. He wrote to Charles Towneley, sometime after 1775, urging that 'the most valuable acquisition a man of refined taste can make is a piece of fine Greek sculpture'. Hamilton sold many statues to Towneley, whose collection of Greek and Roman marbles was then one **165** of the largest in England. Lord Shelburne also bought from Hamilton, whose attraction as a dealer in comparison with such men as Pacetti was that he had a reputation for honesty and fair dealing. The *Wounded Amazon*, found in 1771 at Tor Colombaro, was sold to Lord Shelburne, as was a Hermes found at Hadrian's Villa in 1769. The Towneley collection was purchased in 1805 by the British Museum which had been founded in 1753 on the basis of the vast, miscellaneous collection that Sir Hans Sloane left to the nation on his death. The museum was then in Montagu House, and it was not until 1823, when it became obvious that the building could not accommodate the rapidly expanding collections, that the present building was commissioned from Sir Robert Smirke. Undoubtedly the most important acquisition of Greek antiquities was that of the sculpture from the Parthenon and Erectheum (the Elgin marbles) which were **152** purchased in 1816 for £35,000.

153

THE FURY OF ATHAMAS
1790–92
John Flaxman 1755–1826
marble
Ickworth Hall

This statue, inspired by antique models such as the Laocoön, was commissioned by Lord Hervey while Flaxman was in Rome. Flaxman wrote to Romney, the artist, on 15th of April 1790, 'His Lordship . . . immediately ordered me to execute a group in marble, the figures as large as the Gladiator, from a sketch in clay which I had made.' It must have been a somewhat peremptory demand, for it led him into staying in Rome much longer than he had intended.

154

THE THEOCRITUS CUP
1812
John Flaxman 1755–1826
silver-gilt
h. 9·5 in (24 cm)
Royal Collection, Windsor Castle

Flaxman played a considerable part in popularising the Neoclassical style. As well as his sculptures (**153**) and his Greek designs for Josiah Wedgwood (**150**), he designed several pieces of plate, of which this is one, for the Regency silversmiths Rundell and Bridge. The cup is in the shape of an original Greek krater and the scenes are taken from the *Idylls* of Theocritus; the illustration shows two youths contending for the favours of a maiden.

Gavin Hamilton also dealt in paintings, both of the Renaissance and Baroque periods, and his assiduity and energy is one of the reasons for so many Italian paintings finding their way into English collections. Two of his most sensational hauls were Raphael's *Ansidei Madonna*, bought from the Servite church of San Fiorenzo in 1764 and sold to Lord Shelburne, and Leonardo's *Virgin of the Rocks* from the Hospital of Santa Caterina 163 alla Ruolta which was sold to Lord Lansdowne. The Carracci, Guido Reni and Domenichino also featured prominently in his dealing.

Sir William Hamilton, the British envoy and plenipotentiary in Naples, made a vast collection of Greek vases. His first collection was purchased 151 by the British Museum in 1772 and his second was sent to England for sale in 1798. The designs on these vases had a decisive influence on forming the style of the sculptor John Flaxman, and provided the formal inspiration for his illustrations to the *Iliad* and the *Odyssey*, published in 1793, which were bought up avidly. Flaxman was patronised by Lord Hervey of Ickworth, who commissioned his *Fury of Athamas* in 1794. The owner 153 claimed that it 'exceeded the Laocoön in expression', which is doubtful, but it was greatly admired and is still at Ickworth in Suffolk. He also executed many church monuments. Sculpture was at this time largely confined to such monuments, and foreign-born sculptors such as Rysbrack and Roubiliac had made their living largely by them. Their work can be 155 found in many country churches throughout the British Isles. Flaxman's talents were also used by Josiah Wedgwood before the sculptor went to Italy in 1787, and Wedgwood's Neoclassical pottery was one of the most important factors in the general popularisation of the new style. Flaxman designed the figures on many of Wedgwood's products, ranging from 150 plaques and medallions to vases and teapots. Wedgwood was practical and businesslike, possessed of considerable acumen and foresight, and he employed many contemporary artists in the production of his pottery and earthenware. He was also a patron in his own right, and commissioned the *Corinthian Maid* from Joseph Wright of Derby, a painting of particular interest to him as the girl in the painting was a daughter of a potter.

The Neoclassical style percolated through all forms of the visual arts until it adorned such everyday objects as cups and firegrates. Flaxman designed several pieces of plate for the leading Regency silversmiths, Rundell and Bridge, and his Theocritus Cup of 1812–13 is in the shape of 154 an original Greek krater. English patrons also liked Neoclassical details and motifs in their portraits, which accounts for the success of Mengs and especially Batoni, who both worked in Italy in the second half of the eighteenth century and painted English aristocrats on the Grand Tour. Batoni's portraits of Englishmen, many of which remain in England, include pieces of classical sculpture, often with the Colosseum in the background.

The Scottish-born architect Robert Adam evolved an elegant decorative 157, 1 style from classical sources, and he was widely patronised by the aristocracy and upper middle classes in the second half of the century. The Adam style replaced the Palladian style and brought to English interior decoration a new dimension and lightness. Most houses rebuilt or redecorated in the latter part of the eighteenth century bear the mark, if not of Adam himself, at least of his influence. Adam published in 1764 a book on the ruins of Diocletian's Palace at Split on the Dalmatian coast and his repertory of decorative and architectural motifs is largely culled from Roman sources. Patrons eagerly adopted his pleasing style for their own houses and decorated their walls and ceilings with paintings and panels by Angelica Kauffman, Antonio Zucchi and Biagio Rebecca. His was essentially an unserious style; it was not until the turn of the century that furniture and decoration became severely classical with the Regency style of Thomas Hope, but it was especially attractive to the aristocracy and middle classes at the end of the century with their taste for luxury and elegance. The furniture designer Thomas Chippendale, previously noted for his traditional Rococo designs published in *The Gentleman and Cabinet* **156** *Maker's Director* in 1754, was quick to grasp Adam's Neoclassical principles and apply them to his own work. Some of his finest pieces are those made between 1766 and 1770 for Harewood House, Yorkshire. *The* **171** *Director* stimulated a new interest in furniture, which was characterised throughout the eighteenth century by its high standard of craftsmanship, and also influenced other craftsmen like Hepplewhite and Sheraton.

The Royal Academy and history painting

In 1768 King George III conferred a charter for the foundation of the Royal Academy. But the monarch provided financial backing only initially, and the Academy, unlike the state-controlled Academy of France, was a private institution. The importance of this foundation cannot be over stressed because artists could now show their works at an annual exhibition and moreover could paint the kind of history pictures and landscapes that they wanted to. Sir Joshua Reynolds, the first president, together with artists such as Barry, believed that the Academy would provide the means for the founding of a strong national school of history painting. The style did subsequently increase, but it never thrived in the eighteenth century because patrons were still unwilling to commission such pictures. An important exception to this rule was Alderman Boydell, who opened the Boydell Shakespeare Gallery in Pall Mall in 1786. He commissioned over 150 pictures of Shakespearean subjects, to be treated in a grand historical manner, and he employed such contemporary English and American artists as Reynolds, Fuseli, West, Kauffman and Barry. Engravings of these works were also issued.

Reynold's 'Discourses', delivered from 1768 until 1792 at the Royal Academy, aimed to set down the principles for an academic art. He believed that the finest painting had been produced by the Florentine artists of the Renaissance, and that ideally all art should be based on that of the past. He argued for history painting, but his own art was mainly confined to portraiture, which he attempted to elevate by introducing elements of the 'grand style'. Many of his portraits of the 1770s, especially of women, show his sitters in allegorical guise with classical draperies, but his finest portraits were those of a more informal nature. Gainsborough, who came to London from Bath in 1774, was his greatest rival, and his more spontaneous and unscholarly portraits were often preferred to the weighty works of Reynolds. In the 1780s both artists could command up to 200 guineas for a full-length portrait.

George III was a more active patron than his two Hanoverian predecessors, and although court patronage never reached the proportions it achieved in the early seventeenth century, he did, with the advice and encouragement of his first prime minister, Lord Bute, build up the royal collection in the early years of his reign. In 1761 he bought the collection of pictures belonging to Consul Smith, an Englishman living in Venice, and he used Richard Dalton to obtain pictures for him from Italy. One of his most important purchases was that of Cardinal Albani's collection of drawings, which was engineered by Robert Adam and his brother James. The purchase was completed in 1762. The king also patronised certain contemporary artists such as the American Benjamin West and Gainsborough. It was under George III, too, that the architect James

155
MONUMENT TO JOHN,
DUKE OF MONTAGU
*detail showing Charity with a child on her arm
1752, marble
Louis François Roubiliac 1705?—62
Warkton Parish Church*

The best eighteenth-century sculpture in Britain is in the form of church monuments. It was very common for the family of an aristocrat or magnate to commission an elaborate monument to commemorate him, which was set up in the local church. Sculpture of very high quality is thus found, not only in Westminster Abbey and St Paul's Cathedral, but also in numerous parish churches throughout Britain—churches such as Warkton, which has two monuments by Roubiliac.

Wyatt began to rebuild and extend Windsor Castle in the Gothic style.

Interest in Gothic architecture was stimulated by a number of patrons and architects, despite the fact that the majority of building was then in the classical style. The mania for Gothic was largely frivolous and unscholarly and was mainly restricted to the design of garden pavilions and follies. It was only in the early nineteenth century that the Gothic Revival became a serious movement with a high moral purpose. Designs for Gothic buildings were produced by such men as Batty Langley in the first half of the eighteenth century, and in 1750 Horace Walpole, dilettante and man of letters, started gothicising the small house he had bought at 170 Twickenham which became known as Strawberry Hill. Though this took the nature of a polite and witty 'conceit', Walpole was keen to ensure that the details of his interiors were based on genuine medieval prototypes such as tombs and screens. Also in the middle of the century an interest in Chinese architecture became prevalent and Chippendale introduced what were believed to be Chinese motifs into his chairs and tables. It was this taste for the exotic that was to blossom most extrava-172, 173 gantly in the Pavilion at Brighton.

After the middle of the century, London increased in importance as a centre for the sale of pictures. High prices were recorded, sometimes up to £3000 and over for a genuine old master, and many people from the continent sent their pictures to London to be sold. After the outbreak of the French Revolution in 1789 this practice increased. The important 256 Orléans collection including magnificent paintings by Raphael, Titian and Poussin (now on loan to the National Gallery of Scotland), was sold to a syndicate headed by the 3rd Duke of Bridgewater in the early 1790s. It may be thought that the closing down of the continent to English tourists with the outbreak of the Napoleonic wars would have encouraged English patrons to turn to English artists, but in fact the reverse was the case, at least to start with, and pictures continued to pour into London. The Italians, frightened that their collections would be appropriated by Napoleon, were eager to sell to English agents who brought many pictures back to England. Robert Fagan, the British consul general in Sicily, was an active agent and it was largely through his endeavours that the Altieri Claudes were imported into England in 1799. The important Dulwich Gallery collection was also being amassed at this time, largely by Noel Desenfans, who built up the nucleus of the collection, initially for the King of Poland. Subsequently Desenfans and Sir Francis Bourgeois 147, 168 transferred the paintings to Dulwich and founded a gallery which was built by the architect Sir John Soane and reflected accurately the taste of British patrons of the time.

Recognition of English art

After the turn of the century patrons became gradually more interested in English artists; the patriotism engendered by the Napoleonic wars was a part cause of this, as was the fact that critics and patrons could look back on a century in which there had been English artists of considerable repute. The idea gradually spread that they could compete with and even surpass the work of foreigners. But this change only came about gradually and in 1805, at the sale of the Boydell Gallery, only eleven paintings fetched over £100. However, in the same year the British Institution was founded, which was significant because it was supported financially by almost all the wealthiest patrons of the day. At last a public gallery of British painting was formed and exhibitions were held, though these were not seen in any way as a threat to the Royal Academy exhibitions, which still retained the allegiance of the best artists of the time. A visitor to the British

156
DESIGN FOR A STATE BED
a page from the 'Gentleman and Cabinet-Maker's Director'
first edition 1754
Thomas Chippendale c. 1718–79
British Museum, London

This publication was immensely successful and had run to three editions by 1762. It was the first comprehensive pattern book of furniture design to appear and showed Chippendale's early Rococo designs, often with Gothic and Chinese motifs. Cabinet-makers used it extensively, so that the term 'Chippendale', when used to describe a piece of furniture, usually means that it is in the style of Chippendale's *Director*, rather than by Chippendale himself.

157 left
DINING ROOM, SALTRAM HOUSE

Adam working at Saltram c. 1768–c. 1780
Robert Adam 1728–92

Saltram is one of several houses that had been built earlier for which Adam designed the interiors. He was commissioned by John Parker and his wife Lady Catherine to carry out extensive alterations, and he supervised all the elements of the decorative scheme, from the stucco ceiling and the pattern of the carpet to the placing of the pictures, here painted by Antonio Zucchi. The Parkers were friends of Sir Joshua Reynolds, who was originally a Devon man, and many of the portraits at Saltram are by him. Reynolds often stayed here, once with Samuel Johnson in 1762, and advised the Parkers on the buying of old masters. One of the paintings at Saltram, by Guercino, was formerly in Reynolds's own collection.

158 above
THE KIMBOLTON CABINET

1771
Robert Adam, 1728–92
marquetry work with inlaid marble panels
h. 74·25 in (188 cm)
Victoria and Albert Museum, London

The finished cabinet differs considerably from the original design, which is preserved in the Soane Museum. This was probably because it would have been too expensive to make. The cabinet was commissioned by the Duchess of Manchester as a decorative frame for a set of eleven landscapes in inlaid marble purchased by her in Florence. The marquetry work was carried out by one of the leading London cabinet-makers.

159
SALOON AT HOLKHAM HALL

begun 1734
William Kent 1685–1748

Built in the Palladian style for Lord Leicester, Holkham Hall provided an appropriate home for his important collection of Roman antiquities and fine pictures. The richness in the decorative detail of this interior contrasts with the austerity of the exterior. The side-table on the left has the heavy exuberance which characterises the William Kent style of furniture.

160 *below*

DIDO BUILDING CARTHAGE

1815
Joseph Mallord William Turner 1775–1851
oil on canvas
61·25 × 91·25 in (155 × 232 cm)
National Gallery, London

Exhibited at the Royal Academy in 1815, this is a romantic historical landscape in the manner of Claude (**166**), painted with the clear intention of emulating, if not surpassing, the seventeenth-century French painter's style. The painting was not sold by the artist, but forms part of the Turner Bequest. A very large number of Turner's pictures and drawings were bequeathed to the nation by the painter, but a dispute over the will made a settlement impossible until 1856. The pictures and drawings are now divided between the National Gallery, the Tate Gallery and the British Museum.

161

THE HAYWAIN

1821
John Constable 1776–1837
oil on canvas
51·25 × 73 in (130 × 185 cm)
National Gallery, London

Although it was exhibited at the Royal Academy in 1821, this picture caused far more comment in France in 1824, when it was shown at the Paris Salon and gained a gold medal. Arrowsmith, an Anglo-French dealer, bought this together with two other Constables from the artist in the same year for the small sum of £250. Constable worked on *The Haywain* for probably as long as nine months.

162 *below*

THE SIMONIAC POPE

1824—27
William Blake 1757—1827
pen and watercolour
20·5 × 14·5 in (52·5 × 37 cm)
Tate Gallery, London

Blake's series of illustrations to Dante, of which this is one, was commissioned by John Linnell, who first met Blake in 1818 and was an important friend and patron during the latter's last years. The poet Hayley was one of his earlier patrons, but the artist's marked individuality and isolation in his own visionary world precluded any wide popularity or patronage. He was always poor and only managed to survive by working for publishers as an engraver, and through the generosity of a few close friends.

THE VIRGIN OF THE ROCKS
1483–1506/8
Leonardo da Vinci 1452–1519
panel
74 × 47·25 in (189 × 120 cm)
National Gallery, London

Gavin Hamilton bought this picture from the Hospital of Santa Caterina alla Ruota in 1785. By 1786 he had sold it to Lord Lansdowne, and the National Gallery purchased it from the Earl of Suffolk, a later owner, in 1880. It was originally an altarpiece in the chapel of the Confraternity of the Immaculate Conception in San Francesco Grande at Milan, but there is still a dispute among scholars as to whether this painting, or the version in the Louvre, was the one which was originally commissioned by the confraternity. In any case, it was one of Gavin Hamilton's most sensational purchases.

Institution in 1811 remarked that 'a tasteless and disgraceful preference is no longer given to the wretched fabrications of French and Italian picture dealers. Our artists are no longer entirely confined to portrait painting; but they have some, though not adequate, encouragement to exert their talents in the higher branches of art.'

The Norwich group of landscape painters formed a genuine provincial school which found its patrons in the wealthy merchants and landowners of East Anglia. They owed much to the Dutch naturalistic landscape painters of the seventeenth century, whose works they were able to study in the East Anglian collections. Trade links with the Low Countries and proximity with Holland had helped to encourage the collection of Dutch landscapes in the eighteenth century. The young Gainsborough used to repair and repaint these landscapes for the trade and it was this kind of picture which inspired John Crome, the leading painter of the Norwich **167** School. Crome's most important patron was Thomas Harvey of Catton, whom he met in about 1790, and who owned both Dutch and English landscape paintings. The Norwich Society was founded in 1803 for the purposes of study and discussion and it held its first exhibition in 1805. At this exhibition Crome showed twenty-two pictures, though he only exhibited thirteen paintings at the Royal Academy throughout his life.

English patrons began to build up their own collections of pictures by native artists. In 1804 the landscape painter Joseph Farington said that Sir George Beaumont would have a room devoted to English artists in his new house at Coleorton, and in 1810 Benjamin West informed Farington that 'he had been with the Prince of Wales who seemed much disposed to make a collection of the works of British artists'. The Prince Regent (later George IV) was the most active royal patron of the period. As well as looking favourably on English artists he admired and collected Dutch and Flemish seventeenth-century paintings. His own personal and eccentric creation was the Royal Pavilion at Brighton, where he employed **172, 173** John Nash as architect and eagerly encouraged the adoption of exotic styles, Gothic, Moorish and Chinese, in a theatrical extravaganza that most clearly expresses his buoyant and wayward personality.

Although higher prices were being achieved for English paintings, the more progressive artists still found it difficult to sell their works. Turner died a rich man, but his later works were almost universally derided, and Constable could never make a living from his art. Basically Constable's paintings were regarded as too 'sketchy', and critics and patrons preferred the highly detailed finish of pictures by landscapists such as Callcott and Clarkson Stanfield. Constable was, in fact, more appreciated in France, especially after his *Haywain* had received a gold medal at the Salon of **161** 1824. But neither Constable nor Turner lacked the discerning admiration of a few connoisseurs. Constable was supported by Sir George Beaumont and the Fishers of Salisbury, while both artists received the patronage of the Earl of Egremont at Petworth.

In 1824 the National Gallery was opened in Pall Mall with the collection of John Julius Angerstein, which had been bought by the government for £57,000, and that of Sir George Beaumont who had offered his **166** to the nation as soon as a gallery was built. The pictures were transferred to their present site in 1838. However, the demand for a national collection was one which had to be created rather than met, as the public was not aware of a need and the landowners had their own collections of pictures. It was not until the end of the nineteenth century that British artists themselves were at all adequately represented outside the country houses of the wealthy patrons.

John Sunderland

164 *right*

THE ALE HOUSE DOOR

1792
George Morland 1763–1804
oil on canvas
24·75 × 30·5 in (63 × 77 cm)
National Gallery of Scotland, Edinburgh

Morland's rustic genre scenes were popular
in his time and have remained so. In 1786
he married the sister of William Ward, the
engraver, and subsequently his works sold
widely through the medium of engraving.
Prints after pictures such as this adorned
many of the houses and cottages of the
lower classes and continued to do so
throughout the nineteenth century.

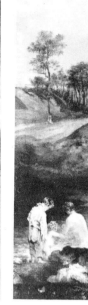

165

CHARLES TOWNELEY
AND HIS FRIENDS

1790
Johann Zoffany 1734/5–1810
oil on canvas
50 × 40 in (127 × 101 cm)
Burnley Art Gallery, Lancashire

Towneley was one of the most avid collectors of antique marbles and statuary
during the eighteenth century. His collection was purchased by the British Museum
in 1808, after his death. Here Towneley is
shown sitting with his dog at his feet; at
the table is d'Hancarville, a well known
antiquary and 'one of the band of virtuosos
who helped to explain the basso-rilievos
on the Portland Vase'.

166 *right*

HAGAR AND THE ANGEL

Claude Gellée, called Le Lorrain 1600–82
oil on canvas mounted on wood
20·75 × 17·25 in (52 × 44 cm)
National Gallery, London

By about 1792–95 this picture was in the
collection of Sir George Beaumont, an
amateur painter and patron of Constable
and Wordsworth. He gave it to the nation
in his gift of 1823 but was allowed to keep
it during his own lifetime. Constable
greatly admired this picture and the composition of his *Dedham Vale* of 1828, in the
National Gallery of Scotland, is based on
the Claude. Claude's paintings were much
coveted in the eighteenth century and
Farington noted in 1794 that one was sold
by the dealer, Vandergucht, for 1500
guineas, a large sum for one painting.

167 *left*

THE PORINGLAND OAK *detail*
c. 1818–20
John Crome 1768–1821
oil on canvas
49·25 × 39·5 in (125 × 100 cm)
Tate Gallery, London

The Norwich school of landscape painters,
of which Crome was the central figure,
was inspired by the naturalistic landscapes
of the Dutch seventeenth century, which
were then being widely collected, particularly by the East-Anglian gentry and
merchants who were Crome's major
patrons. Crome himself was also influenced
by the English landscapist, Richard Wilson.
This may have been the picture that was
exhibited in the Crome exhibition at Norwich in 1821 and was shown at the British
Institution in 1824.

168 *below*

ST JOHN THE BAPTIST
PREACHING IN THE
WILDERNESS

Guido Reni 1575–1642
oil on canvas
88·5 × 63·75 in (224 × 190 cm)
Dulwich College Picture Gallery, London

Many canvases by Guido Reni were bought
in the eighteenth century, as well as copies
and forgeries faked by unscrupulous
dealers to meet the huge demand for
Italian paintings. This picture was included
in the Bourgeois bequest of paintings of
1811 to the Dulwich Gallery, which was
built by Sir John Soane and opened in
1814. Through the generosity of the dealer
Noel Desenfans, his widow and Sir Francis
Bourgeois, the gallery received a
magnificent collection of pictures, all
acquired in the second half of the eighteenth century.

169
THE NEWDIGATE CENTREPIECE

London hallmark for 1743–44
Paul de Lamerie, d. 1751
silver
Victoria and Albert Museum, London

This elaborate centrepiece was a wedding gift. Inside the bowl is inscribed, 'The gift of ye Rt. Honble. Sophia Baroness Lempster to Sr. Roger and Lady Newdigate, AD 1743'. In this year Sir Roger married Sophia Conyers, a grand-daughter of Lord Lempster, and engraved on the silver are the arms of Newdigate impaling those of Conyers. The curvilinear decorative quality of the design shows French influence, which appeared in nearly all branches of the visual arts at this time.

170
STRAWBERRY HILL GALLERY

house started c. 1750; gallery 1759–62
gallery designed by Thomas Pitt
Twickenham

Walpole's Strawberry Hill combines genuine Gothic details–the ceiling of the gallery is adapted from one of the aisles of Henry VII's Chapel at Westminster Abbey –with Walpole's own brand of witty sophistication and just a hint of the macabre, for here he wrote the first Gothic novel, *The Castle of Otranto*. Few of the other Gothic Revival buildings of the eighteenth century followed medieval models so closely, but Walpole took great pains to ensure that his details were correct.

171
SIDEBOARD AND PEDESTALS

c. 1772–75
Thomas Chippendale c. 1718–79
carved rosewood inlaid with other woods and mounted with ormolu
Harewood House

Only a man of wealth could have afforded such a rich and intricate piece of furniture as this sideboard, which was commissioned by the Earl of Harewood. It represents Chippendale's later style, during the time that he was working with the architect Robert Adam, as he was at Harewood. Though this is obviously in the Adam manner, it seems likely that both the design and the execution are Chippendale's own.

172, 173
ROYAL PAVILION

1815–21
John Nash 1752–1835
Brighton

The first Marine Pavilion was built at
Brighton by Henry Holland in 1787. The
complete reconstruction of the exterior in
an 'Indian' style was carried out by John
Nash from 1815 to 1821. The remodelling
of the interior with its many 'Chinese'
features was started in 1802 and carried on
by Nash, Frederick Crace, Robert Jones
and others. George IV used it as a residence
until 1827. The interior view is of the
Saloon, one of the principal rooms in the
original Pavilion. The wallpaper, which is
now framed by late nineteenth-century
mouldings, dates from 1802 and represents
a Chinese formal garden. The mirrors are
probably original and the doors, first hung
in 1818, are of English lacquer work of
exceedingly high quality.

The Victorians had a passion for art which found expression in large international exhibitions and in the social importance attached to, and reflected in, the annual summer exhibitions at the Royal Academy. Artists were able to command large salaries—Millais was reputedly earning £30,000 a year—and recognition was accorded to them not only by peerages or baronetcies but even more flatteringly by the newly established Order of Merit which was conferred by the sovereign on Holman Hunt and G. F. Watts. The place of the collector and connoisseur did not differ very much from earlier years: both continued to be often in advance of fashion and the patron's relationship with an artist might still prove to be as mutually vexatious as in previous centuries. The nineteenth century is of particular interest in the way in which this traditional situation in the world of art was combined with new factors and attitudes. The great increase in the literate public created a demand for magazines and books, which in turn demanded illustrators, so that an artist's work could become more widely disseminated and known than ever before. While Millais objected to one of his paintings being used as an advertisement, other
175 artists like William Nicholson and James Pryde (the 'Beggarstaffs') were only too pleased to have their posters publicly exhibited.

As more and more people had the means to buy works of art so also was there a new development in public patronage. In the past the great European collections had been royal or aristocratic. The foundations of the Louvre and the Prado were the French and Spanish royal collections. In England the royal collection, which had grown since the Commonwealth, remained the queen's, and the National Gallery started with the purchase of a small private collection. During the century the role of the museum director grew in importance as did the collections under his care. In this respect as in many others—the place of the art dealer, of the sale-room, of the critic, and, latterly, the independence of the artist—the art world of the nineteenth century set the pattern for that of today.

In 1837, the year of Queen Victoria's accession, Joseph Neeld M.P. commissioned his portrait bust from Sir Francis Chantrey, who for nearly thirty years had been the leading portrait and memorial sculptor in England. The bust was to take its place with the other marbles in the hall
176 and corridor of Grittleton House in Wiltshire. Neeld had been enabled to make and house his collection by his inheritance in 1828 of a fortune approaching £1,000,000 from his great-uncle, the Regency silversmith Philip Rundell. His taste and collection continued to reflect those Neoclassical canons established early in the century, yet he was also in accord with a change in contemporary fashion, for in 1855 he bought *Eve after the Fall* by Raffaelle Monti (one of the prize-winning exhibits at the Great Exhibition of 1851). In his representation of the natural as
200 opposed to the ideal, Monti's work can be compared with that of the Pre-Raphaelite painters, and this change in taste was further exemplified by Neeld's patronage of Scipione Tadolini, whose naturalistically carved *Pescatrice* he had bought in 1854.

From the last years of the eighteenth century a few connoisseurs had been collecting early Italian paintings. This interest in the early Renaissance was shared by the accomplished diplomatist William Thomas Horner Fox-Strangways, later Earl of Ilchester, who in 1828 gave to Christ Church in Oxford a collection of paintings, chiefly fourteenth and fifteenth-century Florentine works, including those by Sano di Pietro and Jacopo del Sellaio. In 1850 Fox-Strangways made over another such collection to the University Galleries in Oxford, a gift which included Paolo Uccello's
180 *Hunt in a Forest* and predella panels by Bicci di Lorenzo, Fra Filippo Lippi

The National Collections and the Gothic Revival

1837-1910

174

ST GILES' CHURCH
1841–46
Augustus Welby Northmore Pugin 1812–52
Cheadle

The church was originally designed for Lord Shrewsbury in 1841. It was to have been fairly inexpensive—Pugin's work suffered all too frequently from lack of sufficient funds—but fortunately the earl decided to give more money than he had originally intended, and the finished building is one of the most lavish of all Pugin's churches. The exterior is a pleasant enough version of his favourite Perpendicular style, in dull-red sandstone, but the real glory is the interior, where every inch glows with rich patterns and painted decoration. Pugin himself said of the church: 'It is the only place—excepting the hospital at Alton—where I have had an opportunity of showing a *real* revival.'

175

QUEEN VICTORIA AND
HER DOG

1897
William Nicholson 1872–1949
coloured wood engraving
British Museum, London

Whistler complimented William Nicholson on this engraving, calling it a 'wonder-
ful portrait'. This strength and simplicity
of design was also found in the joint work
of Nicholson and James Pryde, who designed posters under the name of J. and W.
Beggarstaff. Nicholson's Jubilee portrait
secured a commission for *Twelve Portraits*,
and between 1898 and 1900 he produced
such books as *London Types*, *An Alphabet*
and *The Book of Animals*.

176

PORTRAIT BUST OF
THE PRINCE CONSORT

1841
Edward Hodges Bailey 1788–1867
marble
Victoria and Albert Museum, London

This bust was one of the numerous marbles
by Bailey, Gibson, Monti and other contemporary sculptors, purchased by Joseph
Neeld M.P. to decorate his hall at Grittleton House in Wiltshire. Neeld's collection,
which was built up over a period of more
than twenty years, reflected both the Neoclassical taste established by Antonio
Canova and the more naturalistic style
introduced in the 1850s.

and Nicola di Maestro Antonio d'Ancona. That these collectors were not
alone in setting a new fashion is clear from the catalogue of the 'Art
Treasures Exhibition' held in Manchester in 1857, where comparable
paintings were shown, from the collections of the Rev. W. Davenport
Bromley, the Rev. John Fuller Russell and Lord Northwick. They were,
however, still ahead of fashion: a note made in his catalogue by a well-
informed visitor to the exhibition refers to a *Virgin and Child* by Pinturicchio as 'a charming tempera painting by a master unknown to me,
details extremely fine'. At this period and in the 1860s one of the most
remarkable collections of Tuscan Trecento and Quattrocento paintings
was being brought together at Highnam Court near Gloucester by Thomas
Gambier-Parry. The latter had started collecting paintings on finishing
his studies at Cambridge in 1837. A list of those bought in 1849 includes a
tondo attributed to Lorenzo di Credi, which provides the first indication of
his taste for the Quattrocento. Two of his most impressive purchases, the
splendid polyptych *Crucifixion with Saints* by Bernardo Daddi and *The
Coronation of the Virgin* by Lorenzo Monaco, were made at the Davenport   **179**
Bromley sale in 1863.

Royal patronage

Among the paintings to be seen at Manchester in 1857 were a number
lent by Albert, the Prince Consort, including the Pinturicchio already
noted. He not only shared the taste for early Italian painting but was also a
pioneer in the revaluation of the early Flemish masters. In 1848 he purchased the collection of one of his relations, Prince Ludwig-Kraft-Ernst of
Oettingen-Wallerstein, which had been sent to London for sale. After his
death the queen, at Prince Albert's wish, presented twenty-two of his
paintings to the National Gallery, among them *An Ecclesiastic Praying*, the   **181**
right wing of a diptych by Gerard David.

Both Prince Albert and Queen Victoria patronised contemporary
British artists. Undoubtedly the royal favourites were William Dyce and
Sir Edwin Landseer. Landseer made numerous sketches and paintings of
the queen's dogs and birds, and among the thirty-nine oil paintings she
owned at his death are *Dash* (1836), *Lory* (1838), *Islay and Tilco with a Red
Macaw and Two Lovebirds* (1839) and *Waldmann* (1841). From William
Dyce, whose scholarly interest in art as well as his friendship for the
German Nazarene artists working in Rome were probably both recommendations, Prince Albert purchased in 1845 the harmonious Quattro-
centist *Madonna and Child*. At the invitation of Sir Robert Peel, himself a
collector and the owner of Rubens's *Chapeau de Paille*, Albert had agreed
in 1841 to act as president of the royal commission set up to consider the
decoration of the new Houses of Parliament, built to the designs of Sir   **201**
Charles Barry between 1837 and 1852. In the open competition for the
frescos three little-known artists, Edward Armitage, Charles West Cope
and the twenty-six-year-old G. F. Watts, won the £300 prizes. Despite
Dyce's expert advice on the technique of fresco painting, this ambitious
attempt at state patronage did not withstand the effects of the London
climate, nor did the commission itself long survive its hard-working and
conscientious president, who died in 1861.

Barry himself described his architectural style as 'late Medieval and
Tudor'. The full, even violent, ardour of the Gothic Revival is to be found
in the work of Augustus Welby Pugin. With such publications as *Contrasts;*   **174, 2**
*or a Parallel between the Noble Edifices of the Middle Ages, and corresponding
buildings of the Present Day; showing the decline of Taste* of 1836 and his
Apology for the Revival of Christian Architecture in England of 1843, Pugin
reinforced the visual example of his buildings such as those for Lord

Shaftesbury at Alton. This enthusiasm for 'true' Christian architecture is clearly evident in the book of designs he made for a Gothic Balliol College, **177** also in 1843. Although the project was unfinished, Pugin's designs formed the basis for those of Alfred Waterhouse which were carried out after 1866. To Pugin's advocacy of an art which expressed the finest aspirations of mankind was soon added that of John Ruskin who published *The Seven Lamps of Architecture* in 1849 and *The Stones of Venice* in 1851 and 1853, becoming thereby a powerful influence on public opinion.

The Pre-Raphaelite Brotherhood and the contemporary scene

Writing of the 'failure' of the English school of painting, Sir E. L. Bulwer, later Lord Lytton, described the prevalent characteristic as 'MATERIAL: nothing raises, elevates, touches or addresses the soul'. Three young artists, William Holman Hunt, John Everett Millais and Dante Gabriel **182, 183** Rossetti, shared this opinion and in the revolutionary year of 1848 formed themselves, with four others, into the Pre-Raphaelite Brotherhood, whose avowed aims were to revive the purity of painting before Raphael, by clarity of colour and line and simplicity of subject. They were initially opposed to the authoritative position of the Royal Academy as an arbiter of contemporary taste, although in 1853 Millais was elected an associate member and became president in the last months of his life. Hunt was never reconciled to the power wielded by the Academy, and Rossetti from the first had preferred to exhibit at the rival British Institution. The short-lived Brotherhood was also opposed to the 'frivolous' standards represented by much contemporary painting, to any continuing influence of Sir 'Sloshua' Reynolds, and to the use of the damaging bituminous varnishes which were already disfiguring some of Wilkie's portraits. Perhaps the Pre-Raphaelites were not really quite as revolutionary as they thought themselves, but their scrupulously careful work, wedded to their declared aims, tended to find them a new class of patron in the provinces. At the sale of the collection of T. E. Plint of Leeds at Christie's in 1863 Chichester Fortescue, for long one of Hunt's metropolitan admirers, noted in his diary that he had 'committed the extravagance' of buying for 200 guineas the finished sketch of Holman Hunt's *Claudio and Isabella*. At the close of the Royal Academy exhibition in 1856 B. G. Windus of Liverpool purchased for 450 guineas Hunt's *The Scapegoat*, painted with **183** such pains at Oosdoom in the Holy Land. In Manchester, too, in the 1857 exhibition, both Millais and Hunt took their place among the 'Modern Masters'. In Oxford, the Printer to the University, the religious and business-like Thomas Combe, was one of the first to patronise and befriend the Pre-Raphaelites. He bought Millais's *The Return of the Dove to the Ark*, which had been hissed at the Academy in 1851, and came to Hunt's rescue in purchasing *Early Britons sheltering a Missionary from the Druids*. Rossetti and the sculptor Thomas Woolner also found patrons in Mr and Mrs Combe. John Ruskin came to the defence of the brotherhood in two long letters to *The Times* as a result of its critic's abuse of *The Return of the Dove to the Ark* and for several years continued his support by his *Academy Notes*, until his severe critique in 1857 of Millais's *Sir Isumbras at the Ford* ('not merely Fall – it is catastrophe'). Such an ally as Ruskin was invaluable to the young artists.

It may seem contradictory that at the same time as the vogue for Gothic architecture artists were increasingly looking to the contemporary scene for their themes. Not only Holman Hunt in *Awakening Conscience* or Rossetti in *Found*, one of his rare essays in narrative art, were painting incidents from daily life. Augustus Leopold Egg, Abraham Solomon and William Maw Egley in *The Travelling Companions, First Class – The*

177

GENERAL PROSPECT OF THE PROPOSED BROAD STREET FRONT OF BALLIOL COLLEGE

1843
Augustus Welby Northmore Pugin 1812–52
pencil and watercolour
Balliol College, Oxford

Of the numerous architects associated with The Gothic Revival none fought for 'true' Christian architecture with more whole-hearted ardour than Pugin. His rejected designs for Balliol are still preserved in the college, among them the general prospect of the college on which the buildings later designed by Alfred Waterhouse are based. The drawings include proposed interiors for a Fellow's room and for an under-graduates' room complete with priedieu, canopied bed and improving text.

Meeting and *Second Class – The Parting*, and *Omnibus Life in London* respectively, reflected the railway age and gave a reminder to visitors to the Academy of the visual impact on landscape and city alike of changes brought about by the industrial and mercantile revolution. The Academy itself was portrayed by William Powell Frith, whose other views of ordinary life included *Derby Day* and *The Railway Station*.

Another development, not so much new as greatly increased in scope and influence, was the part played by dealers such as Ernest Gambart. In 1860 Chichester Fortescue went to visit Gambart's German Gallery to see Holman Hunt's *Christ in the Temple*. On the advice of Charles Dickens, the artist had made an arrangement whereby Gambart was to exhibit the painting and charge for admission, which was expected to bring in £20–£30 a day. The painting was to be engraved (Hunt estimated the cost at £800). Gambart, who was to retain the reproduction rights, would then sell both the painting and the numerous engravings. Hunt, thereby, was able to obtain the 5,500 guineas he wanted for the painting. The engravings reached the homes of hundreds who could not afford nor perhaps even see the original although its exhibition made it easily accessible.

The widespread dissemination of contemporary art in the Victorian period found its widest audience through the work of the illustrators in black and white. Rarely can a mass market have been better served than it was by the artists and engravers during the heyday of the 1860s. Millais illustrated *Framley Parsonage* and *The Small House at Allington* for Trollope; he also contributed, with Hunt's pupil Arthur Hughes, Fred Walker and G. J. Pinwell, to *Once a Week* and *Good Words*. *The Cornhill Magazine*, edited by Thackeray, who took a lively interest in the illustrations, reproduced some of the best of Walker's subjects, and the brothers Dalziel, the engravers, commissioned *The Parables of Our Lord* from Millais. It was at this period, as in the following decades of the century, that *Punch, or the London Charivari* achieved its great popularity and brought the draughtsmanship of Leech, du Maurier and Charles Keene to many who, **178** in enjoying the joke, may yet have missed the artistic skill of the illustrator.

The great years of the national collections

Public instruction and education were precepts dear to the Victorians and the avowed object of their museums and art galleries. That those institutions achieved collections which both in quality and in quantity remain of international importance is due to the connoisseurship, practical resourcefulness and energies of their directors. In 1855 Sir Charles Eastlake was appointed to the newly created post of Director of the National Gallery, where he had already served as keeper since the 1840s. In the relatively short span of ten years Eastlake raised the position of the National Gallery from that of a private collection to one 'of high rank among the public collections of Europe'. Until his death in 1865 he made annual visits to the continent in search of paintings, particularly to parts of Italy previously unvisited by the *cognoscenti* or the Grand Tourist. On these journeys he was accompanied and assisted by his gifted wife, herself a critic and amateur artist, Elizabeth Rigby. During this decade Eastlake purchased 139 paintings for the National Gallery. A large proportion of these were altarpieces with impeccable provenances, coming from the churches for which they had been executed, or from the families of those who had given the commission. From the artist's native town of Borgo San Sepolcro came *The Baptism of Christ* and *St Michael* by Piero della Francesca, and from the Rucellai collection in Florence the altarpiece *The Virgin and Child with SS Jerome and Dominic* by Filippino Lippi. Historically perhaps the **186** outstanding additions were those made in 1857 from the Lombardi-Baldi

178

SELF PORTRAIT
Charles Keene 1823–91
pen and brown ink
Ashmolean Museum, Oxford

Of all the illustrators of the 1860s and the following decades, Charles Keene may be considered the master, and not only for his illustrations to *Punch*, good though they are. It was the quality of draughtsmanship, as seen here, which won him the admiration of his French contemporaries, Pissarro and Degas. Bracquemond, the engraver and critic, ranked him with Daumier and Gavarni, and Sickert called him 'the first of the moderns'.

179

THE CORONATION OF
THE VIRGIN

c. 1390–91
Lorenzo Monaco c. 1370–1425
tempera on wood
72 × 60·5 in (185 × 155 cm)
Courtauld Institute Galleries, London

The first evidence of the awakening of
Thomas Gambier-Parry's interest in early
Italian painting is to be found in his pur-
chase of a Florentine tondo in 1849, twelve
years after he went down from Cambridge.
This picture by the Florentine artist,
Lorenzo Monaco, was included in the Art
Treasures Exhibition in Manchester in 1857
and Gambier-Parry bought it at the
Davenport Bromley sale of 1863. It hung
at Highnam Court until bequeathed to the
University of London in 1966.

180 *below*

HUNT IN A FOREST

c. 1460
Paolo Uccello 1396/7–1475
oil on panel
30·75 × 70 in (73 × 177 cm)
Ashmolean Museum, Oxford

The painting was presented by the Hon.
W. T. H. Fox-Strangways to the new
University Galleries in Oxford in 1850.
Dating from the 1460s, Uccello's animated
and colourful painting is evidence of Fox-
Strangway's advanced taste for Tuscan
Trecento and Quattrocento painting, a
taste which he may have acquired when he
was Secretary at Legation in Florence
between 1825 and 1828. It was a year later
that he made his first gift of early Italian
paintings to his former college, Christ
Church.

181 *below*

AN ECCLESIASTIC PRAYING

Gerard David c. 1460–1523
painted on oak
13·5 × 10·5 in (34 × 26 cm)
National Gallery, London

Prince Albert was not only a connoisseur of early Italian painting, he was also a pioneer in the revaluation of early Flemish masters. In 1848 he bought the collection of Prince Ludwig-Kraft-Ernst of Oettingen-Wallerstein, and after his death the queen, at his wish, presented twenty-two of his paintings to the National Gallery. Among them was this picture, the right wing of a triptych. It was exhibited at Kensington Palace in 1849 and was until 1859 attributed to Hans Memling.

182 *centre*

PORTRAIT OF JOHN RUSKIN

1853–54
John Everett Millais 1829–96
oil on canvas
31 × 26·75 in (74 × 68 cm)
collection of Mrs Patrick Gibson

Millais began the portrait of Ruskin standing beside the stream in Glenfinlas, Perthshire, in 1853, and completed it the following year. Ruskin himself made a drawing of the rock formation behind him; he was deeply impressed by the setting chosen for the portrait. In 1871 he gave the portrait to Dr Henry Wentworth Acland who had been present when it was begun, and had thought it, as Ruskin wrote to his father, 'in every way perfect both for me and Millais'.

183 *right*

THE SCAPEGOAT

1854
William Holman Hunt 1826–1910
oil on canvas
33·75 × 54·5 in (85 × 138 cm)
Lady Lever Art Gallery, Port Sunlight

Holman Hunt had dreamed of Syria since childhood, and he left England in 1853 determined to illustrate the life of Christ. On the shores of the Dead Sea, at Oosdoom, he started to paint *The Scapegoat*. As he later wrote, 'the mountains became more gorgeous with the preciousness of jewels, and each minute I rejoiced more in my work'. On completion in 1854 the work was sent back by sea and was exhibited at the Royal Academy in 1856. There it was purchased by B. G. Windus of Liverpool, one of several provincial collectors of paintings by the Pre-Raphaelite Brotherhood. In Windus's sale at Christies in 1862 the painting fetched 475 guineas.

184
SILVER-GILT TABLE FOUNTAIN
London hall-mark for 1852/3
Messrs. Garrard and Edmund Cotterill
silver, parcel-gilt and enamel
Royal Collection, on loan to the Victoria and Albert Museum, London

Prince Albert, as well as taking a keen interest in fostering and encouraging contemporary artists, was himself a practitioner. Both he and Queen Victoria took drawing lessons and Albert was taught the technique of etching by Landseer. The prince made designs for two table-centres, of which this is one. The other, dated ten years earlier, and also on loan to the Victoria and Albert, depicts his favourite dogs. This piece was exhibited in London in 1862. The kiosk was designed by E. Lorenzo Percy, the base by William Spencer, and the horses were modelled by Edmund Cotterill.

185

ADORATION OF THE MAGI

Sandro Botticelli c. 1445 – 1510
tempera on wood
20 × 55 in (50 × 139 cm)
National Gallery, London

This is a very early painting in the manner of Filippo Lippi, and was formerly catalogued as the work of Filippino Lippi, the son of Filippo, who worked in Botticelli's studio. It was one of the works from the Lombardi-Baldi collection bought by Sir Charles Eastlake for the National Gallery.

186

VIRGIN AND CHILD WITH ST JEROME AND ST DOMINIC

Filippino Lippi 1457 – 1504
tempera on wood
81 × 73 in (205 × 185 cm)
National Gallery, London

The altarpiece was painted for the Rucellai family chapel of San Pancrazio in Vallombrosa, and later removed to the Rucellai Palace. It was bought by Sir Charles Eastlake in 1857. St Jerome kneels on the left, and St Dominic is shown on the right with a lily in his hand.

187 *above*

STATUE OF SEN-NEFER

c. 1500 BC
granite
British Museum, London

This statue from Thebes was bought by the museum in 1829 from the collection of Henry Salt. In 1815 Salt was appointed British consul general in Egypt, where he encouraged excavation and formed three large collections of Egyptian antiquities. In 1818 he wrote to his friend William Richard Hamilton enclosing a priced list of his first collection. His prices were extravagant, as he later admitted, and Sir Joseph Banks discouraged the purchase by the British Museum. However, after prolonged negotiations Salt's agents accepted the sum of £2,000 offered by the museum, but Salt felt that he had been badly treated as the trustees had originally encouraged him to collect for them.

collections in Florence. After months of patient, skilful negotiation Eastlake secured for the National Gallery more than sixty paintings, the cream of the two collections, including such masterpieces as 'a vast altarpeice of Orcagna', Uccello's *The Rout of San Romano*, painted for the Medici Palace, *The Virgin and Child with Saints* by Duccio and Botticelli's *The Adoration of the Magi*, all for the sum of £7,000 with an **185** addition of £35 for banker's commission. To mark her husband's tenure of office, not an enviable one to try to rival, Lady Eastlake gave to the National Gallery in his memory a fitting companion to these acquisitions – *The Virgin and Child with SS George and Anthony Abbot* by Pisanello from **193** the Costabili collection in Ferrara.

Although few people would query the wisdom of Eastlake's policy of buying Italian masterpieces at a time when the prices were so low, there was throughout the nineteenth century a growing feeling that British artists were inadequately represented. In 1890 Henry Tate offered about sixty of his modern British paintings to the nation on condition that they were housed without undue delay in the National Gallery. This generous bequest, together with several articles in the press stressing the desirability of a separate national gallery for works by native artists, provided the motivation for the founding of the Tate Gallery. After prolonged and fierce controversy the present site at Millbank was chosen, and the new gallery was built to the designs of Sidney Smith between 1894 and 1897.

Five minutes walk from Trafalgar Square, John Charles Robinson was making important acquisitions for what was to become the Victoria and Albert Museum. In 1852, at the age of twenty-eight, Robinson was appointed curator of the Museum of Ornamental Art which was then housed in Marlborough House but moved to South Kensington in 1857. In 1854 Robinson bought the Gherardini collection of sculptors' models including an unrivalled series in wax by Giovanni Bologna. He matched this *coup* two years later by the purchase of the Soulages collection of **204** maiolica. Against a background of political unrest, violence and war, and after protracted negotiations with the papal authorities, Robinson succeeded in purchasing in 1860 eighty-four pieces of sculpture from the collections of Ottaviano Gigli and the Marquis of Campana for the sum of £5,836. In adding sculpture by Arnolfo di Cambio, Donatello, Luca **198** della Robbia and Verrocchio, Robinson laid the foundations, as he justly claimed in 1883, of a collection of masterpieces which 'are now the envy of the most celebrated museums'. Unhappily this claim was made after twenty years of lost opportunities which resulted from Robinson's demotion to the post of Art Referee without powers of purchase. The museum was to be further enriched by the collection of English porcelain given by the Lady Charlotte Schreiber whose father, the 9th Earl of Lindsey, had made considerable purchases of Worcester porcelain in the preceding century. It also benefited by the studies of C. D. E. Fortnum who catalogued the maiolica. However, in 1899 Fortnum bequeathed his own collection of Renaissance bronzes, maiolica and other examples of the applied arts, together with funds for new galleries, to the Ashmolean Museum in Oxford, thereby earning the title of 'second founder'.

The British Museum collections were also being considerably enlarged. Sir Henry Layard himself financed his original excavations at the Palace of Nimrud on the Euphrates, but in 1852 he was repaid the money by the trustees of the museum, who urged him to continue his work. In 1847 he brought back one of the great winged bulls from the palace, and after 1848 he uncovered more bas-reliefs showing hunting scenes. Early in the **206** century, the British consul general in Egypt, Sir Henry Salt, had amassed a collection of colossal sculpture, which was bought by the museum and was later joined by the sculpture from such sites as Abydos and Amarna, excavated by Sir Flinders Petrie. Sir Augustus Wollaston Franks devoted his own resources to building up the collection of oriental antiquities, and presented the museum with the hoard of Achaemenian goldwork known as the Oxus treasure.

William Morris and his contemporaries

In the art history of the nineteenth century the decade of the 1850s may be considered as pivotal. The Pre-Raphaelite Brotherhood gained its greatest degree of publicity, divided and ended. It was succeeded by a second wave of artists which formed around Dante Gabriel Rossetti and absorbed some of the sense of purpose and seriousness of the brotherhood. William Morris and Edward Burne-Jones met as undergraduates at Exeter College, Oxford, in 1852. Both came under the influence of Rossetti, some five years their senior, with whom they worked on the decoration of the ceiling of the Oxford Union Society in 1857. The other latter-day Pre-Raphaelites who worked with them to such brief effect (the 'frescos' on distemper soon faded away) were Arthur Hughes, Spencer Stanhope, Val Prinsep and Hungerford Pollen. When he had finished his studies at Oxford, Morris worked in the offices of the architect George Edmund Street and met Street's senior clerk Philip Webb. The latter, in 1859, designed for Morris the Red House at Bexleyheath in Kent, a relatively simple example of domestic Gothic. Webb also designed much of the furniture for the Red House, and Burne-Jones was responsible for the stained glass.

Artists and architects were themselves becoming patrons. William Burges, the architect of St Finbar's Cathedral, Cork, spent the last six years of his life building and adorning his own Tower House in the artists' colony at Melbury Road, Kensington, in a personal blend of high Victorian fairytale and thirteenth-century Gothic style. Not far away Sir Frederick Leighton R.A., with that thoroughgoing eclecticism that was characteristic of the Victorians, installed a patio and an Arab hall decorated with tiles purchased for him in Damascus, skilfully strengthened where necessary by those made in London by William de Morgan. At 11 Melbury Road Richard Norman Shaw built a house for Sir Luke Fildes R.A. In 1858 Shaw had succeeded Philip Webb as chief draughtsman to the dedicated Gothic-Revivalist architect G. E. Street. Despite this inauspiciously fashionable beginning Shaw, as his biographer Sir Reginald Blomfield wrote, 'devoted his immense ability to the development of the English tradition in architecture'. In addition to his country houses such as Bryanston and those in London in Queensgate, Shaw was commissioned by Jonathan T. Carr in about 1877 to make designs for 'a settlement of small houses in Turnham Green'. Shaw designed the Tower House for Carr himself, the Tabard Inn and stores and the church of St Michael and All Angels, a group which thus composed the first garden suburb in England.

It had been the practical difficulties of finding the kind of furnishings he wanted for the Red House that spurred William Morris, who had already taken up architecture, poetry, carving and illuminating, into founding Morris, Marshall, Faulkner and Company (later known simply as Morris and Company) in 1861. In the ensuing five years Morris made his first designs for wallpapers, but the firm's chief product was stained glass, which in 1867 brought in more than two thirds of the year's takings. However, Morris is probably best known as a designer through his patterns for wallpapers and chintzes, which in 1873 he again started to design, as well as patterns for other printed and woven textiles including carpets and tapestries. In 1891 he turned to printing: he founded the

210, 21

188

PAYSANNE FRANCAISE

1873
Jules Dalou 1838–1902
terra-cotta
h. 53·75 in (136 cm)
Tate Gallery, London

Dalou completed *Paysanne Française* in six weeks. In 1873, the second year of his nine-year exile from France, it was exhibited at the Royal Academy and then bought by Sir Coutts Lindsey, the founder of the Grosvenor Gallery, for 300 guineas. The subject was a great success; numerous replicas including those in the Victoria and Albert Museum and the Hermitage, Leningrad, testify to its popularity.

189

THE RED HOUSE

1859
Philip Webb 1831–1915
Bexleyheath

In 1859 William Morris asked his friend and colleague Philip Webb to design a house for himself and his wife. The Red House is an unpretentious example of Domestic Gothic, a style quite opposed to those which prevailed in the previous century. The designs naturally had to conform to the theories of Morris, who avoided any connection with Italy and the Baroque style both in architecture and in his decorative work. Much of the furniture for the house was also designed by Webb, and Burne-Jones was responsible for the stained glass.

190

THE WORKS OF GEOFFREY CHAUCER

detail, 1896
William Morris
British Museum, London

Morris was far from being the only social and artistic reformer of his day, but he was the first to hold the belief that the artist must himself turn craftsman-designer instead of being reliant on machine production. The Kelmscott Press was founded in 1891, and the works that came from it, with type-faces based on those of the fifteenth and sixteenth centuries, caused a revolution in typography. The exquisite decoration of the pages of *The Works of Geoffrey Chaucer* bears witness to Morris's absorption of the medievalist ideals of Pugin and Ruskin.

Kelmscott Press, designed two founts of type and produced fifty-three books including the famous *The Works of Geoffrey Chaucer*. These works **190** influenced not only numerous private presses but also the design of typography. In his writings too, Morris, like Pugin and Ruskin before him, had a strong influence on contemporary taste, an influence which did not end with his death in 1896.

Charles R. Ashbee, founder and chief designer of the Guild of Handicraft, published in 1901 *An Endeavour Towards the Teaching of John Ruskin and William Morris*. In his jewellery and metalwork, like Arthur H. Mackmurdo in his advanced title-page for *Wren's City Churches* of 1883, Ashbee had produced work which must be considered as belonging to the style known as Art Nouveau. If its characteristic can be accepted as the prevalence of the sinuous line, a flowing, undulating movement, then Morris's patterns and Burne-Jones's paintings and designs can be considered the precursors of what became an international style. Their influence is as intertwined in the later movement as are Morris's own patterns for chintzes, *Honeysuckle* (1875) or *Wandle* (1884) and the foliage **211** in Burne-Jones's *Pelican*. Their work, together with that of their juniors Charles Voysey and Walter Crane, both of whom professed to dislike Art **194** Nouveau, had a widespread influence on the development of this new style on the continent, 'Stile Liberty' as it was known in Italy after the metalwork, furniture and ceramics made for, and sold by, Liberty and Company. Such developments are, of course, intimately connected with the theme of patronage; the difference from the more traditional practice already considered being that now the artists themselves were trying to instruct the public in what it should buy or, at least, producing what conformed with their own aims and standards in the hope that the public would buy their artefacts. Of the public manifestations of Art Nouveau in England, two of the best-known and most accessible examples are the memorials designed by Alfred Gilbert, those to Lord Shaftesbury in Piccadilly Circus (Eros) and to Queen Alexandra opposite the Friary Court of St James's Palace. In Scotland the University of Glasgow Art Collections preserve furniture and designs by Charles Rennie Mackintosh, **205** the leader of the Glasgow School and of the internationally known group, The Four. Between 1897 and 1910 Mackintosh designed tea rooms in Glasgow, together with several houses and the Scottish pavilion for the international exhibition at Turin in 1902.

Artist, patron and collector

Having followed the movement in the decorative arts through the last decades of the nineteenth and into the twentieth century, it is necessary to go back to the time of the Franco-Prussian War and once again consider the roles of artist, patron and collector. High Victorian art is distinguished by a group of artists who, having studied on the continent, were painting subjects inspired by their conceptions of ancient Egypt, Greece and Rome. At the Royal Academy of 1871, Alma-Tadema, who had just settled in England, showed *Grand Chamberlain to King Sesostris the Great*; the previous year he had sent in from Brussels *Un Interior Romain*. Among the three paintings by Frederic Leighton was *Greek Girls picking up Pebbles by the Sea*, while Edward Poynter, who later also became President of the Royal Academy, exhibited *Feeding the Sacred Ibis in the Halls of Karnac*. In contrast two exiled French artists, Jules Dalou and Jacques-Joseph Tissot, exhibited there two years later subjects drawn from the domestic life of the day. Dalou's *Paysanne Française* was purchased by Sir **188** Coutts Lindsey and is now in the Tate Gallery. By the time he returned to France as a result of the amnesty of 1879, Dalou had exhibited terra-cotta portraits of Alma-Tadema, Leighton and Poynter. Tissot, who had fled the Commune in Paris, exhibited *Too Early* (which 'made a great sensation') and *The Last Evening*. Both paintings were included in the bequest of Charles Gassiot, a city merchant, to the Guildhall Art Gallery in 1902. Monet, Camille Pissarro and Sisley also escaped the Prussian invasion and the effects of the Commune in England. Manet had paid a brief visit in 1868 and Toulouse-Lautrec made several in the 1890s. However, only the influence of Degas, 'without doubt the greatest artist of the period' as Camille Pissarro wrote to his son Lucien in 1883, reached the English through the work of Walter Sickert. 199

French painting and works of art of an earlier period, however, were far from being neglected by Victorian collectors. The creation of those collections which have since become an inseparable part of the nation's heritage was in contrast to the paucity of interest in contemporary French painting. During his long residence in Paris the 4th Marquess of Hertford amassed a collection of French pictures, furniture and porcelain of the 195, 2 eighteenth century which passed on his death to his illegitimate son Sir Richard Wallace. Lady Eastlake recorded in her diary her visit to Lord Hertford's storehouse in Paris in October 1860 where Wallace showed 'his father's treasury'. The clocks she thought 'of great beauty', the furniture 'priceless, such things as would adorn, and have adorned, royal chambers in the most luxurious times'. After the Commune in Paris Wallace moved the collections to Hertford House in Manchester Square, and after his death in 1890 his French wife willed the larger part of the inheritance to the British nation.

Both the taste and the financial resources of the prodigiously rich Lord Hertford were rivalled by those of the Rothschild family. Three houses in Buckinghamshire – Waddesdon, Ascott Wing and Mentmore – bear witness to the impact of '*le gout* Rothschild' (the first two now belong to the National Trust). Building at Waddesdon began in 1879 to the designs of the architect Gabriel-Hippolyte Destailleur. The house (built in the style of the châteaux of the Touraine, Blois and Chambord) and its contents exemplify the homogeneity of Rothschild taste. Alongside and in addition 196 to the founding collections of Baron Ferdinand de Rothschild (1839–98) are those of his two successive heirs: his sister, Alice, and great-nephew, James de Rothschild and also of Baron Edmond, the latter's father. In his *Reminiscences* Baron Ferdinand claimed: 'Whether it is to the credit of my family or not may be a matter of opinion, but the fact remains that they first revived the decoration of the French eighteenth century in its purity, reconstructing their rooms out of old material, reproducing them as they had been during the reigns of the Louis …' By the purchase of tapestries and boiseries from hôtels in Paris then being pulled down, Baron Ferdinand provided the perfect setting for Sèvres porcelain, Savonnerie carpets, commodes by Riesener and Cressent, and sculpture by Caffieri, Clodion and Falconet. To these he added English full-length portraits of the same period, among which are those of the *Prince of Wales* by Gainsborough and *Colonel St Leger* by Reynolds. There are Dutch and Flemish masterpieces by Albert Cuyp, Pieter de Hooch and Jan van der Heyden, and Baron Edmond's painting by Rubens, *Garden of Love*. Clocks, barometers, illustrated books and bindings, pieces of Oriental and Meissen porcelain in their eighteenth-century ormolu mounts, and superb tapestries make up a collection which, together with that at Manchester Square, presents a comprehensive picture of the arts of France in the eighteenth century.

The Camden Town Group

Continued opposition to the Royal Academy found expression in the

191
PORTRAIT OF
CHICHESTER FORTESCUE,
LORD CARLINGFORD

1871
oil on canvas
Jacques-Joseph Tissot 1836–1902
Examination Schools, Oxford

The portrait was presented to the sitter's wife Frances, Lady Waldegrave, by a body of Irish subscribers, to mark Fortescue's tenure of office as First Secretary of Ireland. The fans on the mantelpiece recall the enthusiasm for Japonaiserie begun in Paris in 1856 by Bracquemond. Although this influence is more marked in Whistler's work, the portrait of Lord Carlingford, painted soon after Tissot's arrival in England, must then have seemed noticeably modern and Parisian.

192

BUDDHA IN PRAYER *detail*

T'ang, mid-eighth century
painting on silk, British Museum, London

The painting, representing the Buddha praying under the Tree of Enlightenment, was found by Sir Aurel Stein in 1907 in the Cave of the Thousand Buddhas in China. In 1899, after having been principal of the Oriental College in Lahore, Stein was appointed to the Indian Education Service, and until 1908 he carried out archaeological explorations for the Indian government in Chinese Turkestan, central Asia and western China. This is one of some 6,000 oriental manuscripts and paintings which found their way into the British Museum as a result of his travels.

193

THE VIRGIN AND CHILD WITH ST GEORGE AND ST ANTHONY ABBOT

Pisanello, living 1395 – c. 1455
oil on panel
18·5 × 11·5 in (47 × 29 cm)
National Gallery, London

Lady Eastlake gave this painting to the National Gallery in 1867, in memory of her husband Sir Charles Eastlake, its first director. Sir Charles, who had bought the picture from the Costabili Collection in Ferrara in 1858, was well aware of its sadly damaged condition, but as a reminder of Eastlake's purchases in Italy over a period of ten years the gift remains a fitting one.

194
WRITING DESK
1896
Charles Francis Annesley Voysey 1857–1941
oak
Victoria and Albert Museum, London

Voysey was the most creative of all his contemporaries in the field of domestic architecture. He also designed furniture and fittings, including this desk made by W. A. Tingey in 1896 for W. Ward Higgs. Made of plain oak, the vertical emphasis and the elaborate hinges are characteristic of Voysey. His influence is indicated by a reviewer of the Paris Exhibition of 1900 who wrote, 'If one is to have l'art nouveau the proper course is to go to the fountain-head and though Mr Voysey has had many imitators nevertheless he remains *par excellence* the prophet of that school of artistic expression.'

195 *far left*
THE TILSIT TABLE
c.1760–70
René Dubois
Wallace Collection, London

What we now know as the Wallace Collection was largely formed by the 4th Marquess of Hertford, who inherited from his father and grandfather a considerable knowledge of art and an avid taste for collecting as well as a huge fortune. He was passionately fond of French eighteenth-century furniture, and this table, bought in 1866, is only one of the many superb examples acquired by him. It was possibly made for Louis XV, who gave or sold it to Catherine II of Russia. Tradition holds that the Franco-Russian Treaty of Tilsit was signed at it, hence the name.

196
WEST GALLERY, WADDESDON MANOR

The west gallery at Waddesdon reflects that search for the purity of French eighteenth-century decoration which, as Baron Ferdinand de Rothschild justifiably claimed, characterised his family's taste. The boiseries and tapestries provide the period setting which is in keeping with the Boulle furniture, the Sèvres porcelain, and the paintings by Watteau representing characters from the Italian Comedy.

opening of the Grosvenor Gallery by Sir Coutts Lindsey. Here Burne-Jones, Tissot and Whistler shared the honours. Whistler exhibited three *Arrangements* and four *Nocturnes*, the latter a general title suggested by his patron, the collector and shipping magnate F. R. Leyland, for whom Whistler had just completed the decoration of the Peacock Room at 49 Princes Gate (now reconstructed in the Freer Gallery, Washington, D.C.) and whose portrait he had painted earlier. Whistler's paintings enraged Ruskin who had 'never expected to hear a coxcomb ask 200 guineas for flinging a pot of paint in the public's face'; although he found Tissot's paintings 'mere coloured photographs of vulgar society', Ruskin praised their 'dexterity and brilliancy'. In 1886 the New English Art Club was set up by a group of young artists who had completed their studies in Paris, again with the intention of attacking the prestige of the Academy. Although the Academy proved a lure to some of its members, including Clausen and Sargent, the N.E.A.C., under the leadership of Sickert and a small group of 'Impressionists', among them Wilson Steer, attracted two teachers at the Slade School of Art, Fred Brown and Henry Tonks. Many of the latter's most gifted pupils, including Augustus John, McEvoy and Orpen, were soon to join.

1905 was a year of importance in three respects. Frank Rutter, the art critic, was asked to found the Allied Artists Association, which in imitation of the Salon des Indépendants in Paris, was to hold its first exhibition at the Albert Hall in 1908 without a jury; each artist was free to select his own work. While this new outlet for artists' work represents a development by now familiar, one of the results of the Allied Artists exhibition was the meeting of a number of artists hitherto unknown to one another. Sickert, the pupil of Whistler and the follower of Degas, had returned from Dieppe to London in 1905, setting up house in Fitzroy Street. Around him grew a circle of young artists which included Harold Gilman and Spencer Gore. As a result of the exhibition, Robert Bevan, who had worked at Pont Aven and known Gauguin, also joined the group, as did Charles Ginner, who had recently come over from Paris. They met at Sickert's house on Saturday afternoons to exhibit and sell their paintings. In 1911 they formed the short-lived Camden Town Group, which two years later was to grow into the London Group. These artists were therefore true heralds of the new century, in that they worked for themselves, following through their own stylistic experiments, rather than with an eye to a patron or to a sale, and were increasingly dependent on forward-looking or sympathetic owners of such galleries as Carfax, Chenil and Goupil to create the necessary outlet and market for their work.

Finally, 1905 was a significant year in the history of English patronage – if only, sadly, in a negative sense. Despite the French influences discussed here it was not until 1905 that the first exhibition of paintings by the Impressionists was seen in England. The 315 paintings shown by Durand-Ruel at the Grafton Galleries included those by Boudin, Sisley, Manet, Monet, Pissarro, Renoir and Berthe Morisot but only ten by Cézanne. The exhibition, as Frank Rutter wrote, 'made very little impression on London or England. The general public was hardly aware of its existence' and it came too late. Viewed not only in the light of the subsequent high prices but also art-historically, this oversight on the part of British collectors has left a deficiency in collections, public and private, the effects of which are still felt and may never be remedied. If this is a sad close to a chapter of remarkable achievement it is also a reminder of how dependent the public has been, and is likely to remain, on individual taste and enterprise.

John Doig

197

THE ALBERT MEMORIAL

1863–72
George Gilbert Scott 1811–78
London

Scott's architectural practice was originally
founded on workhouses; he designed more
than fifty of these in partnership with
William Moffat. He won international
fame in 1845 through his prizewinning
designs for the Nikolaikirche in Hamburg.
The Albert Memorial was begun two
years after Prince Albert's death, the queen
having invited proposals for a national
monument, and it is generally regarded as
the epitome of High Victorian ideals and
style. With its rich mosaics, marble,
granite and bronze, together with a wealth
of sculptural decoration, it cost more than
£120,000. The bronze statue of Prince
Albert, beneath the canopy, is the work of
J. H. Foley.

200 *below left*

THE SLEEP OF SORROW
AND A DREAM OF JOY

1861
Raffaelle Monti 1818–81
Victoria and Albert Museum, London

This elaborate allegory of the Italian
Risorgimento was included in the International Exhibition of 1862 where its
success equalled that of the sculptor's *Eve
after the Fall*, which Joseph Neeld had added
to his collection at Grittleton the year
before he died. Monti's sculpture was also
commissioned by the Copeland factory
and was reproduced in biscuit or parian
porcelain in the 1860s and 70s.

198 *bottom*

THE DEAD CHRIST
TENDED BY ANGELS

late 1430s
Donatello c. 1386–1466
Victoria and Albert Museum, London

One of the finest pieces of sculpture of the
fifteenth century in the Victoria and Albert
Museum is that purchased by John Charles
Robinson from the Gigli Campana Collection in December 1860. Despite the
unrest in Rome and the surrounding
countryside, Robinson successfully con-
cluded the protracted negotiations and so
secured the Donatello relief for £1,000.
The head, left side and arm of Christ are
considered to have been carved by Donatello himself, and the remainder to have
been finished in his studio.

199 *bottom centre*

ST MARK'S, VENICE

1895–56, Walter Richard Sickert 1860–1942
oil on canvas, 35·75 × 47·5 in (100 × 120 cm)
Tate Gallery, London

After briefly attending the Slade School in
1881 Sickert entered Whistler's studio as an
apprentice. He learned a great deal from
Whistler, particularly about the technique
of etching, but by far the most formative
influence in his life was that of Degas, whom
he first met in Dieppe in 1885. Sickert first
visited Venice in 1895, and this is one of
several impressions of the city that were
painted in London after his return.

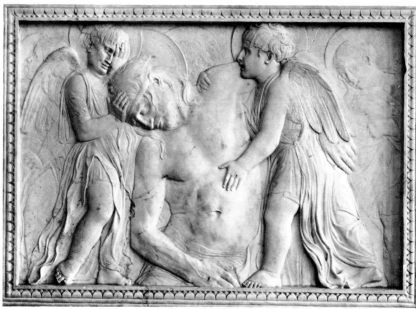

201
HOUSES OF PARLIAMENT
1837–60, designed 1836
Charles Barry 1795–1860 and
Augustus Welby Northmore Pugin 1812–52
London

In 1834 the old Houses of Parliament were burnt down and a committee was set up to consider the new scheme for the building, which was to be either Gothic or Elizabethan. Classical designs were entirely excluded. By this time the Neo-Gothic style was well established: as early as 1818 the Church Commissioners had allotted £1,000,000 for the building of 214 churches; 174 of these were Gothic. The competition was won by Barry, and Pugin collaborated with him, being responsible for the exterior detail and decoration. Barry did not have the same devotion to the Gothic style as Pugin, who equated it with Christianity, but he was a highly skilled architect and manged to create a building which is the most remarkable example of Gothic Revivalism in secular architecture.

202 *centre*
DERBY DAY
1856–58, William Powell Frith 1819–1909
oil on canvas, 40 × 88 in (101 × 223 cm)
Tate Gallery, London

Frith's scenes of everyday life were so popular during his lifetime that when they were first exhibited at the Royal Academy they required special railings for protection. *Derby Day* was commissioned by Jacob Bell in 1856, and bequeathed by him to the National Gallery two years later, but due to some difficulties with the owner of the engraving rights, it did not enter the gallery until 1865. It was one of the paintings of special beauty and interest lent by the National Gallery to the Tate shortly after it opened.

203 *below*
ALL SAINTS, MARGARET STREET
1849–59
William Butterfield 1814–1900
London

William Butterfield was a willing recipient of Pugin's ideas concerning the true Christian architecture. The church of All Saints, built under the auspices of the Ecclesiological Society, embodied these ideals, and introduced many features foreign to English architecture. The most outstanding of these was the incorporation of decorative coloured brickwork and tiles, used lavishly on the exterior as well as the interior, which was widely imitated by other High Victorian architects. Ironically, the organ of the Ecclesiological Society, *The Ecclesiologist*, called the building ugly, though forceful and powerful.

204

MAIOLICA WARE

dated 1530 and 1531 respectively
diameter 9 in (23 cm)
Victoria and Albert Museum, London

The purchase of the huge collection of maiolica amassed by M. Soulages of Toulouse was the result of a major campaign on the part of Henry Cole, Director of the South Kensington Museums, and John Charles Robinson, Curator of the Museum of Ornamental Art. The Treasury three times refused a grant for the purchase; indeed Lord Palmerston, when inspecting the collection, had inquired, 'what is the use of such rubbish to our manufacturers?' It was sold to the city of Manchester who had asked for its loan for the 'Art Treasures Exhibition', on condition that if the exhibition yielded no balance, it was to be auctioned. When its auction seemed inevitable, Cole played his last card. The Manchester Committee was requested to rent the collection to the Practical Art Department and to give it the right to buy individual objects whenever funds were available. This was done, to the fury of the Treasury, and purchases began immediately at the rate of about £2,000 a year.

205 *right*

CHAIR WITH OVAL BACKRAIL

Charles Rennie Mackintosh 1868–1928
oak with upholstered seat
h. 53·5 in (136 cm)
Victoria and Albert Museum, London

In 1889 Mackintosh entered the firm of Honeyman and Keppie where he worked as a draughtsman. Here he met J. Herbert MacNair, also a draughtsman, and together they attended evening classes at Glasgow School of Art. The head of the school, F. H. Newbury, introduced them to two other students, Margaret and Frances Macdonald, and they formed the group known as 'The Four'. The work that they did together – book illumination, posters, watercolours, metalwork and furniture – became much admired abroad, particularly after the International Exhibition at Turin in 1902. During the 1890s Mackintosh began to make his way as an architect, and in 1896 his designs for the new Glasgow School of Art won a competition. The School of Art is his most famous building, marking a turning point in the history of architecture. As well as the exterior, Mackintosh designed all the interior details including the furniture, most of which can still be seen today.

206 *below*

KING ASSURNASIPAL HUNTING

relief from the north-west Palace of Nimrud
883–59 BC
British Museum, London

Henry Layard is best known as the excavator of the Palace of Nimrud on the Euphrates between 1845 and 1853. He was, however, also a close friend of Sir Charles Eastlake, to whom he gave much valuable assistance in the purchase of early Italian paintings for the National Gallery. He was made a trustee in 1866, on Eastlake's death, and remained active until his own death in 1894. This relief is one of many superb Assyrian sculptures now in the British Museum that are a testimony to his tireless enthusiasm, but his own words on the two lions guarding the north-west palace at Nimrud sound a cautionary note. 'It seemed almost sacrilege to tear them from their own haunts to make them a mere wonder-stock to the busy crowds of a new world. They were better suited to the desolation around them . . .'

207

HARMONY IN GREY AND GREEN

1873
James Abbot McNeill Whistler 1834–1903
oil on canvas, 74 × 38 in (188 × 99 cm)
Tate Gallery, London

Whistler's nonchalant custom of distinguishing his paintings by chromatic and numerical titles, together with their technique, enraged Ruskin, and the resulting publicity ensured that the artist's *Arrangements* and *Nocturnes*, shown at the Grosvenor Gallery in 1877, proved one of the 'prime social events of the London season'. The portrait of Miss Cicely Alexander was painted by Whistler in his 'little house at Chelsea' in 1873 and exhibited at 48 Pall Mall the following year.

208 *below*

LES CHAMPS ELYSEES

Antoine Watteau 1684–1721
oil on panel, 12·5 × 16·5 in (32 × 42 cm)
Wallace Collection, London

This painting was purchased by Richard, 4th Marquess of Hertford at the Comte de Morny's sale of 1848. He paid the sum of £945, a figure described by the critic of the Art Union as an 'outrageous price'. He continued, 'It would be the climax of imbecile judgement to say that such a picture was worthy of the sum.' Lord Hertford's taste was for what he called 'pleasing pictures'; in addition to Watteau, other favourite artists of his were Boucher, Greuze, Bonington, Rubens, Velasquez and particularly Murillo.

209 *bottom centre*

ST MICHAEL

detail from the Clarence Tomb
1898
Alfred Gilbert 1854–1934
polychrome bronze
h. about 17 in (43 cm)
St George's Chapel, Windsor

The tomb was commissioned shortly after the duke's death in 1892 but was not finished until 1926, when the sculptor returned from Bruges at the request of George V. The design was suggested by the tomb of Henry VII in Westminster Abbey, although in his treatment of the figures Gilbert was clearly influenced by the prevalent style of Art Nouveau. The sarcophagus itself is made of Mexican onyx, and the figure of the duke is bronze. The whole tomb is surrounded by an elaborately worked grille with statues of the Virgin and twelve saints placed in niches.

210
THE ADORATION
OF THE MAGI

Edward Burne-Jones and William Morris
tapestry
Exeter College, Oxford

The tapestry was woven on the loom at
Merton Abbey and was presented by the
artists in 1890 to the college where they
had first met as undergraduates in 1852.
The subject was a popular one. Ambrose
Poynter proposed it for the high altar of
King's College chapel in 1903, and other
examples are in Eton College chapel and in
the Castle Museum, Norwich. The cartoon was presented to the Victoria and
Albert Museum.

211
WANDLE CHINTZ

1884
William Morris 1834–96
Victoria and Albert Museum, London

In 1881 Morris and Company moved out
of London to Merton Abbey in Surrey,
and from the looms set up there came
carpets, woven textiles (**210**) and woollens.
Chintz painting began in 1883, and a year
later Morris designed *Wandle*, named after
the river on which the works stood.

'The patronage at present enjoyed by the arts is probably greater in amount than at any previous time in European history. In the past fifty years vast sums have been expended on the purchase, not only of old masters, but also of contemporary works of art of all schools', wrote Sir Herbert Read in *Art and Alienation* (1967). He was reviewing the enormous increase in government spending in support of the arts, the continuing existence of the private patron to commission and collect works of art, the patronage effected by the church, particularly after the Second World War, and by industry. Art is fashionable today as it never has been before; the public is presented with more and new opportunities to see it and learn about it, while artists themselves are able to attend art schools with financial support from the state, and are given an increasingly large chance to display their work in competitions and exhibitions.

Sir Herbert Read's assessment of contemporary patronage is accompanied by a warning. 'There is', he wrote, 'no demonstrable connection between the quality of art in any period and the quantity of patronage: patrons for the most part have been whimsical, inconsistent, and sometimes positively tasteless or reactionary'. It is certainly true that in the 1930s the most talented artists of the day, with whom Read was closely associated, received humiliatingly little recognition and encouragement. These are the artists who are now considered responsible for dispersing the provincialism of English painting and sculpture. The work of Ben Nicholson, Henry Moore and Barbara Hepworth has found a place in many great international collections in the past two decades. Yet, in spite of this apparent lapse on the part of English connoisseurs, there have been a great number of inspired acts of patronage. Some of the most advanced painters of the 1910s were chosen to be official war artists, for example, and it would be impossible to condemn Samuel Courtauld's collection or Coventry Cathedral as 'tasteless or reactionary.'

The influence of Roger Fry

In the early years of the twentieth century there was one man in particular who passionately wanted to encourage the arts in England. Roger Fry's ambition was to direct the attention of both artists and the public towards contemporary painting, to which he was exceptionally sympathetic. The first major step in his campaign took the form of an exhibition at the Grafton Galleries in London called 'Manet and the Post-Impressionists'. To most people the paintings by Cézanne, Gauguin and Van Gogh seemed disconcerting or merely ridiculous, but from then onwards some of the most advanced of the young English artists grouped themselves around Fry. In 1912 he furthered the cause with a second Post-Impressionist exhibition which included examples of Picasso's Cubism and the work of Braque and Matisse, together with an English contribution. Eric Gill, Wyndham Lewis, Stanley Spencer and Duncan Grant were among those of Fry's disciples who exhibited.

Fry was himself a painter and he knew how hard it was to obtain commissions and to sell work. In 1913 he founded the Omega Workshops, a studio where objects of everyday use were to be designed and decorated with bold Post-Impressionist colours, and where the works were to be shown and sold. The communal style that was evolved by Fry, Duncan Grant, Vanessa Bell and Wyndham Lewis is now considered exaggeratedly brash, yet despite the obvious amateurishness of the furniture and ceramics they have a forcefulness and originality that contrasts with the thin tastelessness of late-Victorian and Edwardian decorative art.

When war broke out in 1914 Fry decided to hold together his artistic community in Bloomsbury, but by that date he had been deserted by the

Art and Society in the Twentieth Century

1910 to the present day

212

MADONNA AND CHILD

1943–44
Henry Moore, born 1898
Hornton Stone
h. 59 in (150 cm)
St Matthew's Church, Northampton

The *Madonna and Child* was commissioned by the Reverend Walter Hussey for the north transept of St Matthew's. He also commissioned a Crucifixion from Graham Sutherland for the south transept of the same church, and, in his present appointment as Dean of Chichester, a *Noli me Tangere* for Chichester Cathedral. In working on this project Moore made a series of twelve maquettes from which small sculptures in bronze were made (some examples of his bronze maquettes are in the Tate Gallery). Moore returned to the Madonna and Child theme in a stone group for St Peter's Church, Claydon, Suffolk, developed from these earlier maquettes.

213

SELF-PORTRAIT

1930–34
Roger Fry 1866–1934
oil on canvas
23·5 × 19·5 in (60 × 49 cm)
National Portrait Gallery, London

Fry's career as a painter is overshadowed by his championship of Post-Impressionism. He studied under Sickert in the 1890s, and his artistic output includes still-lifes, landscapes and portraits as well as the decorative paintings executed at the Omega Workshops which he founded in 1913.

214

THREE WOMEN

c. 1914, Vanessa Bell 1879–1961
oil on canvas, 34 × 32 in (86 × 81 cm)
Courtauld Institute Galleries, London

Vanessa Bell, wife of the critic and author Clive Bell, worked at the Omega Workshops where she designed textiles, screens and a mosaic floor for a house in Hyde Park Gardens. Her painting in the 1910s shows that she was very aware of the continental schools of Fauvism, Cubism and Futurism that were becoming known in London at this period and her work is strongly eclectic.

more progressive of his followers. In the same year, one of them, Wyndham Lewis, founded the Rebel Art Centre and published *Blast, a Review of the Great English Vortex.* Vorticism was an angular, severe style of drawing and painting which was connected with the international Cubist movement and in particular with Italian Futurism (in 1912 there had been an exhibition of Futurist painting at the Sackville Gallery, and in 1914 Marinetti had produced an English Futurist Manifesto). Lewis and C. R. W. Nevinson, the best-known official artists of the First World War, both described scenes of action or the tension of waiting for the attack in the peculiarly menacing vocabulary of Vorticism. Lewis's drawing, *A Battery in a Wood* and Nevinson's *Roads of France, Field Artillery and Infantry* are powerful records of the fearful destruction.

By no means all the officially commissioned war painters were Vorticists, however, and not all the commissions were for battlefield scenes. Portraits were painted and sculpted – Jacob Epstein's bust of Admiral of the Fleet Lord Fisher of Kilverstone, for example – to commemorate the organisers of the campaigns. The Imperial War Museum in London and the National Gallery of Canada in Ottawa own most of the great war paintings by artists such as William Roberts, Paul and John Nash, Stanley Spencer, Sir William Rothenstein and Sir William Orpen.

In 1910, the year of Fry's first Post-Impressionist exhibition, the Contemporary Art Society was founded. Characteristic of the present century has been the foundation of societies and committees to encourage appreciation and practice of the fine arts and to preserve buildings and works of particular historic or artistic interest. Organisations such as the National Trust (founded in 1895), the Royal Fine Art Commission (appointed by royal warrant in 1923 to give guidance to the government on the design and siting of buildings and memorials), the Institute of Contemporary Arts (founded in 1948 to promote the best and the most creative in the arts and to provide a meeting place for artists and members of the public) and the Arts Council, must rank among the most important and active patrons of the arts in England. The aim of the committee members of the Contemporary Art Society was to acquire works by living artists for loan or gift to public galleries. Their aim has been achieved year by year ever since; the society is responsible for the presence of Matthew Smith's *Reclining Woman* in the Art Gallery, Bradford, and 221 Ben Nicholson's *Guitar* design in the Tate Gallery, Graham Sutherland's 215 *Fallen Tree against the Sunset* in the Art Gallery, Darlington, and Vuillard's lithograph *La Couturière* in the British Museum.

In the 1910s and 20s there were some spectacular collectors at work, two of whom made an identifiable mark on English art. The first was Hugh Lane (later Sir) who began to collect French nineteenth-century paintings in 1905, the year that he bought Renoir's *Les Parapluies* from the dealer Durand-Ruel. He intended to start a gallery of modern art in Dublin to which he would give his pictures, but only on the condition that the city of Dublin undertook to build the gallery. At the time of his death in the Lusitania disaster of 1915 his collection was on loan to the National Gallery, London. Dublin did not fulfil Lane's wishes and in accordance with his will the collection remained in London, where it was simply an embarrassment. In 1917 the four new rooms at the Tate Gallery, specifically intended for modern foreign art and paid for by Lord Duveen, were opened, and the National Gallery thankfully handed the thirty-nine pictures over to the Tate. The National Gallery of Ireland, however, continued to press its claim, and the works are now divided into two groups, and are exhibited alternately in London and Dublin.

In 1917, when Lane's pictures were revealed to the public, there was perhaps no more astonished visitor than Samuel Courtauld. He had attended Fry's two exhibitions and had been unimpressed, like so many of his contemporaries. His complete conversion to French painting took place at an exhibition in 1922 at the Burlington Fine Arts Club. Miss Gwendoline Davies of Llandinam, Wales, had been collecting late-nineteenth and early-twentieth-century paintings for some years and it was her *Provençal Landscape* by Cézanne that quite overwhelmed Courtauld. (In 1952 most of the Davies collection was given to the National Museum of Wales, Cardiff.) He formulated a plan to build up a collection of Impressionist and Post-Impressionist paintings and to publicise the brilliance and originality of these schools. In 1923 he donated to the Tate £50,000 for the purchase of modern French pictures, a fund which enabled the gallery to take its place among the major collections of modern French painting. Among the most important purchases were Seurat's *Une Baignade,*
217 *Asnières,* Manet's *La Servante de Bocks* and Cézanne's *Paysage Rocheux,* to mention only a few masterpieces in the national collection. He continued to acquire pictures for himself too, buying among other works Monet's
8, 220 *Gare St Lazare,* Renoir's *La Loge,* Gauguin's *Nevermore* and Cézanne's *Lac d'Annecy.* In 1932 he fulfilled his ambitions as an educator of British taste by giving the lease of his house in Portman Square to the University of London to be the home of the Courtauld Institute of Art, and at the same time he presented an important part of his collection to the Institute where it was to be accessible to the public.

He also contributed a large sum of money towards the cost of building the Courtauld Institute Galleries in Woburn Square, where the greater part of his collection is housed. It has since been enlarged by the addition of Roger Fry's collection of early-twentieth-century art, Viscount Lee of Fareham's paintings by old masters, a selection of drawings from Sir Robert Witt's collection and, quite recently, the Gambier-Parry collection of Florentine paintings, oriental metalwork, glass, enamels and ivories, formed in the nineteenth century. Lord Lee and Sir Robert Witt were both key figures in planning the teaching activities of the Institute: the study of the history of art, they believed, led to a true understanding and appreciation of art, and in the early days they were encouraged and assisted by Roger Fry who gave a course of lectures there.

Lord Lee was a notably brilliant collector; he seemed above all to look for rich, clear colour in his acquisitions, such as can be seen in the *Portrait*
219 *of a Man* by Joos van Cleve or the panels of a Florentine *cassone* that belonged to him. He also left to the institute a *Descent from the Cross* by Rubens that is related to the large altarpiece in Antwerp Cathedral. Sir Robert Witt's main contribution was his collection of drawings, but he also bequeathed his uniquely valuable collection of photographs of European paintings that is being consistently enlarged. Fry's bequest contains the work of his own contemporaries—a personal selection that represents Vuillard, Sickert and some Bloomsbury artists.

Painters and illustrators

If Roger Fry has seemed to dominate this account of patronage in England in the early part of the century it is because his influence as a patron, collector, writer and teacher was so widely felt. Matthew Smith was perhaps the most obvious product of the Post-Impressionist climate created by Fry in England. Smith had attended briefly the school opened by Matisse in Paris and thereafter divided his time between France and
221 England, painting landscapes, nudes and still-life pictures in thick reds, purples and blacks. But if Smith was one of the most interesting artists

215
GUITAR
1933
Ben Nicholson, born 1894
oil on panel
32·75 × 7·75 in (83 × 19 cm)
Tate Gallery, London
Presented to the Tate in 1940 by the Contemporary Art Society, *Guitar* is typical of Nicholson's work of the period when he was an editor of *Circle* and a member of the Abstraction-Création Group. Nicholson made several trips to Paris in the early 1930s, where he visited the studios of Picasso and Brancusi, and he was a key figure in practising and furthering internationalism in art. He is today one of the most respected of living English painters; in 1956 he won the first Guggenheim International Painting Prize.

working in the 1920s, he was by no means one of the most sought-after. He did not receive commissions and he did not immediately sell his work. The commissions, the money and the reputation went to the portrait painters, to the American John Singer Sargent and Sir William Orpen. Many men who can afford works of art prefer to sit for their portraits rather then to buy ready-made pictures.

216   Sargent's sitters tend to be described as confident, carefully dressed aristocrats, aloof but not unfriendly members of the ruling class. Orpen, in contrast, favoured a more straightforward approach. His sitters have the air of successful men, but of a drearier type than Sargent's subjects.

Augustus John, the master of understatement in draughtsmanship, the observer of gypsies and tramps and spontaneous supporter of casual, carefree living, was also the maker of supremely dignified, gentle yet
236   authoritative portraits. His response to facial expression and gesture reveals a true assessment and often appreciation of his models and sitters; his simplicity enabled him to show the robustness and at the same time the wistfulness of a single character. John did a great number of portraits, particularly towards the end of his life, and he painted two grand, officially posed portraits: *Portrait of His Honour H. C. Dowdall, K.C., as Lord Mayor of Liverpool*, 1908–09 (rejected by Liverpool and now in the National Gallery of Victoria, Melbourne), and *Portrait of Viscount d'Abernon*, 1931, together with numerous less formal characterisations in pencil and paint. His skilful placing of the subject and superb technique outclass any other portrait painter in the early part of this century.

Stanley Spencer, like Augustus John, who was his senior by thirteen years, was trained at the Slade School. Unlike most of his contemporaries and friends he was a religious man, and he released his intuitive ability to paint by depicting scenes from the Bible in the setting of his native village, Cookham in Berkshire. When he returned from the battlefields of
228   Macedonia he desperately wanted, and needed, to use his experiences of the war to decorate a chapel, and he prepared cartoons for this hypothetical project. While staying with the painter Henry Lamb in 1922, Spencer was visited by Mr and Mrs J. L. Behrend who had already acquired his *Swan Upping*. They saw the cartoons and offered to commission him to execute them as a memorial to Mrs Behrend's brother who had been killed in the war. He eventually accepted, and by 1927 the walls of the Oratory of All Souls at Burghclere in Berkshire were ready for him to carry out his longed-for illustrations of the First World War. The side walls of the chapel are painted with scenes of the domestic aspect of military life – wounded soldiers arriving at a hospital, soldiers washing and
226   drinking. The end wall represents *The Resurrection of Soldiers*, his epic triumph of the god-fearing over war and destruction. The altar wall, the traditional place for a panoramic display of the victory of Christianity, is a maze of crosses and confused figures, with the severe form of the Macedonian hills in the background.

The murals at Burghclere were completed in 1931 and in 1946 the chapel was accepted by the National Trust, an unusual action, as the trust seldom acquires pictures and works of art of a contemporary character.

Another pupil from the Slade who made a name for himself as a decorator was Rex Whistler. In 1926 and 1927 he decorated the restaurant at the Tate Gallery as part of a scheme devised by Henry Tonks, Slade Professor of Fine Art, to give encouragement and practical experience to young artists. This project was financed by Lord Duveen. Whistler under-took a number of commissions for wallpaintings in the 1930s, working at,
230   among other places, Haddon Hall and Plas Newydd in Wales.

216

PORTRAIT OF
SIR PHILIP SASSOON

1923
John Singer Sargent 1856–1925
oil on canvas, 37·5 × 22·75 in (95·5 × 58 cm)
Tate Gallery, London

The portrait, shown at the Summer Exhibition of the Royal Academy in 1924, was commissioned by the sitter and bequeathed by him to the national collection in 1929. Sir Philip Sassoon, private secretary to Field-Marshal Sir Douglas Haig during the First World War, was a wealthy patron and connoisseur who gave exhibitions in his house in Park Lane and owned several paintings by Sargent. He was also a trustee, and later chairman, of the National Gallery. Sargent studied in Paris in the 1870s and was later much influenced by his friend, Monet. As a portraitist he was traditional, deriving his formal, grandiose style from Velasquez, Manet and the English school of the eighteenth century. This is an unusually late example of Sargent's portraiture, as in the latter part of his life he concentrated on landscapes and was occupied with murals for the Boston Museum and the Widener Library at Harvard.

217

UNE BAIGNADE, ASNIERES

1883–84, Georges Seurat 1859–91
oil on canvas, 79 × 118 in (201 × 301 cm)
National Gallery, London

In 1923 Samuel Courtauld set up a Trust Fund of £50,000 for the acquisition of Impressionist and Post-Impressionist art for the Tate (with provision for transfer to the National Gallery). This painting was purchased through the Fund in 1924. In the Courtauld Collection, comprising Samuel Courtauld's private collection, his gifts to the Courtauld Institute and the works purchased for the national collection, there are no fewer than twelve oil paintings by Seurat.

218 *above*

LA LOGE

1874
oil on canvas
Pierre-Auguste Renoir 1841–1919
31·5 × 25 in (80 × 64 cm)
Courtauld Institute Galleries, London

This painting was bought by Samuel
Courtauld in 1925 and was presented by
him to the institute in 1932. Courtauld
was for several years a trustee of both the
National Gallery and the Tate Gallery as
well as being Chairman of Courtaulds
Ltd., the textile firm. In 1931 he endowed
the Courtauld Institute of Art in the
University of London, and in the following year he made over the lease of his
house in Portman Square. It was at this
time that he gave some of his nineteenth-
century paintings to the institute.

219 *above left*

PORTRAIT OF A MAN

sixteenth century
attributed to Joos van Cleve
active 1511–40/1
oil on panel
18·75 × 15 in (47 × 39 cm)
Courtauld Institute Galleries, London

This painting, which has also been attributed to Dirck Jacobsz, was bought by Lord
Lee of Fareham in Frankfurt in 1928. It
formed part of his gift to what later became the Courtauld Institute, which he
instigated and partly financed. His project
was taken up and expanded by Samuel
Courtauld and a generous donation towards the cost of founding it was made by
Sir Joseph Duveen. Lord Lee also presented his collection of metalwork to Hart
House, Toronto, and bequeathed some
illuminated manuscripts to Cambridge. In
1921 he left a collection of portraits at
Chequers, the house he gave to be used as
the country home of the prime minister.

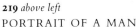

220

NEVERMORE

1897
Paul Gauguin 1848–1903
oil on canvas
23·75 × 45·5 in (59·5 × 116 cm)
Courtauld Institute Galleries,
London

Nevermore was painted in Tahiti, and was inspired by Manet's *Olympia*, of which Gauguin possessed a photograph. Gauguin's work was known to the British public after the 1910 exhibition, 'Manet and the Post-Impressionists', which was organised by Roger Fry at the invitation of the directors of the Grafton Galleries. His work was also included in the exhibition of 1912 at the Grafton Galleries, devoted to the 'classic' artists of the modern movement, which was Fry's second attempt to bring artists and connoisseurs into contact with continental art. Of all the French Post-Impressionists Cézanne was the most admired in England, but the decorative simplifications in Gauguin's work were eventually absorbed into British art.

221

RECLINING WOMAN

Matthew Smith 1879–1959
oil on canvas
25·75 × 34·25 in (65 × 87 cm)
Bradford City Art Gallery, Yorkshire

In spite of having studied–unsatisfactorily –under Henry Tonks at the Slade School, and very briefly under Matisse in Paris, Smith was largely self-taught. He did not achieve a break-through as a painter until his middle thirties, when he quite suddenly seemed to find his own idiom with a flower piece called *Lilies*, which he exhibited in 1915, backed by Epstein who became both a friend and a collector of his work. Smith's paintings are clearly in the tradition of the Fauve artists, who stressed the beauty of colour in its own right, and his work is characterised by the obvious delight he took in the texture and quality of the paint itself. The painting was presented in 1946 by the Contemporary Art Society, to which the gallery has subscribed since its inception.

Throughout the twentieth century there has been a demand for book illustrators. Although the great period of the illustrated book and periodical was at the end of the last century there have been a number of exceptionally talented illustrators at work in England. Edward Ardizzone, as well as providing the illustrations for several of his own children's books, elucidated the texts of *My Uncle Silas* by H. E. Bates, published in 1939, and editions of Anthony Trollope's *The Warden* and *Barchester Towers*, with lively pen and ink drawings. In 1932 Paul Nash illustrated Sir Thomas Browne's *Urne-Buriall* and *The Garden of Cyrus*. For this, an *edition de luxe*, the illustrations were printed by collotype and hand stencilled. His architectural fantasies with wafting clouds are totally different from the naive style adopted by John Nash, his brother, for Walter de la Mare's *Seven Short Stories*.

Towards an international style

222 Barbara Hepworth lived and worked close to Henry Moore, Ben Nicholson, Herbert Read, Paul Nash and John Piper in Hampstead in the 1930s. The arrival in England of Piet Mondrian, Naum Gabo and Walter Gropius, who were escaping from the strictures of official art and patronage in eastern Europe – such as prevailed in post-revolutionary Russia and Germany under the National Socialist Party – helped to create an international artistic climate within the community. Societies such as Unit One were founded and a variety of art books and magazines appeared, including *Axis* and *Circle*. Two distinct but not entirely incompatible tendencies began to emerge in British painting and sculpture, whose character was clearly defined in two major London exhibitions in 1936 – 'Abstract and Concrete' and 'The International Surrealist Exhibition'.

However exciting and significant this period of art may seem in retrospect, the thirties were difficult years for all but a few fashionable artists. At the beginning of the decade potential buyers of works of art were feeling the pinch of the Depression, and as time progressed the inevitability of another world war diverted the attention of dealers and the public alike. To persuade a gallery to show the work of young artists was undeniably difficult, and to sell directly from an exhibition almost exceptional. Edward Wadsworth, together with several designers and craftsmen, was employed by the Cunard shipping line to decorate the Queen Mary, but such commissions were rare. Some earned a living as book illustrators and fabric and poster designers; others, like Henry Moore, accepted teaching posts in the ever-increasing number of art schools.

The principal collectors of paintings at this time were Lord Henry Bentinck, brother of Lady Ottoline Morrell, who was the friend, patron and hostess of the Bloomsbury set, and Sir Edward Marsh. Marsh, who was the particular friend and patron of the poet Rupert Brooke, knew, helped and corresponded with innumerable artists including Eric Gill, Mark Gertler and Stanley Spencer. Professor Michael Sadler, Sir Leslie and Lady Martin and Nicolette Gray were admirers and occasional purchasers of the work of the Hampstead artists, and Sir Kenneth Clark, Director of the National Gallery from 1934 to 1945, was a special sup-
223 porter of Henry Moore and of the Euston Road painters, Victor Pasmore and William Coldstream.

The Second World War interrupted and destroyed. Apart from the actual loss of life many artists lost their enthusiasm, and while the development of individuals was often arrested, a more general development was also ruined – that of the easy exchange of ideas that had previously been taking place between one European country and another.

222
SINGLE FORM
Barbara Hepworth, born 1903
bronze
h. 10 ft 3 in (3·12 m)
Battersea Park, London

This was purchased from the artist by the London County Council and now occupies a position by the lake in Battersea Park. A counterpart to *Single Form* stands outside the United Nations Secretariat building in New York as a memorial to Dag Hammarskjöld, a former secretary-general. Hepworth was one of the first British artists to understand the developments of the School of Paris. In the 1930s she visited France and met Picasso, Braque and Brancusi and was a prominent member of the Abstraction-Création Group. Her commissioned work includes two sculptures for the Festival of Britain in 1951 and an aluminium winged figure for the John Lewis department store in Oxford Street, London.

However, there were a few painters who in a sense benefited from their experience of the war years, thriving on the type of work that they were commissioned to do by the War Artists Advisory Committee. Henry Moore, John Piper and Graham Sutherland were notably successful in adapting themselves to the subject matter of war. Perhaps it was the prevailing undercurrent of traditional English romanticism that led each of these three to minimise the immoral and violent aspects of the war, to the extent that their paintings and drawings seem less shocking and more objective than the comparable work of Wyndham Lewis or Nevinson.

224 Henry Moore was specifically asked by the committee to make drawings of sleeping, sheltered figures in the London underground. In these drawings he worked the main masses in white wax chalk, a medium which gives his bundled figures an eerie texture; the same textural quality characterises his studies of miners, commissioned in 1941.

212, 240 From the beginning of his career Moore had been preoccupied with the subjects of the reclining figure and the mother and child, and in 1943 he started on a Madonna and Child group for the Church of St Matthew, Northampton, a sombre, hefty image in stone that is indebted to his wartime figure studies. Since that time he has undertaken several commissions –among them *Three Standing Figures*, which is situated in Battersea Park, for the Contemporary Art Society, and a screen-wall for the Time and Life Building in Bond Street. It is remarkable that in each case he should interpret his habitual themes in such a manner as both to reflect and affect their predestined environment.

John Piper was committed as an official war artist to describing bomb damage. His work with John Betjeman on the *Shell Guide to Oxfordshire*, the first guide book of a series, had interested him in photography, particularly of architectural detail. This, and his writing and illustrations for the *Architectural Review*, were important factors in his abandonment of abstract painting in favour of a topographical style that owes much to the appearance and romantic mood of Samuel Palmer's drawings. It is in this style that Piper portrayed intricate Gothic tracery and the Georgian **225** terraces of Bath in his war paintings. At this time he was also commissioned to execute two series of watercolours of Windsor Castle for Queen Elizabeth, now the Queen Mother.

Graham Sutherland was directed by the War Artists Advisory Committee, headed by his friends and his patron, Sir Kenneth Clark, as to what subjects he should paint and draw; but he was under no obligation to submit his work to the committee, nor was it automatically accepted. Sutherland specialised in a more positive comment on the devastation than Piper, who was primarily concerned with the romantic decay that set in after the catastrophe. Especially impressive are his scenes of buckled machinery, distorted man-made objects rendered useless by their own deformity and the horrifying absence of human beings to direct them.

The Church as patron

In 1944 Sutherland was invited by Canon Hussey to paint an *Agony in the Garden* for the same church as Moore's *Madonna and Child*, St Matthew's, Northampton. He welcomed the commission, for he felt that he had responded well to the discipline of working to satisfy a patron in his official wartime activities; but he was not happy with the choice of subject. In the same way that Stanley Spencer longed to express his feelings by decorating a chapel, Sutherland felt himself compelled to consolidate his experiences of the war in a painting of the Crucifixion.

He made a great many studies for the Northampton commission, and he was fascinated afterwards by some of the objects and shapes that he

223

THE EVENING STAR; EFFECT OF MIST

1945–47
Victor Pasmore, born 1908
oil on canvas
30 × 40 in (76 × 101 cm)
collection of Sir Kenneth Clark

The title is taken from Turner's *The Evening Star* from which the composition is partially derived. Until 1948 Pasmore painted in a naturalistic style; in 1937 he had established a teaching studio in the Euston Road to promote a revival of interest in the French Impressionists. This picture bears witness to his gradual development towards abstraction. During his early life he was employed as a clerk to the London County Council, but in 1938, through the patronage of Sir Kenneth Clark, he gave up this job to work as a full-time artist. Sir Kenneth is one of the most remarkable collectors, patrons, lecturers and writers on art in this century. He worked with Bernard Berenson in Florence and was Director of the National Gallery from 1934 to 1945. He has also held the posts of Chairman of the Arts Council of Great Britain and Surveyor of the King's Pictures.

224

SHELTER SCENE: BUNKS AND SLEEPERS

1941
Henry Moore, born 1898
pen, chalk, watercolour and gouache
19 × 17 in (48 × 43 cm)
Tate Gallery, London

Henry Moore found it impossible to work as a sculptor during the Second World War because of the lack of space and the difficulty of obtaining materials. He filled two sketch-books with drawings of London air-raid shelters, totally unrelated to any sculptural project. The huddled, impersonal forms of the shelterers do, however, reappear in his post-war reclining figures and his mother and child groups. Between 1940 and 1942 he worked as an official war artist and in this capacity he did a second series of shelter drawings of which this scene is one. It was presented to the Tate by the War Artists Advisory Committee in 1946.

225

ALL SAINTS CHAPEL, BATH

1942
John Piper, born 1903
watercolour and chalk
16·75 × 22 in (42·5 × 56 cm)
Tate Gallery, London

Piper visited the church four days after it was mutilated in the air-raid on Bath in which many of the Georgian terraces were partially destroyed. The picture was presented to the Tate Gallery by the War Artists Advisory Committee. Piper has made a very considerable contribution to British art not only as a painter and designer but also as a trustee of the Tate Gallery and a member of the Arts Council panel. In 1951 he supervised the design of the Battersea Pleasure Gardens in collaboration with Osbert Lancaster.

studied for the *Crucifixion* – particularly the crown of thorns, a motif which matured into paintings of thorn trees and thorn heads.

Sutherland has undertaken other commissions for the Church: *Noli Me Tangere* for Chichester Cathedral, a *Crucifixion* for St Aidan's, Acton, and the design of the magnificent altar-wall tapestry in Coventry Cathedral. **229** He is among the few twentieth-century artists who have overcome the difficulties of re-interpreting the traditional Christian themes in a manner that is both acceptable to the patron and in accord with their own stylistic inclinations.

Since 1904 no less than four cathedrals have been begun and at least partially completed. This is an indication that the Church's activity as patron of the arts has not ceased even though religion – or church-going, at least – is a less important feature of everyday life than previously. The architect of the Anglican cathedral at Liverpool, Giles Gilbert Scott, was twenty-two when he won the design competition. Built of stone in an adapted – or modernised – Gothic style, it is most imposing in terms of space, solidity and dignity. When finished it will be the second largest cathedral in the world, the largest being St Peter's in Rome.

Maufe, who designed Guildford Cathedral, was one of three assessors to the chairman and members of the Coventry Cathedral Reconstruction Committee, who examined the 219 designs submitted and judged that of Basil Spence to be the most suitable and imaginative. Built between 1956 and 1962, it co-exists with the bombed ruins of an earlier cathedral.

Coventry Cathedral could not be described as startlingly modern in **244** appearance, but it is undoubtedly expressive of contemporary taste in art. It is made of reinforced concrete, pink Staffordshire sandstone and green slate, with rough-textured white plaster on the inside walls. These materials have a character of their own which also shows to advantage the structural features of the exterior – the circular form of the Chapel of Christ the Servant and the shallow breadth of the porch steps – and the decorative details of the interior. Many artists apart from Graham Sutherland were invited by Spence to contribute to the decoration: Elizabeth Frink modelled the lectern eagle; John Piper, Lawrence Lee, Geoffrey Clarke and Keith New were among those who worked on the stained-glass windows; John Hutton engraved with saints and angels the screen of glass dividing the porch from the nave, and Epstein modelled **243** the St Michael and Lucifer group outside the east entrance.

The newest cathedral is the Roman Catholic cathedral at Liverpool, **245** which departs from the traditional cross plan in having a circular base with the walls tapering upwards through a lantern tower to a crown of stainless-steel spokes. The effect is bold and colourful, fascinating rather than imposing.

Industrial patronage

In the past the most skilled and adventurous architects were employed to build churches, universities, and large country houses. In the twentieth century the first two types of commission have continued, but the third has died out. In fact almost the last large country house was built at Gledstone, Yorkshire, in 1930 by Sir Edwin Lutyens, principal architect of New Delhi. The highest architectural achievements of the present age are town-planning schemes such as Peterlee in County Durham, and office buildings, whose prototype is of course the American skyscraper. Work for festivals and exhibitions has given architects the opportunity for more exciting work; the Royal Festival Hall, originally built for the Festival of Britain in 1951, is now part of a permanent complex of **248** exhibition and concert halls.

If industry and commerce have been responsible for some of the most exciting architectural commissions, they have also played a prominent role in sponsoring the arts in general. Miss Jennie Lee, Minister for the Arts, regards industrial patronage as 'a form of enlightened self-interest', a statement which refers as much to the public-spirited aspect as to the prestigious and profitable. Many businesses sponsor exhibitions and award prizes and scholarships to improve local or national facilities, in much the same spirit as they would donate money to a new youth centre. In fact, they consider the encouragement of the arts to be a genuinely good cause.

John Moores of Littlewoods mounts a biennial competition and exhibition at the Walker Art Gallery, Liverpool. His aims, as defined, are 'to give Merseyside the chance to see an exhibition of painting and sculpture embracing the best and most vital work being done today throughout the country' and 'to encourage living artists, particularly the young and progressive'. The competition was started in 1957 and has since acquired a reputation approaching that of the Venice or São Paulo *Biennales*, although in general only English artists are eligible for entry.

The Peter Stuyvesant Foundation, which derives its income from the manufacture of cigarettes, sponsors 'The New Generation' exhibitions as well as concerts, awards scholarships, and is in the process of forming a collection of modern British painting rivalling that of the Tate Gallery. The directors of the foundation claim that the industrial patron can afford to be more adventurous than the government and may be less influenced by personal prejudice in selecting works than a private patron.

The Calouste Gulbenkian Foundation was established in 1958. A committee was set up to ascertain the requirements of the arts in Britain, and it was reported that, among other things, patronage on the official level was directed away from the provinces. Accordingly, the foundation has spent more than £100,000 on the purchase of works of art, mostly in grants to provincial public galleries. These galleries have received large grants on condition that a matching sum is raised from local sources. It also sponsors isolated projects, one of which was an exhibition at the Tate in 1964 called 'Painting and Sculpture of a Decade: 54/64'. There the current heroes of modern, and especially of Pop art, were well represented.

Apart from these spectacularly enterprising and generous schemes devised by individual philanthropists or philanthropic organisations, industry and commerce patronises the arts in a variety of other ways. Barbara Hepworth's *Winged Figure* in aluminium dominates the south-east wall of the John Lewis department store in Oxford Street, and behind the headquarters of the Bowater Paper Company in Knightsbridge stands Epstein's last work, a large bronze group of humans and animals. A remarkable example of stained glass used in a commercial context is the window designed by John Piper at the showrooms of Sanderson the wallpaper manufacturers, and John Hutton, who also worked at Coventry Cathedral, has engraved relevant designs for the windows of New Zealand House. Artists are also employed to design advertisements, packaging and trade symbols. Certain rooms in every office and factory, such as the board-room and the canteen, require decoration. If the decoration is well chosen—and the Institute of Directors has set up an Arts Advisory Council to assist in these matters—the firm gains a reputation for providing pleasant surroundings as one of the 'extras', which might include exhibition space and even an art club. In the past, colour reproductions were used for livening up office accommodation, but today original prints are favoured, and murals, mosaics and tapestries are

250

226 *right*
RESURRECTION OF SOLDIERS
1928—29
Stanley Spencer 1891—1959
oil on canvas
20 ft × 17 ft 6 in (6·09 × 5·33 m)
Burghclere Chapel, Berkshire

Spencer had served with the R.A.M.C. in Macedonia, and it was this experience which provided him with subject matter for the imposing epic painting which covers the altar wall of the chapel built by Mr and Mrs Louis Behrend in commemoration of a member of their family. The side walls are divided into segments each containing a scene from army life. The confusion of overlapping planes, stolid, curiously-balanced figures, and the irregular perspective are characteristic of Spencer's paintings.

227
CANDELABRUM
1966
silver, partly gilt
Stuart Devlin, born 1931
diameter 13 in (33 cm)
City University, London

Born in Australia, Stuart Devlin came to Britain in 1958. He is acclaimed as one of the most experimental designers working in silver today; his designs for cutlery and tableware are evidence of a new look at the function of the objects and are not mere adaptations of an eighteenth-century design. The decimal coinage of Australia was designed by Devlin as were maces for the universities of Bath and Melbourne, Australia. The candelabrum was given to the new City University by its past and present students.

228 *below*

WOUNDED ARRIVING AT A DRESSING STATION AT SMOL IN MACEDONIA

1919
Stanley Spencer 1891–1959
oil on canvas
72 × 86 in (183 × 218·5 cm)
Imperial War Museum, London

In 1918 Stanley Spencer and Paul Nash were commissioned to execute paintings of the First World War for the national collection. The pictures were to hang in a national war museum, the creation of which had been approved by the War Cabinet the previous year. Spencer had served in the army in Macedonia and this work, painted at Cookham after his return, shows the mountain ambulance transport in Macedonia. In 1940 Spencer was commissioned by the War Artists Advisory Committee to paint scenes of shipbuilding on the Clyde; some of these panels are in the Imperial War Museum which was permanently moved to the old Bethlem Royal Hospital in 1936.

229 *below*

CHRIST IN GLORY

1952–62
Graham Sutherland, born 1903
tapestry
74ft 8in × 38ft (22·55 × 11·58m)
Coventry Cathedral

In his design submitted to the judges of the cathedral competition
Sir Basil Spence specified a monumental tapestry to cover the wall
behind the high altar. It was his intention from the beginning that
Sutherland should be persuaded to undertake the work. Of all the
decorative features inside the cathedral (**244**) this superb tapestry
is the most eloquent expression of the spirit of victory and hope
that brought about the building of a new cathedral beside the old.
It depicts Christ surrounded by the beasts symbolic of the Four
Evangelists, and on the right, St Michael, the patron saint of the
cathedral, overcoming the devil. Between the feet of Christ is
Man, and beneath him the chalice and serpent and the Crucifixion
with a weeping sun and moon. It was woven by Pinton Frères in
the Aubusson factories at Felletin, France, and took some 3000
hours to make.

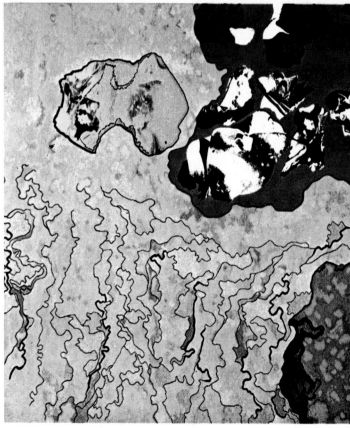

230
MURAL AT PLAS NEWYDD *detail*
1936–38
Rex Whistler 1905–44
oil on canvas and oil on plaster
h. 12 ft 6 in (3·80 m)
Isle of Anglesey

The mural decorations, commissioned by the Marquess of Anglesey, cover three walls and the ceiling of the dining-room at Plas Newydd. The classical harbour scene on the main wall was designed to complement the view of the Menai Straits and the mountains of Snowdonia from the windows opposite. Rex Whistler was a master of the *trompe l'oeil* and his decorative style is imitative of the eighteenth century. One of his first important commissions was the decoration of the restaurant in the Tate Gallery. He was a fashionable painter in the thirties, working as a portraitist, book-illustrator and stage designer as well as a decorator.

231 *below*
TAPESTRY FOR BRITISH PETROLEUM COMPANY
1965–66
Harold Cohen, born 1928
Britannic House, London

Besides painting, Harold Cohen designs furniture and textiles and is a lecturer in the history of art. He studied at the Slade and in 1959 went to America on a Harkness Commonwealth Fellowship. He belongs to a generation of British artists who turned for excitement and guidance to New York rather than Paris, and he gained much from the study of Jackson Pollock and Willem de Kooning, the principal American exponents of Abstract Expressionism. This tapestry, which was commissioned for the coffee room of the new BP building, is laid out like a map of the world with shapes that may be identified as Canada and Australia. The company formed a collection of mainly British twentieth-century paintings, sculptures and prints which includes the work of Graham Sutherland, John Piper and Sidney Nolan.

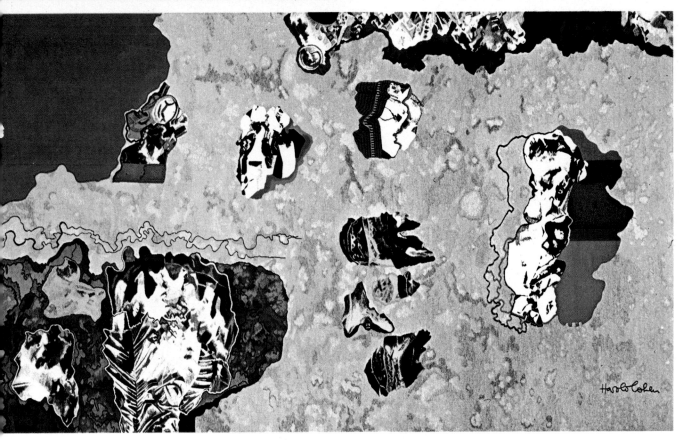

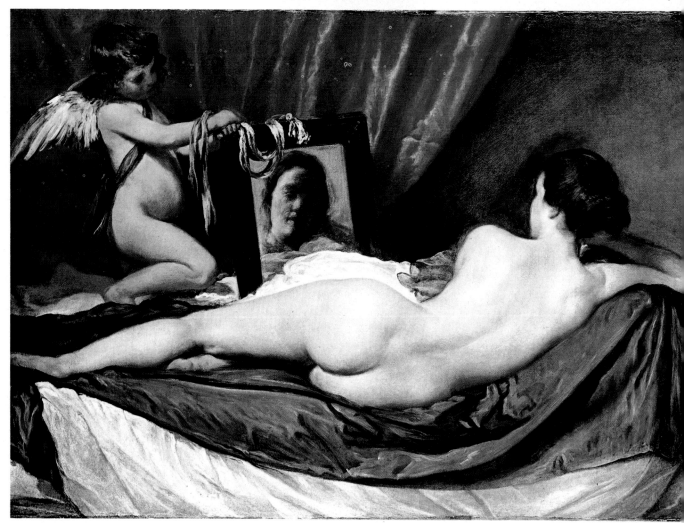

232 *far left*

TORSO OF A BODHISATTVA

fifth century
red sandstone
h. 34·25 in (87 cm)
Victoria and Albert Museum, London

This figure is in the Gupta style, of the fifth to sixth centuries, the classic period of Indian art, when sculpture reached its highest peak of development. The Bodhisattva is wearing princely dress and ornaments and a broad necklace of stylised floral design. The perfect proportions show the mastery of the sculptors of this time in depicting the human figure. It was originally bought in 1910 for the old India Museum, which was merged with the Victoria and Albert Museum in 1955.

233

SEATED COURT LADY

T'ang, 618–906
terra-cotta with coloured glazes
h. 12·5 in (31·8 cm)
Victoria and Albert Museum, London

This delicate piece, one of the ceramic figurines which were made as grave goods during the period, is a reminder of the elegance and sophistication of life in China under the T'ang rulers. It is one of the pieces from the huge Eumorfopoulos collection of early Chinese art, bought for the nation in the late 1930s. Half the collection is now in the British Museum.

234

THE ROKEBY VENUS

before 1651
Diego Velasquez 1599–1660
oil on canvas
48·25 × 69·75 in (122 × 177 cm)
National Gallery, London

In 1651 the painting belonged to a Spanish nobleman, Don Gaspar Mendez, who may even have commissioned it. It later passed to his daughter, who married the 10th Duke of Alba, and it remained in the Alba collection until it was sold on the order of Charles IV to his prime minister, Godoy. It came to England as a result of the looting during the Peninsular War, and was owned by J. B. S. Morritt of Rokeby Hall from about 1813. Finally it was bought by the National Art Collections Fund in 1906 for £45,000. This purchase was made in the teeth of furious opposition. The price was considered huge, the Treasury refused a grant, and the fund had to launch an appeal, with the result that protesting voices were raised, some claiming that the picture was a forgery, others that it was wrongly attributed. Various artists were suggested as its author, among whom were Mengs, Titian and Boucher.

gaining popularity for large wall areas. There are paintings by Lowry and Sutherland in some London offices, a mural by Edward Bawden in the Morgan Crucible Company headquarters, and one by Victor Pasmore in the staff dining-rooms of Pilkington's, the glass manufacturing firm at St Helens. Patronage of this type also extends to the minor arts; many firms own elaborate silver ink-stands, cutlery, china, and furniture of **227** simple design.

The activities of commerce and industry are supplementary to those of the government, which, together with local authorities, provides subsidised training for artists and craftsmen in the numerous art schools throughout the country, and finances the upkeep and acquisitions of the museums. The Arts Council, created under royal charter in 1946 to develop 'a greater knowledge, understanding and practice of the fine arts exclusively, and in particular to increase the accessibility of the fine arts to the public throughout our realm, to improve the standard of execution of the fine arts and to advise and co-operate with our government departments, local authorities and other bodies on any matters concerned directly or indirectly with these objects', bears heavy responsibilities. It has its faults and failures and among its difficulties is that of supplying the public with what is known to be appreciated, and at the same time of fostering unknown talent. The encouragement of art is almost a part of the welfare state, and in 1964 the Labour government appointed a 'Minister with special responsibility for the Arts'.

Recent years of the national collections

In order to discuss the national collections in the twentieth century it is necessary to return briefly to the latter part of the nineteenth, when many British national and private collections were being slowly drained of their works by collectors from other countries, notably Wilhelm von Bode, who was then building up the Kaiser Friedrich Museum in Berlin. When the American millionaires such as Pierpont Morgan entered the field of art collecting, the situation rapidly reached the proportions of a crisis, and in 1903, when repeated appeals to the government had met with no success, the National Art Collections Fund was founded, both to check the flow of works of art from the country, and wherever possible to assist the museums and galleries in the purchase of further works. In 1905 the N.A.C.F. bought Whistler's *Nocturne in Blue and Silver* for the Tate Gallery, and in the same year they made what was at the time a highly controversial purchase, that of Velasquez's *Rokeby Venus*, for **234** which the Treasury had refused a grant. These began a long series of purchases of major paintings for the nation with financial assistance from the fund. The various collections of sculpture have also been enlarged: among many gifts and assisted purchases are reliefs by Agostino de Duccio and Desiderio da Settignano and Bernini's *Neptune and Glaucus*, all at the Victoria and Albert Museum, bronzes from Nigeria at the British Museum, and works by Maillol and Degas at the Tate Gallery. The most important purchase in the field of ceramics was that of part of the famous Eumorfopoulos collection which ensured for the Victoria and **233** Albert Museum a strong representation of early Chinese art, neglected in the nineteenth century in favour of later examples. In 1952 the museum was also presented by the N.A.C.F. with fifteen pieces of Islamic pottery from the Kelekian collection.

The Victoria and Albert Museum began collecting in the 1840s. By 1910, the year of the massive Salting Bequest, which added pieces of outstanding quality to almost every section of the collections, it had already by far the most comprehensive assemblage of works of applied art and

235

THE PROPHET HAGGAI
last quarter of the thirteenth century
Giovanni Pisano, born c. 1250 died after 1314
marble
Victoria and Albert Museum, London

This formed part of a full-length statue
carved as one of a series of fourteen
prophets and prophetesses for the façade
of Siena Cathedral. All the sculptures were
executed between 1284 and 1296 which
was the date of Pisano's departure from
Siena. The work was purchased in 1963.

sculpture in the world, and was able to pursue a policy of slower and
more selective acquisition. By 1910 many of the greatest masterpieces
were already in the collection, but some really major works of art have
been added from time to time. A few outstanding random examples are
Bernini's famous bust of Thomas Baker, acquired in 1921; the Butler-
Bowden Cope, the most important surviving example of English
medieval embroidery, in 1955; the beautiful jade drinking-cup of Shah
Jehan in 1962, and one of the greatest treasures of the whole collection,
Giovanni Pisano's statue of the prophet Haggai, in 1963. These quite   235
exceptional pieces were acquired against a background of steady purchasing, to make the existing representation of less spectacular works more
complete. A few areas of the museum's collections have, however, been
quite transformed within the last fifty years. For instance, it is only since
1936, when the Buckley collection was acquired, that the whole history of
glass manufacture has been fully represented, while by far the greater part
of the now immense collection of English furniture has come to the
museum piece by piece over the years since 1930. To the same years are due
most of the English silver and practically all of the very complete collection
of English post-Renaissance sculpture. The unique collection of jewellery
has been mainly built up only in the last twenty years, and the large and
definitive collection of English medieval alabaster carvings came only in
1946 as a gift from Dr W. L. Hildburgh, who throughout his life was a
constant benefactor of the museum in all fields. The most important event
in the field of oriental art was, besides the purchase of the Eumorfopoulos
collection, the merging into the Victoria and Albert in 1955 of the old
India Museum; the richest single collection of Indian and south-east   232
Asian art in the world.

In contrast to the munificence of industrial patronage, and in spite of
the generosity of private benefactors, the funds available to the National
Gallery have for some time been inadequate to allow it to compete with
the great American museums, though in recent years the government has
taken on a new degree of responsibility for the purchase of works of art.
The practice of special grants was revived in 1955 to save from export
El Greco's sketch for *The Adoration of the Name of Jesus* and Poussin's
Adoration of the Shepherds. The Finance Act of 1956 allowed the Chancellor
of the Exchequer to accept works of art in payment of estate duty, and by
this means the gallery acquired the superb *Pietà* by Rogier van der
Weyden, as well as three paintings from the Duke of Devonshire's
collection: Memling's *Donne Triptych*, Rembrandt's *Old Man* and the
Portrait of a Man and his Wife by Jordaens. The *Portrait of a Notary* by
Quentin Metsys was also acquired in this way by the National Gallery of
Scotland.

The importance of the Courtauld Fund has already been discussed, but
certainly the most important event to affect the Tate Gallery since the
Second World War has been the National and Tate Gallery Act, which
was passed in 1954 and came into effect the following year. This Act
transferred the legal responsibilities for the Tate collections from the
trustees of the National Gallery to those of the Tate, and made provision
for transfers between the two galleries. Thus the Tate, for the first time
since it was opened in 1897, became fully independent. The Massey
Committee, whose recommendations had led to the clauses included in
the act, was set up in 1944 'to examine the functions of the National
Gallery and the Tate Gallery, and, in respect of paintings, of the Victoria
and Albert Museum, and to consider the workings of the Chantrey
Bequest'. The committee recorded its opinion about the poor quality of

the purchases under the bequest and suggested that the administration of this income should be transferred to the Tate. Discussions led to an agreement whereby the Tate was allowed three instead of two representatives on the selection committee, and the Royal Academy agreed to purchase no work which was not acceptable to the Tate. The various compromises arrived at over the years did not entirely settle the vexed question; however, several important works have entered the gallery under the bequest, among which are one of John's portraits of W. B. Yeats, Matthew Smith's *Nude, Fitzroy Street No 1*, Gaudier-Brzeska's *Brodsky* and several bronzes by Epstein.

The British collection has been considerably increased since the war, a good representation of the works of Constable has been assembled, and, owing to the generosity of W. Graham Robertson, the collection of works by Blake has been more than doubled.

Undoubtedly the most outstanding expansion has been in twentieth-century works. During the war the Montague Shearman Bequest of 1940 had made it possible to acquire major paintings by Matisse, Rouault and Utrillo, and peace allowed for a more systematic attempt to represent recent developments in art. Although the funds available have never been sufficient to keep abreast of the constantly rising prices of works of art, the Tate has never lacked generous benefactors, and many important acquisitions have been made, including the two fine examples of Analytical Cubism, Picasso's *Femme Nue Assise* (1909) and Braque's *Still-life with Fish* (1909–11).

When in 1937 the Duveen sculpture gallery was opened, the Tate actually possessed very little with which to fill it, other than the remarkable collection of Rodin bronzes. This has now been rectified; indeed the enlargement of the sculpture collection is one of the most important developments of recent years. Acquisitions include four more bronzes by Degas, two by Renoir, several works by Rodin and Maillol, no less than twenty carvings by Henry Moore and a good selection of the work of Brancusi, Arp, Giacometti, Paolozzi and Gabo, to name but a few artists represented.

Art and society

In spite of some inevitable misunderstandings between artist and public, it can be said that patronage flourishes in Britain in the twentieth century. The quantity of interest in the arts appears to increase year by year and the popular demand for more exhibitions and art education is constantly attended to in schools and universities, and through the media of radio, television, newspapers and books. Dealers' galleries make a vital contribution in promoting and encouraging young artists, who may be the accepted masters of tomorrow. At the same time, during the last fifty years the country has been by no means deprived of individual, independent benefactors and enthusiastic connoisseurs and collectors. The private patron still exists: Mr and Mrs R. J. Sainsbury have amassed a formidable collection of paintings by Francis Bacon, and both Sir Roland Penrose and Sir Colin Anderson are renowned collectors. Two world wars and several economic disasters have not destroyed the activities of these people.

Although quality in art is often hard to distinguish at the time of its creation, the fact that this account involves some of the most beautiful and impressive works of art ever created either in Britain or abroad lends authority to the statement that some of the patronage and collecting of this period has been both enlightened and enduringly important to patron, artist and public.

Elizabeth Bridgeman

254

236
W. B. YEATS
1907
Augustus John 1878–1961
oil on canvas
29·5 × 19·5 in (75 × 49 cm)
Manchester City Art Gallery

In 1908 A. H. Bullen at the Shakespeare Head Press brought out an edition of Yeats's *Collected Works*. This occasion gave rise to a whole group of portraits of the poet by several artists apart from John, including Sargent, Mancini, Shannon and Ricketts. John himself went to Yeats's home, Coole, in the summer of 1907 and there did several drawings and paintings at Yeats's request in preparation for an etching which was to be used in the book. However, none of these portraits pleased the poet, who was remarkably particular about his appearance, and he refused to allow the inclusion of any of John's work in the edition. Although he admired the quality of the etching, he insisted that John had shown him as 'a gypsy, grown old in wickedness and hardship'.

237 *Left*

PORTRAIT OF SOMERSET MAUGHAM

1949
Graham Sutherland, born 1903
oil on canvas, 54 × 25 in (137 × 63·5 cm)
Tate Gallery, London

Commissioned by Somerset Maugham, the author and playwright, this was Sutherland's first attempt at portraiture. His later portraits include those of Sir Winston Churchill and Lord Beaverbrook. Sutherland also worked as a poster designer and illustrator and he undertook to illustrate a limited edition of Maugham's *Cakes and Ale* to commemorate the author's eightieth birthday. This painting was presented to the Tate Gallery in 1951 by Maugham's daughter.

238 *right*

GIRL

1953–54
Reg Butler, born 1913
bronze, h. 70 in (178 cm)
Tate Gallery, London

This is the fourth of seven casts of *Girl;* others are in the British Museum and in the collection of the Museum of Modern Art, New York. Butler was first trained as an architect, a fact which may account for the pleasing balance and disposition of mass which is typical of his sculpture. In the 1940s he worked as a blacksmith and also as an assistant to Henry Moore; the knob-shaped head and taut drapery binding the underlying form in this piece are reminiscent of Moore. In 1953 he attained recognition when he won the grand prize in the competition and exhibition for *The Unknown Political Prisoner*, sponsored by the Institute of Contemporary Arts.

239

THREE DANCERS

1925
Pablo Picasso, born 1881
oil on canvas 84·5 × 56·25 in (215 × 143 cm)
Tate Gallery, London

The painting, which was in the artist's possession until 1965, was bought for the Tate largely through the efforts of Mr Roland Penrose, who spent some months urging Picasso to part with it. Picasso attaches a special value to it; its occasion was the death of his close friend, the painter Ramon Pichol, whose profile appears in the painting. The purchase was not approved in all quarters: the picture has been regarded by some as a disconcerting one. Indeed, it is not an easy painting, but it represents a turning point in Picasso's art, when his distortion of forms ceased to be formal and became violent and emotional. Seen in this context it becomes clear that the apparent grotesqueness is essential to the picture's purpose.

240 *right*

RECLINING MOTHER AND CHILD

1960–61
Henry Moore, born 1898
bronze, 86·5 in (220 cm), London

The bronze was bought from the artist by Minerals Separation Limited, who decided in 1965 to place an important piece of sculpture in the garden of their new offices in Queen Anne's Gate. This combination of Moore's recurrent themes of the reclining figure and the mother and child had previously only appeared in a few drawings, in which the subject was treated naturalistically. Here the sculptor has not attempted a representational treatment; his chief preoccupation is with the relationship of forms and space.

241 *below*

TOTES MEER (DEAD SEA)

1940–41, Paul Nash 1889–1946
oil on canvas, 40 × 60 in (101 × 152 cm)
Tate Gallery, London

Paul Nash was a pupil at the Slade School, worked with Roger
Fry at the Omega Workshops and did special duty as a war artist
in the First World War. He was a prominent member of the
Surrealist faction in England, exhibiting, like Henry Moore, at
the International Surrealist Exhibitions in London and Paris.
Apart from painting, he worked as a book illustrator and theatrical
designer. This picture was painted during the Second World War
in his capacity of official war artist, and it was presented to the
national collection by the War Artists Advisory Committee. The
subject, a heap of wrecked aircraft, reminded him of a strongly
swelling sea by moonlight. A white owl scans the wreckage lit up
in a ghostly, cold light.

242 *below*

EDITH SITWELL

1923–35
Wyndham Lewis 1882–1957
oil on canvas
34 × 44 in (86 × 112 cm)
Tate Gallery, London

Lewis's association with the Omega Workshops, founded by Fry,
was brief and stormy; in 1914 he broke away to found the Rebel
Art Centre with, among others, Edward Wadsworth and
Frederick Etchells. In the same year he founded the Vorticist
Group, responding to the introduction into England of Cubism
and Italian Futurism, and he edited the Vorticist magazine *Blast*.
During the First World War he was official war artist to the
Canadian Corps Headquarters and applied the cold, mechanical
manner of his Vorticist compositions to figurative work. He had a
close friendship with the Sitwell family, and he worked on the
portrait of Dame Edith, the poet, for several years.

243
ST MICHAEL AND THE DEVIL
1956–60
Jacob Epstein 1880–1959
bronze
h. 35 ft (10·66 m)
Coventry Cathedral

244 *centre*
COVENTRY CATHEDRAL
1954–62
Basil Spence, born 1907

On the left this view shows part of the remains of the old cathedral, bombed in 1940. In June 1950 a competition for the design of the new cathedral was announced, open to any architect in the British Commonwealth or the Republic of Ireland. Spence was declared the winner in August 1951. Previously he had worked with Lutyens on the design for New Delhi; he is also the architect of Sussex University and the Hampstead civic centre. The nave windows are the work of Lawrence Lee, Geoffrey Clarke and Keith New. Between the porch steps and the baptistery window, designed by John Piper, is Jacob Epstein's *St Michael and the Devil*, symbolising the triumph of the spiritual over the animal instincts of man. Born in New York, of Polish-Jewish parentage, Epstein settled in London in 1905. He worked mainly as a portrait sculptor; one of his earliest commissions was the Oscar Wilde Memorial in Paris, and the head of St Michael is derived from his portrait bust of Wynne Godley. He was engaged on another religious work, *Christ in Majesty*, for Llandaff Cathedral, when he was invited to undertake this project, and he died before the bronze cast of *St Michael* was finished.

245
METROPOLITAN CATHEDRAL OF CHRIST THE KING
1962–67
Frederick Gibberd, born 1908
Liverpool

Several attempts were made to build a cathedral for the Catholic community of Liverpool, the first being in 1853 when A. W. N. Pugin was commissioned to make designs in the Gothic style. More recently the foundation stone of the Cathedral designed by Sir Edwin Lutyens was laid in 1933. In 1959 a competition was announced: two of the conditions defined by the committee were that Lutyens's crypt should be incorporated in the new structure and that the high altar should be visible to the entire congregation. The result is a sixteen-sided building of simple tent form with the high altar in the centre, with a conical roof and a concrete-ribbed lantern of stained glass tapering to a crown of pinnacles. The stained glass in the lantern is by John Piper and Patrick Reyntiens and the bronze crucifix on the high altar is by Elizabeth Frink.

246 *right*
THE VIRGIN AND CHILD WITH ST ANNE AND ST JOHN THE BAPTIST
c. 1495, Leonardo da Vinci 1452–1519
black chalk, heightened with white, on paper
53·75 × 41 in (141·5 × 104 cm)
National Gallery, London

By 1779 this cartoon was in the possession of the Royal Academy, and in 1962 it was presented to the National Gallery by the National Art Collections Fund. It was acquired for the astonishing sum of £800,000, the money being raised partly by public subscription, from the N.A.C.F. itself, from the gallery's annual grant and the Pilgrim Trust and by a Special Grant from the Exchequer. The acquisition was facilitated by the power given in 1952 to the Reviewing Committee on the Export of Works of Art, both to refuse an export licence for a work of this kind, provided that its considered price can be raised, and to recommend a government grant.

247

DESIGN FOR THE
EAST WINDOW OF
ETON COLLEGE CHAPEL

1949–51
Evie Hone 1894–1955
gouache on paper
47·5 × 34·5 in (121 × 88 cm)
National Gallery of Ireland, Dublin

The window for which this is a study illustrates the Crucifixion in the upper panels, and the Last Supper flanked by the Sacrifice of Melchizedec and the Sacrifice of Isaac in the lower panels. It was commissioned in 1949 to replace a window that was destroyed during the Second World War, and completed in 1952. The medieval squareness of the composition and the figures is in keeping with the architecture of the chapel. The influence of Rouault, the greatest twentieth-century painter of religious subjects, is evident. Born in Dublin, Evie Hone studied under Sickert in London and under Gleizes in Paris. She designed stained-glass windows for the cathedral in Washington, D.C. and for several churches in Ireland.

248

THE QUEEN ELIZABETH HALL

1961–67
Hubert Bennett, born 1909
London

The Queen Elizabeth Hall forms part of the new arts complex on the South Bank, London. In 1961 the London County Council announced plans for improvements to the Royal Festival Hall, designed by Robert H. Matthew and J. L. Martin as the one permanent building of the 1951 Festival of Britain. It also referred to a new art gallery (which opened in 1968 as the Hayward Gallery and is rented for a large part of the year by the Arts Council of Great Britain) and two new concert halls. The smaller of these is the Purcell Room, a recital room designed for Chamber Music; the larger, the Queen Elizabeth Hall, had 1106 seats and is intended to accommodate a full orchestra.

249

CREST

1964
Bridget Riley, born 1931
emulsion on board, 65·5 × 65·5 in (166 × 166 cm)
Peter Stuyvesant Foundation, London

Bridget Riley arrived at her canvases of vibrating lines and
relentless ambiguities through the study of nineteenth-century art
theory. She began by painting figure compositions in a semi-
Impressionist manner and by 1960 had evolved a type of
Pointillism. She is now the leading exponent of Op art in this
country and her influence is widespread. The Peter Stuyvesant
Foundation has set out to form a collection of contemporary
British art rivalling that of the national collection. In 1964, the
foundation sponsored, for the first time, a major exhibition at the
Whitechapel Art Gallery, and in the following year the exhibition
of contemporary sculpture called 'The New Generation 1965'
was shown.

250

ON THE BALCONY

1955
Peter Blake, born 1932
oil on canvas, 47·75 × 35·75 in (121 × 91 cm)
Tate Gallery, London

Peter Blake is a pioneer of Pop art in Britain. He studied at the
Royal College of Art, London, between 1953 and 1956, and this
picture was his diploma composition. It was begun after he had
seen *Workers and Pictures*, an experiment in social realism with
trompe l'oeil effects, by the American artist, Honoré Sharrer,
which was included in an exhibition from the Museum of Modern
Art, New York, at the Tate Gallery. Blake won first prize in the
junior section of the John Moores Liverpool Exhibition in 1961.
He works in collage as well as simulated collage, often combining
the two techniques. One of his best-known works is a collage construction, over six foot long, entitled *The Lore Wall*, which is in the
collection of the Calouste Gulbenkian Foundation.

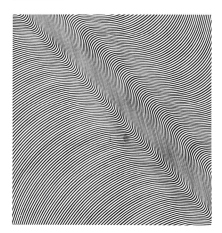

251

HORNPLAYER

fifteenth to sixteenth century
bronze
British Museum, London

This fine bronze figure is one of the many
examples of Benin art brought back to
England in the nineteenth century as a
result of British expeditions to West
Africa. This particular expedition, of 1897,
was a punitive one following the massacre
of an earlier party. The objects taken were
within the palace; it was the practice for
the king to reserve the right of bronze-
casting. It was bought for the British
Museum in 1949 from the Oldman
collection.

252

THE LITTLE DANCER
AGED FOURTEEN

1880–81
Edgar Degas 1834–1917
bronze
h. 39 in (99 cm)
Tate Gallery, London

Because of its familiarity the uniqueness of
this work tends to be overlooked; there is,
however, nothing quite like it in the history
of sculpture. In order to give the figure the
authenticity which he sought, Degas made
what were at the time startling innova-
tions – the dancer wore a real bodice,
shoes and tutu and her skin was tinted.
This statue was the only one of Degas's
sculptures to be publicly seen during his
lifetime; it was exhibited at the Impressionist Exhibition of 1881. When he died
about a hundred and fifty pieces of sculpture were found in his studio, many in a
state of ruin. *The Little Dancer* was bought
by the Tate in 1952 for £9076, £6000 of
which came from the National Art
Collections Fund.

253

THE SNAIL

1953
Henri Matisse 1869–1954
gouache on cut and pasted paper
8 ft 4·75 in × 8 ft 5 in (2·56 × 2·57 m)
Tate Gallery, London

Matisse produced about thirty-five of these *gouaches découpées* in his last years when he was too ill to stand at his easel. The paper was hand-coloured in gouache and then cut with scissors. When he began these 'drawings with scissors' Matisse wrote, 'cutting into living colour reminds me of the sculptor's direct carving.' *The Snail* was purchased from Jean Matisse with financial assistance from the Friends of the Tate Gallery in 1962.

254 *bottom left*

STILL-LIFE WITH FISH

c. 1909–11
Georges Braque 1882–1963
oil on canvas
29·25 × 29·5 in (74 × 75 cm)
Tate Gallery, London

Braque and Picasso can be said to have invented the Cubist style in 1908, and they were the most consistent exponents of its later development, known as Analytical Cubism. This canvas, together with Picasso's *Bust of a Woman* of 1909, and his *Seated Nude* of 1909–10, provided the Tate Gallery with its first examples of the style. *Still Life with Fish* was bought in 1961.

255

LES GRANDES BAIGNEUSES

c. 1902
Paul Cézanne 1839–1906
oil on canvas, 51 × 76 in (129 × 193 cm)
National Gallery, London

Cézanne painted nearly a hundred small scenes of bathing figures in the open air which led to the three large-scale compositions executed during the last ten years of his life; one is in the Barnes Foundation, Pennsylvania, the other in the Philadelphia Museum. The National Gallery was anxious to purchase this work, despite a certain amount of public criticism, as it represents a summing up of Cézanne's experiments and ambitions. He wanted to create a type of painting that is monumental, strongly subjective and as true in the interpretation of nature as an Impressionist painting. Shown at an exhibition in Paris in 1907, *Les Grandes Baigneuses* assisted Picasso and Braque (**254**) in their development towards Cubism.

Museums and Monuments

An index of museums, churches, palaces and country houses, listing some of the major treasures they contain.

ABERDEEN, Aberdeen

1 **Cathedral of St Machar** Founded 1157, but earliest extant work is 14th C. Flat ceiling of panelled oak c.1530; many tombs and effigies.

2 **Art Gallery and Museum** Paintings by Raeburn, Zoffany, Romney, John, Toulouse-Lautrec, Monet, Boudin, Vlaminck, Conder.

3 **University Anthropological Museum** Archaeology from all over the world, classical vases, Egyptian collection, ancient Chinese art.

ABERYSTWYTH, Cardiganshire

4 **National Library of Wales** Collections relating to Wales; prints, watercolours, drawings, etchings.

ABINGDON, Berkshire

5 **Abbey** Founded 675, demolished 1538, remaining buildings include Long Gallery of stone and timber, 13th C Checker building.

ADLINGTON HALL, Cheshire

6 Begun 1315, continued until 1581; Georgian s front and Palladian portico. Great Hall has carved ceiling and murals.

ALCESTER, Warwickshire

7 **Ragley Hall** 17th C mansion built by Hooke c.1680–90, with some alterations to exterior by Wyatt and possibly Gibbs. Fine interiors by Gibbs (Great Hall) and Wyatt. Paintings, furniture, porcelain etc; valuable library.

ALNWICK, Northumberland

8 **Castle** Main part dates from 14th C, but present building much restored.

ALTHORP, Northamptonshire

9 Great house begun c.1580; altered c.1670; 18th C exterior and suite of rooms by Holland; Long Gallery with Stuart portraits. Collection of Italian and Dutch masters, portraits.

ARBURY HALL, Warwickshire

10 Quadrangular Elizabethan mansion altered 1670s (chapel with stucco work by E Martin) and again in Gothic style, 1748–1800. Pictures, furniture, china, glass.

ARUNDEL, Sussex

11 **Castle** Massive, much-restored Norman stronghold. Living quarters partly rebuilt in the 18th C (Gothic library). Castle almost entirely rebuilt in a 13th C style by C A Buckler in 1890–1903. Furniture, portraits.

ASCOTT WING, Buckinghamshire

12 Contains Anthony de Rothschild's important collection of pictures, French and Chippendale furniture and oriental porcelain.

ASTBURY, Cheshire

13 **Little Moreton Hall** Black and white half-timbered Elizabethan moated manor house.

ATTINGHAM PARK, Shropshire

14 Late 18th C mansion designed by G Stewart in 1784. State rooms in manner of Wyatt; picture gallery by Nash (1807) containing works of Italian and Spanish schools; drawing-room contains Louis XVI and Empire furniture.

AUDLEY END, Essex

15 Huge Jacobean mansion built 1603–16. Great Hall with 2 classical porches, ornate Jacobean screen, woodwork, plasterwork, English portraits and other paintings. Principal rooms redecorated in Adam and Jacobean styles by Rebecca c.1776.

AVEBURY, Wiltshire

16 **Alexander Keiller Museum** Neolithic, Bronze Age and other finds from the Avebury and Windmill Hill excavations.

17 **Stone circle** Largest in Europe, circle of megaliths 450 yds across. Bronze Age, c.1800 BC.

AYLSHAM, Norfolk

18 **Blickling Hall** Gabled and turreted brick Jacobean mansion built from designs by R Lyminge 1616–24. Furniture, pictures, Chinese wallpapers and St Petersburg tapestries.

AYNHOE PARK, Northamptonshire

19 17th C mansion in style of Inigo Jones. Paintings of the Spanish (Murillo), Dutch, Italian and French schools, glass, porcelain, French and Italian furniture.

BADMINTON, Gloucestershire

20 **Badminton House** Palladian mansion built 1682, altered and enlarged c.1740 by Kent. Furniture and carvings.

BAKEWELL, Derbyshire

21 **Haddon Hall** Medieval manor house of

12th–15th C, probably the most complete example of its type in England. 12th C chapel with 15th C murals.

BARFRESTON, Kent

22 **St Nicholas** Small Norman church with profuse Romanesque carving.

BARNACK, Northamptonshire

23 **St John the Baptist** Partly Saxon church with late Saxon tower of the early 11th C crowned by 13th C spire. Saxon relief carving of Christ in Majesty, 13th C font, monuments.

BARNARD CASTLE, County Durham

24 **Bowes Museum** European art of late medieval period to 19th C. Paintings of Spanish (El Greco, Goya), Italian, French, Flemish, Dutch and English schools. Furniture notably French 18th C, porcelain, tapestries, glass, jewellery, sculpture, metalwork.

BARNSLEY, Yorkshire

25 **Cannon Hall Art Gallery and Museum** 18th C house by Carr containing collections of furniture, painting, china and silver in period rooms.

26 **Cooper Art Gallery** Paintings of 17th–19th C, English watercolours of 19th–20th C, English drawings.

BATH, Somerset

27 **Abbey** Present building begun 1501 to the design of R and W Vertue. Not completed until 19th C. Style consistently Perpendicular, notable for its fan-vaulting.

28 **American Museum in Britain** In Claverton Manor (Wyatville). American decorative arts of 17th–19th C. Complete furnished period rooms.

29 **Assembly Rooms and Museum of Costume** Public rooms designed by J Wood Junior (1771). Important collection of costume and costume accessories from 1580.

30 **Holburne of Menstrie Museum of Art** Paintings: Guardi, Brueghel, Gainsborough, Ramsey, Stubbs etc, drawings, miniatures, silver, porcelain, furniture, glass, maiolica.

31 **Roman Museum** Important Roman relics found in and around Bath.

32 **Victoria Art Gallery** Paintings (mainly 18th and 20th C), early English watercolours, etchings, English and Bohemian glass, Delftware.

BATTLE, Sussex

33 **Abbey** Benedictine abbey founded by William the Conqueror in 1066. 14th C turreted gatehouse and partly ruined dormitory and scriptorium still survive.

BEAULIEU, Hampshire

34 **Palace House** Former great gatehouse of the Cistercian abbey founded 1204.

BEAUMARIS CASTLE, Anglesey

35 Concentric building of great symmetry, founded 1293 by Edward I, work never completed. Large gatehouse, beautiful small oratory.

BEDFORD, Bedfordshire

36 **Cecil Higgins Art Gallery** English watercolours and drawings of 17th C to present day; prints from Dürer to present day; English and continental porcelain and glass of the 18th C; furniture, sculpture (Moore, Epstein, etc).

BELFAST, Antrim, Ireland

37 **Ulster Museum and Art Gallery** Sculpture, Irish metalwork and glass, ceramics, silver, paintings.

BELVOIR CASTLE, Leicestershire

38 Formerly a fortress, rebuilt during 17th C; private apartments reconstructed c.1800 by Wyatt, who also added a new range. Mausoleum in Norman style built by Thoroton 1826–28.

BERKELEY, Gloucestershire

39 **Berkeley Castle** Historic medieval castle with massive circular keep (1155–60). State apartments contain furniture, paintings, tapestries and silver. Elizabethan terraced gardens.

BERWICK-ON-TWEED, Northumberland

40 **Museum and Art Gallery** Paintings, silver, bronzes, ceramics.

BEVERLEY, Yorkshire

41 **Minster** Chancel and transepts of present church fine examples of Early English, 1190–1210, with many original features. Nave continued in the same style in the 1st half of the 14th C. W front of about 1400 one of the best in

England, with 2 tall towers and high gable. Interior contains the Percy tomb c.1340, good series of 16th C misericords.

BIGNOR, Sussex

42 **Roman Villa and Museum** Villa of 2nd–4th C (mosaic floors). Museum contains finds from recent excavations.

BIRKENHEAD, Cheshire

43 **Williamson Art Gallery and Museum** English watercolours, paintings by Raeburn, Steer etc, pottery, porcelain.

BIRMINGHAM, Warwickshire

44 **Cathedral of St Chad** Built 1839–41 by A W N Pugin.

45 **Aston Hall** Red brick, gabled and turreted Jacobean mansion built 1618–35. Furniture, paintings, tapestries etc.

46 **Barber Institute of Fine Arts** Works of art up to 1900: paintings by Bellini, Botticelli, Martini, Rembrandt, Rubens, Murillo, Poussin, Claude, Watteau, Gainsborough, Constable, Turner, Manet, Monet and Toulouse-Lautrec; drawings and miniatures; sculpture by Giov. della Robbia, Barye, Rodin and Degas; furniture, tapestry, gold, silver, ivory and enamels.

47 **City Museum and Art Gallery** Paintings of the English and continental schools: Martini, Botticelli, Rembrandt, Rubens, Claude, Gainsborough, Reynolds, Pissarro, Courbet, Sisley, etc. Paintings and drawings of the Pre-Raphaelites: Millais *Blind Girl*, Ford Madox Brown *The Last of England*. English watercolours of the 18th C onwards; sculpture by Donatello, Rodin, Renoir, Epstein and Moore; silver, pottery and porcelain. Exhibits from Europe, the East, S. America and the South Seas.

BLACKBURN, Lancashire

48 **Museum and Art Gallery** English watercolours of the 18th–20th C, Japanese prints, coins, manuscripts, paintings, pottery, glass, archaeology.

BLAIR CASTLE, Perthshire

49 Fortress during 13th C; main feature is the Cummings Tower, a copy of the former tower with stepped gable and battlements. Furniture, tapestries, Sèvres china, jewellery etc.

BLENHEIM PALACE, Oxfordshire

50 Masterpiece of Sir John Vanbrugh, built 1705–22 in Baroque style, with 2 storeys, arranged round a huge courtyard. State apartments contain portraits, china, furniture, tapestries.

BLICKLING HALL, Norfolk

51 Red-brick Jacobean house built 1616–28 by R Lyminge. Furniture, tapestries, paintings.

BODIAM CASTLE, Sussex

52 Built between 1385 and 1389 – the last of the great English military castles. Restored 1919.

BOLSOVER CASTLE, Derbyshire

53 17th C castle on emplacement of Norman stronghold. Keep rebuilt in a Jacobean Gothic style by Cavendish and Smythson, 1613–1617. Wallpaintings, unique chimneypieces.

BOSTON, Lincolnshire

54 **St Botolph** One of the largest parish churches in England famous for its 272 ft high tower, the 'Boston Stump' crowned by an octagonal lantern.

BOURNEMOUTH, Hampshire

55 **Rothesay Museum** Early Italian paintings and pottery, English paintings, furniture and ceramics, Victoriana, armour.

56 **Russell-Cotes Art Gallery and Museum** Watercolours; drawings, sculpture, miniatures, ceramics, works from China, Japan, Burma, Thailand, Tibet, India.

BRADFORD, Yorkshire

57 **Bolling Hall** Earliest part of present house is defensive tower dating from 15th C. In 1779 N wing remodelled by Carr in Adam style. Hall has fine panelling, plasterwork and furniture.

58 **City Art Gallery and Museum** British and foreign paintings (Vasari, Reni, Reynolds, Gainsborough, Corot, Sickert, Pissarro and Spencer), British watercolours, drawings, Chinese pottery and porcelain, local archaeology.

BRADFORD-ON-AVON, Wiltshire

59 **St Laurence** Early Anglo-Saxon church; lower part probably dates from c.705.

BRADING, Isle of Wight
60 **Roman Villa** Remains of villa with mosaic pavements, hypocaust etc.
BRECON, Brecknockshire
61 **Cathedral** Cruciform building with central tower, originally Norman, now mainly Gothic.
BRIDLINGTON, Yorkshire
62 **Burton Agnes Hall** Late Elizabethan manor house with turreted gatehouse and lavishly decorated interior. Paintings, oriental porcelain.
BRIGHTON, Sussex
63 **Art Gallery and Museum** Paintings; watercolours, miniatures, prints and drawings. Pottery, Worcester porcelain, ancient jewellery, musical instruments, French and English furniture, antique glass, local antiquities and archaeology.
64 **Royal Pavilion** Residence of the Prince Regent, begun 1787 by Holland and enlarged and transformed by Nash in the Moghul style between 1815 and 1822. N Gate with a Saracenic arch and green bubble dome was added (to a design by Nash) in 1832. Sumptuous interiors in the Regency Chinese taste (with some Indian detail).
65 **Thomas-Stanford Museum** In Preston Manor, rebuilt in 1738 on a 13th c foundation, preserved as country house. Silver from England (Paul Lamerie), Portugal and Scandinavia; Georgian, 16th c and 17th c furniture.
BRISTOL, Gloucestershire
66 **Cathedral** Original buildings begun in 1140, of which the chapter house remains. Early English lady chapel. East part rebuilt from about 1300–20, and forms a remarkable example of the Decorated style. The 'star-recesses' for tombs and 'skeleton vault' in side chapel are unique.
67 **St Mary Redcliffe** Perpendicular parish church (one of the largest in England).
68 **City Art Gallery and Museum** Paintings of English school, Hogarth's altarpiece from St Mary Redcliffe; continental schools, *Withypool Triptych* by Andrea Solario, works by Bellini, Carpaccio, Robert, Courbet and the Impressionists. Contemporary paintings and sculpture. Bristol glass and Delftware, Chinese ivories, ceramics, glass.
BRIXWORTH, Northamptonshire
69 **All Saints** Church begun *c.*675 showing Saxon work of 3 distinct pre-Norman periods. Saxon sculpture and a monument of a cross-legged knight of *c.*1300.
BURGHLEY HOUSE, Huntingdonshire
70 Largest and grandest of Elizabethan houses, built 1552–87 by William Cecil, Lord Burghley, probably to a large extent to his own design. Wall and ceiling-paintings by Verrio ('Heaven Room') and Laguerre; furniture, plasterwork, carving, tapestries. Paintings, chiefly of the Italian and British schools.
BURNLEY, Lancashire
71 **Towneley Hall Art Gallery and Museum** 14th c mansion altered 18th c. Paintings, watercolours, furniture, ivories, glass and ceramics.
BURTON AGNES HALL, Yorkshire
72 Elizabethan mansion, built 1598–1610. Oriental china; paintings by Renoir, Cézanne, Corot, Gauguin.
BURY, Lancashire
73 **Art Gallery and Museum** English paintings, engravings, sculpture.
BURY ST EDMUNDS, Suffolk
74 **Abbey** Norman gateway and 14th c Great Gateway survive intact from the former Benedictine abbey. Remaining abbey buildings now mainly ruins, though parts of the huge abbey church (w front) and cloister buildings together with the 13th c Abbot's Bridge survive.
75 **Hengrave Hall** Originally built 1525–38; now a convent. Oratory has 16th c window with 21 lights showing biblical scenes.
BUSCOT PARK, Berkshire
76 Georgian mansion built 1780 to his own designs by E L Townsend with Wyatt-type ceilings and chimneypieces. Paintings, contemporary furniture. Saloon contains the remarkable *Briar Rose* picture-sequence of 1871 by Burne-Jones in settings designed by the artist.

CAERNARVON, Caernarvonshire
77 **Castle** Begun in 1285 for Edward I, completed in 1322 under Edward II; considerably restored.
CAERPHILLY, Glamorganshire
78 **Castle** The largest in Wales, built *c.*1272. Good example of early military architecture; very well reconstructed.
CAMBRIDGE, Cambridgeshire
79 **Church of the Holy Sepulchre** One of the few round Norman churches to survive in England; vaulted ambulatory. Restored in 19th c.
80 **St Benet** Fine Saxon tower.
81 **Christ's College** Tudor Court with chapel altered in 18th c. 17th c Fellows' Building.
82 **Clare College** Founded 1326, but all buildings 17th c, largely by Robert Grumbold.
83 **Corpus Christi** Old Court basically 14th c, oldest in Cambridge. Second court with hall and chapel added by Wilkins 1823–27. Library: important MSS and paintings.
84 **Downing College** Founded 1800. All designed by Wilkins in classical style. Completed by Sir Herbert Baker 1929.
85 **Emmanuel College** Buildings mostly 16th and 17th c; chapel by Wren. Extensive early 20th c buildings by Leonard Stokes.
86 **Fitzwilliam Museum** Outstanding collections of paintings: English, French, Italian, Dutch, Flemish and Spanish schools. Miniatures, sculpture, 600 medieval MSS, furniture, ceramics, glass etc.
87 **Gonville and Caius** One range and chapel of the 14th c, but much altered in 16th c. Dr Caius's Gates of Virtue and Honour are among the earliest Renaissance works in England. Large assertive additions by Waterhouse in 19th c. Harvey Court by L Martin and S G Wilson is among the most notable Cambridge modern buildings.
88 **History Faculty Building** 1963–68, by Stirling; bright red brick, steel and glass.
89 **Jesus College** Founded 1497 using the 12th and 13th c buildings of a Benedictine nunnery of which part of the church survives as the chapel. Glass by Burne-Jones, ceiling by Morris, furniture by Pugin. 19th c range by Waterhouse and modern block by D Roberts.
90 **King's College** Founded 1441, but only the chapel was built, one of the major Perpendicular churches of England. Mainly by J Wastell, it combines large traceried windows, fan-vaulting and lavish sculpture; 16th c Flemish glass; stalls and screen probably Italian. The chapel now contains Rubens's *Adoration of the Magi*. The 18th c Fellows' Building by Gibbs, the screen to street and hall range by Wilkins in the early 19th c.
91 **Magdalene** College Main court is 15th c, with the Pepys Library added in the 17th c. Contains Pepys's collection of books and MS of his diary.
92 **New Hall** Founded 1954, built 1962 onwards by Chamberlain, Powell and Bon.
93 **New University Library** Built in 1931–34 by Giles G Scott.
94 **Old University Library** Built 1836–42, by C R Cockerell in an inventive Greek style.
95 **Pembroke College** Founded 1346, hall redecorated with good plasterwork in the 17th c Chapel by Wren.
96 **Peterhouse College** Founded in the 13th c. Court basically 15th c with hall and Combination Room decorated by Morris and Co. 17th c extensions, including chapel. New building by Leslie Martin and St John Wilson.
97 **Queens' College** Principal court with hall is 15th c. Other parts, including President's Lodge are Tudor. Walnut Tree Court, with chapel, by Bodley, 1890. Erasmus building, 1959–60, by B Spence.
98 **St John's College** 3 large courts, all basically 16th c. Rickman's New Court (1825) was built across the river and connected by the Bridge of Sighs. Large Neo-Gothic chapel by George G Scott, 1863. New extensions of high quality by Powell and Moya, 1963–67.
99 **Senate House** Built 1722–30 by Gibbs in Palladian style; fine plasterwork.

100 **Trinity College** Largest college in Cambridge. Great Court and Neville's Court 16th and 17th c. Library, added by Wren 1676–90 contains valuable medieval MSS and carving by Gibbons. New Court added by Wilkins 1823.
101 **University Centre** Built 1963–67 by Howell, Killick, Partridge and Amis, one of the best modern buildings in Cambridge.
102 **University Museum of Archaeology and Ethnology** Archaeology of prehistoric to medieval periods; ethnographical material from Africa, America and Oceania.
CANTERBURY, Kent
103 **Cathedral** E end rebuilt by William of Sens, who introduced the Gothic style of the Ile-de-France into England; completed by William the Englishman in 1184. Nave rebuilt in Perpendicular style by Henry Yevele, 1379–1405, the crossing tower, 'Bell Harry', by J Wastell, 1485–1515. Fine Romanesque wallpainting (St Anselm's chapel); the best 13th c stained glass in England; notable tombs, including that of the Black Prince.
CARDIFF, Glamorganshire
104 **Castle** Begun 1090 on the site of a Roman fort. 13th c shell keep and domestic quarters in sw corner. The latter were almost entirely rebuilt by W Burges in the 19th c.
105 **Welsh National Museum** Paintings include works by Wilson, Burne-Jones, John. Archeological collections, particularly relating to Wales. Ivories, church plate, metalwork.
CARISBROOKE CASTLE, Isle of Wight
106 12th c keep and ramparts, chapel (remains) of *c.*1270, Great Hall with chimneypiece of 1390, 14th c gatehouse, 16th c well house.
CARLISLE, Cumberland
107 **Castle** Built *c.*1092, enlarged 12th c. Large parts destroyed during 19th c. Most important remains are 14th c main gate, Queen Mary's Tower and central keep.
108 **Museum and Art Gallery** Local prehistoric and Roman antiquities, Pre-Raphaelite paintings, English porcelain.
CASHEL, Tipperary, Ireland
109 **Cathedral** Built 13th c, unroofed 1749. Porch with Gothic doorway, good 16th c tombs. On s side is Cormac's Chapel (1127–34), perfect example of Irish Romanesque.
CASTELL COCH, Glamorganshire
110 Rebuilt on ruin of 13th c castle by Burges, 1865–75. Walls and ceilings painted with scenes from Aesop's Fables, birds, butterflies etc. Burges also designed the furniture.
CASTLE ASHBY, Northamptonshire
111 Quadrangular Elizabethan mansion begun *c.*1575; continued in Jacobean style; 4th side completed in Neoclassical manner in 1635 and is almost certainly the work of Inigo Jones. State Rooms redecorated *c.*1675 with furniture of the period and tapestries. Italian, Dutch and English paintings.
CASTLE HEDINGHAM, Essex
112 Well-preserved, massive, rectangular Norman keep, with square turrets, built *c.*1140.
CASTLE HOWARD, Yorkshire
113 Built 1700–14 by Vanbrugh assisted by Hawksmoor. Central block, surmounted by a dome, between 2 wings. Fine furniture, paintings by Rubens, Tintoretto, Poussin, Van Dyck, Gainsborough etc.
CHATSWORTH HOUSE, Derbyshire
114 Present building commenced by William Talman (s and E fronts) in 1687 and completed by Thomas Archer (N front) in 1707. A vast N wing was added, and alterations made by Wyatville 1820–30. Ceiling-paintings by Verrio, Laguerre and Thornhill, sculpture by Cibber, wrought-iron by Tijou and wood-carving by S Watson. Paintings, tapestry, objets d'art, old master drawings.
CHEADLE, Cheshire
115 **St Giles** Built 1841–46 by A W N Pugin. The chief exterior feature is an enormous w tower and spire. Interior is richly painted.
CHEDWORTH, Gloucestershire
116 **Roman Villa and Museum** Well-preserved villa of AD 150–350 with mosaic pavements. Museum contains numerous finds.

CHESTER, Cheshire

117 **Cathedral** Founded in 1093. N transept is Norman; choir Decorated, nave and cloister Perpendicular. Its most interesting part is the mid 13th C vestibule to the chapter house.

118 **St John** Fine early Norman nave with Transitional triforium and aisles and early English clerestory and N porch (restored). Unusual skeleton monument by Pierce.

119 **Roman Amphitheatre** Discovered 1929, dates from *c.* AD 80, believed to be largest Roman building in Britain.

CHICHESTER, Sussex

120 **Cathedral** Founded in 1075. Nave Norman with later vaulting; retrochoir Early English with interesting sculpture. Central tower and steeple rebuilt by George G Scott after collapse in 1861. Notable works of modern art including Sutherland's *Noli me Tangere*; 2 Romanesque carved panels: the Raising of Lazarus and Christ's Entry into Bethany. In the Bishop's Palace is the famous 13th C fresco, the Chichester Roundel.

CHIRK, Denbighshire

121 **Castle** Completed 1310; domestic quarters have mullioned windows inserted 1595. Badly damaged during Civil War, extensively repaired after 1660. Further alterations by Pugin in 1835. Long Gallery of 1680; state rooms redecorated in the Adam style 1763–73. 17th C portraits, landscapes, Mortlake tapestries.

CHRISTCHURCH, Hampshire

122 **Priory Church** Norman building (the longest parish church in England) with a fine N porch of *c.*1300 and a late 15th C choir and W tower. Notable late 14th C stone reredos showing the Tree of Jesse; fine misericords of 1200–1500; good monuments including one by Flaxman.

CLAYDON HOUSE, Buckinghamshire

123 18th C mansion begun 1752 and continued 1768–80 to the designs of Sir Thomas Robinson (W front). State rooms are outstanding for their extraordinary carved Rococo decoration by a local craftsman, Lightfoot (notably the Chinese Room) whose only known work this is. Magnificent inlaid staircase. Furniture, paintings.

CLONMACNOISE, Offaly, Ireland

124 **The Seven Churches** Complex remaining from the monastic 'city' founded by St Ciaran in 6th C. Great Church built 904, rebuilt in 14th C, choir vault and elaborately ornamented N doorway were built *c.*1460 by Dean Odo. Great Cross 15 ft high. Remains of other smaller churches, of 11th C onwards. Macarthy's Tower 1124 retains its conical cap. O'Rouke's Tower 62 ft high, built soon after the Great Church.

COLCHESTER, Essex

125 **Colchester and Essex Museum** In castle. Local late Celtic and Roman antiquities etc.

COMPTON WYNYATES, Warwickshire

126 Pink brick, battlemented Tudor mansion. Panelled Great Hall with remarkable carved screen.

CONISBROUGH CASTLE, Yorkshire

127 Wall of inner bailey has largely survived, 90 ft tall circular keep, walls supported by heavy buttresses.

CONWAY, Caernarvonshire

128 **Town walls and Castle** Of 13th C. Part of the same scheme of fortification.

129 **Plas Mawr** (the Great Mansion) Elizabethan house, with crow-stepped gables and octagonal tower; contains elaborate plaster ceilings and striking fireplaces.

COOKHAM-ON-THAMES, Berkshire

130 **Stanley Spencer Gallery** Paintings, drawings and relics of the artist.

CORK, Ireland

131 **St Finbar's Cathedral** Designed by Burges, built 1865–76.

CORSHAM COURT, Wiltshire

132 Elizabethan mansion built 1582; Georgian additions. Picture gallery: old master paintings; Chippendale and Adam furniture.

COVENTRY, Warwickshire

133 **Cathedral** The present cathedral, designed by Spence, is built at right-angles to the old. The S entrance wall is entirely of engraved glass by John Hutton. Over the altar is the huge tapestry *Christ in Glory* by Sutherland. Contains stained glass by various artists, including John Piper, and sculpture by Epstein.

134 **Herbert Art Gallery and Museum** Modern paintings and sculpture, Sutherland sketches for the cathedral tapestry, topographical watercolours of the 18th C onwards (Cox, Holman-Hunt, etc) local archaeology.

CULZEAN, Ayrshire

135 **Castle** Gothic structure built by Adam round an ancient tower. Round drawing-room with circular carpet and special furniture also designed by Adam.

DEERHURST, Gloucestershire

136 **St Mary** Saxon church with a carved Saxon font and curious triangular-headed windows; 14th C stained glass.

DERBY, Derbyshire

137 **Cathedral** Mainly demolished in the 18th C, replaced by a building designed by Gibbs, showing Italian Baroque influence. Contains good monuments.

138 **Museum and Art Gallery** Derby porcelain, paintings by Joseph Wright of Derby.

DEVIZES, Wiltshire

139 **Museum and Art Gallery** Neolithic, Bronze Age and Iron Age antiquities from sites in Wiltshire.

DODINGTON HOUSE, Gloucestershire

140 Neoclassical house built to designs of Wyatt.

DOVER, Kent

141 **Castle** Main fortifications date from 12th and 13th C; keep built 1180s.

DRYBURGH ABBEY, Berwickshire

142 Founded 1150; remains include ruined church and parts of conventual buildings.

DUBLIN, County Dublin, Ireland

143 **Christ Church** Almost entirely restored 1870–78; the only old work remaining is the N wall of nave transepts and W bay of choir. N wall Early English, *c.*1230; transepts and crossing with their mixture of pointed and round arches are typical of Transitional work of *c.*1170; huge crypt with rough arches.

144 **St Patrick's Cathedral** Built largely before 1260, much dilapidated during 17th and 18th C, restored 19th C.

145 **Chester Beatty Library** MSS, including those from India, Tibet, China. Some oriental objects, Japanese sword guards, Chinese jade.

146 **Custom House** Masterpiece of J Gandon, 1781–91. Fine Doric portico, pavilion on each wing, central dome 125 ft high.

147 **Four Courts** Second masterpiece of J Gandon 1786–1802, incorporating work by Cooley 1776–84.

148 **Municipal Art Gallery** Portraits; paintings by Constable, Fantin-Latour, Sargent, Monet, Boudin, Corot, Whistler, Degas, Ingres, Jack Yeats, John, Vuillard, Daumier, Renoir, Manet, Puvis de Chavannes, Utrillo, Picasso, Lurçat, Piper, Bonnard.

149 **National Gallery of Ireland** Important collection of paintings; portrait collection, early English watercolours, Dutch school, French Impressionists and later Italian schools.

150 **National Museum of Ireland** Irish antiquities, sculpture, jewellery, silver, bronze, etc, from prehistory to Middle Ages.

151 **Trinity College** Built 1755–59 by Keene and Sanderson; front with Corinthian portico. Library contains MSS including Book of Kells, Book of Durrow, Book of Dimma.

DUNFERMLINE, Fife

152 **Abbey Church** Norman nave 1150, Gothic choir of 1817–22 by William Burn, great buttresses added in 16th C. Elaborate Norman carving on N porch. Below pulpit is sepulchre of Robert the Bruce.

DUNKELD, Perthshire

153 **Cathedral** Fabric dates partly from 12th C, but most of remains are 14th–15th C. Flamboyant tracery, 15th C wallpaintings.

DUNSTABLE, Bedfordshire

154 **St Peter and St Paul** Fine parish church incorporating remains of the church of the former 12th C Augustinian priory.

DUNSTER CASTLE, Somerset

155 Dates partly from 13th C with many subsequent additions and alterations. 17th C carved staircase and plaster ceilings, remarkable Spanish leather decoration panels depicting the story of Antony and Cleopatra, family portraits.

DURHAM, County Durham

156 **Cathedral** Main fabric built between 1093 and 1133; choir vaults of early 12th C are among the earliest rib-vaults in Europe. Galilee Porch added about 1170, Chapel of the Nine Altars mid 13th C, central tower late 13th C. Considered the masterpiece of English Romanesque.

157 **Gulbenkian Museum of Oriental Art and Archaeology** (University of Durham) Chinese ceramics, jade and ivories, Egyptian and Mesopotamian antiquities, Chinese, Japanese, Indian and Tibetan art etc.

EARLS BARTON, Northamptonshire

158 **All Saints** Famous for its important Saxon W tower of *c.* 1000.

EDINBURGH, Midlothian

159 **Holyrood Abbey** Founded 1128 by David I, restored by Charles I in 1633. W front finest part of remains.

160 **Magdalen Chapel** Founded 1547 together with a hospital. Steeple added 1618–28. Important stained glass in central window.

161 **St Giles's Cathedral** Built between about 1390 and 1450. The tower with its 'crown' dates from 1495.

162 **St Margaret's Chapel** Tiny building, only Norman work in Edinburgh.

163 **St Mary's Cathedral** Built 1876–79 to designs by George G Scott. One of the largest Neo-Gothic churches in the world.

164 **National Gallery of Scotland** Paintings by Bernado Daddi, Filippino Lippi, Perugino, Van der Goes, Veronese, Tiepolo, Tintoretto, Guardi, Hals, Rembrandt, Van Dyck, Ruisdael, Rubens, El Greco, Velasquez, Zurbarán, Poussin, Lancret, Vermeer, Goya, Chardin, Watteau, Boucher, Corot, Monet, Degas, Van Gogh, Gauguin, Fantin-Latour.

165 **National Portrait Gallery of Scotland** Pictures by Lely, Kneller, Wilson, Ramsay, Raeburn, Gainsborough, Romney, Reynolds.

166 **Palace of Holyroodhouse** Built in French style surrounding a quadrangle, begun *c.*1500, by James IV. Picture gallery.

167 **Parliament Hall** Gothic building with timber roof. Portraits by Raeburn, Kneller, statue by Roubiliac.

168 **Royal Scottish Museum** Departments of Art, Archaeology and Ethnology. Silverware, glass, French ivories, wood-carving, armour, coins, Egyptian collection, Japanese pottery.

ELY, Cambridgeshire

169 **Cathedral** Contains outstanding architecture of the Norman period (nave), Early English (presbytery) and above all Decorated (lady chapel and octagon over the crossing). The Prior's Door of about 1150 is a major work of Romanesque sculpture.

ESCOMB, Durham

170 **St John the Evangelist** Notable small early Saxon church of 7th or 8th C.

ETON COLLEGE, Buckinghamshire

171 Founded 1440 by Henry VI as a chantry chapel with school and almshouse attached.

EWENNY PRIORY, Glamorganshire

172 Founded 1141, perfect specimen of early Norman architecture.

EXETER, Devonshire

173 **St Peter's Cathedral** The 2 transepts, with towers, are Norman (1112–33), nearly all the rest Decorated (1288–1342).

FAIRFORD, Gloucestershire

174 **St Mary the Virgin** Fine late 15th C church with a complete series of 28 stained-glass windows painted between 1495 and 1505.

FALKLAND, Fife

175 **Palace** 16th C, only S wing tolerably preserved. Ornamental façade, gatehouse with loopholed round towers, Flemish tapestries.

FISHBOURNE, Sussex

176 **Roman Palace** Largest in Britain, recently excavated. Fine early 3rd C mosaic floor.

FOUNTAINS ABBEY, Yorkshire

177 Founded 1132; reconstructed 1148–79 after being destroyed by fire. Ruins form the

most complete set of Cistercian buildings to survive Dissolution.

FOWLIS EASTER, Angus
178 **Church** Built 1453; restored. Contains 4 pre-Reformation paintings on oak.

GAINSBOROUGH, Lincolnshire
179 **Old Hall** Present building, of brick with half-timbering, dates from c. 1500.

GALLARUS, Kerry, Ireland
180 **Oratory of Gallarus** Fine relic of early Irish Christianity c. 8th c. Development of beehive hut construction but rectangular.

GALWAY, County Galway, Ireland
181 **St Nicholas** Largest medieval church in Ireland. Fine carving including gargoyles on s aisle; 16th c font.

GARWAY, Herefordshire
182 **St Michael and All Angels** One of the round churches of Knights Templars, dates from 12th c. Present nave 13th c; Norman chancel-arch remains.

GLAMIS, Angus
183 **Castle** Present form built 1650–96 in French château style.

GLASGOW, Lanarkshire
184 **St Mungow's Cathedral** E end, with very large crypt (Laigh Kirk) dates from 13th c; nave and spire over crossing 15th c. Restored 19th c.
185 **City Art Gallery and Museum** Dutch and Italian paintings (Rembrandt, Titian and Giorgione); modern French and Scottish pictures; art treasures.
186 **Hunterian Museum and Library** Pictures by Chardin, Rembrandt, Reynolds, Veronese, Titian, Whistler and others.
187 **Pollock House** Collection of paintings, mostly Spanish (El Greco, Murillo, Goya, Velasquez). Also works by Signorelli, Jordaens, Blake, Hogarth, Kneller.

GLASTONBURY, Somerset
188 **Abbey** Founded in Saxon times. The oldest and best-preserved part is St Mary's Chapel, at the w end, 1184–86.

GLOUCESTER, Gloucestershire
189 **Cathedral** The nave, mid-12th c, is remarkable for its tall cylindrical piers and small triforium and clerestory. Early Perpendicular work in s transept and choir. Cloisters contain the earliest of all fan-vaults (c. 1370). Tomb of Edward II.

GOODWOOD HOUSE, Sussex
190 Unusually shaped Georgian house with domed towers. Wyatt interiors; paintings (mainly portraits).

GUILDFORD, Surrey
191 **Cathedral** Begun 1936 to the designs of E Maufe; completed 1962.
192 **Losely Park** Early Elizabethan mansion built 1562–68.

HADDON HALL, Derbyshire
193 Oldest parts date from 13th c. Excellent 20th c restoration. Panelled Long Gallery.

HARDHAM, Sussex
194 **St Botolph** Small 11th c church with notable wallpaintings of c. 1120–40.

HARDWICK HALL, Derbyshire
195 Great Elizabethan mansion, famous for its huge windows, built by Elizabeth, Countess of Shrewsbury 1590–97. Portraits, tapestries etc.

HAREWOOD HOUSE, Yorkshire
196 Built 1759–71 by J Carr; interior by Adam. Adam and Zucchi ceilings. Furniture by Adam and Chippendale.

HARLECH, Merionethshire
197 **Castle** Founded 1285, complete example of Edwardian system of concentric fortification.

HATCHLANDS, Surrey
198 Contains the earliest known ceilings and decorations by Adam, dating from 1750.

HATFIELD HOUSE, Hertfordshire
199 Great brick and stone Jacobean mansion built 1607–11. State rooms contain an unrivalled collection of 16th and 17th c historical portraits.

HEATON HALL, Lancashire
200 Georgian mansion in the Neoclassical style designed by Wyatt in 1772. Contains one of the few surviving Etruscan rooms, with painted decoration by Rebecca. Paintings, furniture and ceramics (chiefly 18th c), English silver.

HEREFORD, Herefordshire
201 **Cathedral** Norman building begun 1079, of which much remains in the choir, transepts and nave. Fell into ruin in the 18th c. Nave revaulted and w front completely rebuilt by Oldrid Scott 1902–28. Contains the best example of a medieval *mappamundi* in England.

HERSTMONCEAUX, Sussex
202 **Castle** 15th c fortified house. Main architectural feature is the gatehouse.

HEVENINGHAM HALL, Suffolk
203 Imposing Palladian mansion built 1779 by Sir Robert Taylor. Interior by Wyatt completed by 1784.

HOLKHAM HALL, Norfolk
204 Palladian mansion built by Kent 1734–60. Paintings, furniture, tapestries and sculpture.

HOLYCROSS, Tipperary, Ireland
205 **Abbey** Founded 1180, enlarged and altered in 14th c. Remarkable window tracery.

HULL, Yorkshire
206 **Ferens Art Gallery** Old master paintings, English paintings of the 17th–19th c, sculpture by Moore, Hepworth and Paolozzi, contemporary British paintings.

IFFLEY, Oxfordshire
207 **St Mary** Small Norman parish church, built c. 1170.

ICKWORTH, Suffolk
208 Elliptical mansion, with curving corridors leading to flanking wings, built to his own designs by Frederick Hervey, Bishop of Derry and Earl of Bristol, 1796–1830.

IONA, Argyll
209 Ruins of Romanesque priory church and several interesting carved crosses.

IPSWICH, Suffolk
210 **Christchurch Mansion** Tudor mansion altered after fire in 1670s with extensive collections of local antiquities, furniture. Pictures by Gainsborough, Constable and others.

KEDLESTON HALL, Derbyshire
211 Classical mansion built 1757–65. Entrance front and wings by J Paine 1761; s front by Adam. Adam interior of 1760–70; collection of old masters and contemporary furniture, silver, ivory.

KENDAL, Westmoreland
212 **Abbot Hall Art Gallery** 18th c furnished rooms; paintings by Romney, Reynolds, Devis etc; modern paintings and sculpture.

KENILWORTH CASTLE, Warwickshire
213 Ruins of medieval castle begun c. 1125.

KILKENNY, County Kilkenny, Ireland
214 **Cathedral** Begun 1251–56, restored pre-1360. Fan-vault of tower erected 1465. Aisled nave of 5 bays with many monuments, 12 c font.

KILLALOE, County Clare, Ireland
215 **Cathedral** Built 1182, restored 1887. Zigzag moulding and corbels; blocked s doorway with rich carving and grotesque heads.

KILPECK, Herefordshire
216 **St Mary and St David** Small Norman church built c. 1145 with elaborate and extraordinary carved decoration showing some Viking elements. Stained glass by Pugin 1849.

KIMBOLTON CASTLE, Huntingdonshire
217 Late 17th c house built on the original Tudor foundations (some remains) c. 1690. Courtyard retains its William III façades but exterior was remodelled by Vanbrugh c. 1714. Murals by Pellegrini in the chapel, boudoir and staircase hall. Gatehouse by Adam.

KING'S LYNN, Norfolk
218 **Guildhall of the Holy Trinity** Dates from 1421; additions in 18th c. Treasury contains regalia including King John's Cup, King John's Sword and goldsmiths' work.

KIRBY HALL, Northamptonshire
219 Elizabethan mansion in Renaissance style begun 1570; work continued after 1575. Unique use of giant order of pilasters. N range altered 1638–40.

KNOLE, Kent
220 Built 1456; extended and transformed internally by Thomas Sackville, 1st Earl of Dorset. Outstanding Jacobean interior with furniture of 17th and 18th c.

LACOCK, Wiltshire
221 **Abbey** Convent buildings, which were mainly completed in 1247, form the most complete example of an English nunnery to survive. Turned into dwelling in 1540 and a number of additions made. Great Hall remodelled in the Neo-Gothic fashion 1754–56.

LAVENHAM, Suffolk
222 **St Peter and St Paul** Mainly Perpendicular, (c. 1580–85) with a 14th c chancel and huge flint w tower (also Perpendicular). s porch and Spring Chapel are particularly fine.

LAYER MARNEY, Essex
223 **Layer Marney Towers** House is early 16th c. Gatehouse is largest of its kind, with Renaissance decorations in terra-cotta.

LEEDS, Yorkshire
224 **City Art Gallery** Paintings of the Italian, Flemish, Dutch, French and English schools, English watercolours, sculpture, pottery, silver.

LEICESTER, Leicestershire
225 **City Museum and Art Gallery** English paintings and sculpture, particularly modern.

LICHFIELD, Staffordshire
226 **Cathedral** Mostly 13th and 14th c, but drastically restored in 17th and 19th c. Tall windows, 3 spires and warm reddish-yellow stone.

LINCOLN, Lincolnshire
227 **Cathedral** Founded as cathedral 1073. Of the original Norman building the lower part of the w front remains, with interesting sculpture. Rest of the church rebuilt 1192–1250, and the Angel Choir added 1256–80, all in the Early English style of which Lincoln is one of the most perfect examples The circular window of the s transept ('the Bishop's Eye') is a superb example of curvilinear tracery.

LIVERPOOL, Lancashire
228 **Anglican Cathedral** Designed by Giles G Scott, begun 1904, still unfinished. The style is a free and inventive Neo-Gothic.
229 **Roman Catholic Cathedral** Begun in 1933 to the designs of E Lutyens, only crypt was built. After the war the present building was erected over the old crypt, to the design of F Gibberd. It is entirely modern in conception: steel frame; circular (with altar in the centre) rising to a high cylindrical crown.
230 **City Museum and Library** Egyptian, Babylonian, Assyrian, Greek and Roman antiquities, ivories, Limoges enamels, Anglo-Saxon art, prints, MSS, rare books.
231 **St George's Hall** Built 1834–54 in Greek classical style by H L Elmes; decoration by C R Cockerell.
232 **Sudley Art Gallery and Museum** 18th and 19th c paintings, mainly of the British School, pottery, costume, etc.
233 **Walker Art Gallery** European paintings (Roscoe collection of old masters of the early Italian and Flemish schools). Foreign artists represented include Martini, Ercole de' Roberti, Bellini, Jan Mostaert, Rembrandt, Rubens, Murillo, Fragonard, Monet, Courbet, Cézanne and Seurat. British schools from 16th c to present: Hogarth, Zoffany, Stubbs, Turner, Constable, Millais, Hunt, Watts, Sickert and John. Sculptures, ceramics, tapestries.

LLANDAFF, Glamorganshire
234 **Cathedral** Originally mostly 12th c, largely rebuilt 19th c and again 1950s. Contains several interesting works of modern art, including Epstein's *Christ*.

LONDON AND GREATER LONDON
235 **All Hallows By The Tower** Saxon work visible in lower parts of tower; Saxon arch. Brick upper part of tower only example of Cromwellian church architecture in London.
236 **St Bartholomew the Great** Impressive interior in pure Norman style.
237 **St Bride** Rebuilt by Wren 1670–84. The tallest of Wren's steeples.
238 **St Clement Danes** Designed by Wren and built 1680–82; tower added by Gibbs, 1719–20.
239 **St Ethelburga, Bishopsgate** One of the smallest and oldest churches in London; dates in its present form from c. 1400.
240 **St Helen, Bishopsgate** One of the largest and most interesting of the city churches.

Belonged to Benedictine priory founded c.1212.

241 St James, Piccadilly Built by Wren 1684, rebuilt after blitz of 1940–41.

242 St Margaret, Lothbury Rebuilt by Wren 1686–90.

243 St Margaret, Westminster Dates from late 15th C; repeatedly altered and restored.

244 St Martin in the Fields Built 1721–26, finest work of Gibbs. Richly decorated interior.

245 St Mary, Abchurch Rebuilt by Wren 1681–86, with wood-carvings by Gibbons. Dome paintings by Thornhill.

246 St Mary, Aldermary Rebuilt by Wren after 1681 (tower 1704). Plaster fan-vaulting.

247 St Mary-le-Bow Built by Wren 1670–83. The steeple a very fine Renaissance campanile. Norman crypt of c.1090.

248 St Mary-le-Strand Built by Gibbs in 1714. Ionic portico and graceful steeple.

249 St Mary, Woolnoth A building of some originality by Hawksmoor 1716–27.

250 St Paul's Cathedral Built by Wren between 1675 and 1710. Severely classical choir and nave roofed by shallow domes, and high dome (paintings by Thornhill) on drum over the crossing. Carving in wood and stone by Gibbons, wrought-iron by Tijou, some notable tombs.

251 St Paul's Covent Garden By Inigo Jones (1638). Rebuilt after a fire in 1795.

252 St Peter, Cornhill Rebuilt by Wren 1677–81. Carved wooden choir screen the only one known to be by Wren.

253 St Stephen, Walbrook Rebuilt by Wren 1672–79. Interior, with circular dome supported on 8 arches, is one of his masterpieces.

254 Temple Church Most important of the 4 remaining round churches in England. Round part of church in transitional Norman style with handsome ornamentation. Chancel (1240) is fine Early English.

255 Westminster Abbey Of Edward the Confessor's abbey of 1060–66 only a chapel in the S transept and some monastic buildings (E side of cloister) remain. New church was begun in 1243 under the patronage of Henry III. The nave was completed only in the late 14th C by H Yevele. The Henry VII Chapel added about 1505–15. W towers, early 18th C, by Hawksmoor. Notable paintings: Westminster Retable (14th C), portrait of Richard II (c.1390), sculpture, remains of the 13th C Italian shrine of Edward the Confessor and an unrivalled collection of royal tombs, including bronze effigies of Henry III, Edward III and Richard II, Henry VII and his queen by Torrigiani and Elizabeth I by Colt.

256 Banqueting House, Whitehall Superb example of Palladian architecture, built by Jones, 1622. Ceiling paintings by Rubens.

257 British Museum Departments: Coins and Medals (including Greek and Roman); Egyptian Antiquities (Rosetta Stone, sculpture, Coptic antiquities, etc); Western Asiatic Antiquities (Sumerian, Babylonian, Assyrian, Hittite, etc, human-headed winged bulls from Khorsabad; sculptures from Nimrud, Nineveh and Persepolis etc); Greek and Roman antiquities (Elgin marbles, Portland Vase, etc); British and Medieval Antiquities (Mildenhall Treasure, Lycurgus Cup, Battersea Shield, Sutton Hoo ship burial etc); Oriental Antiquities (including ceramics); Ethnography (rock crystal Aztec skull, Benin bronzes, etc). Also Ilbert collection of clocks and watches. Library contains over 6,000,000 printed books (first folio of Shakespeare), its other departments being Manuscripts (Codex Sinaiticus, Lindisfarne Gospels, Magna Carta, the Anglo-Saxon Chronicle, illuminated MSS etc) and Oriental Printed Books and Manuscripts (Diamond Sutra, etc). Department of Prints and Drawings; major collections of woodcuts, engravings and etchings and drawings.

258 Buckingham Palace Built 1703. Sumptuously decorated apartments; a large collection of paintings of which a selection can be seen in the Queen's Gallery.

259 Chiswick House Palladian villa designed by Lord Burlington with the assistance of Kent 1725–29, closely modelled on Palladio's Villa Rotonda at Vicenza.

260 Courtauld Institute Galleries Works by Bellini, Botticelli, Veronese, Rubens, Van Dyck, Goya and Gainsborough; the Gambier-Parry collection of early Italian paintings and sculpture, maiolica, Venetian glass, medieval ivories and Limoges enamels; Samuel Courtauld collection of Impressionist and Post-Impressionist paintings (Cézanne, Manet, Renoir, Gauguin, etc); the Roger Fry collection of paintings (Seurat, Sickert, Fry, etc); Witt collection of old master drawings.

261 Dulwich College Picture Gallery Building by Soane. Paintings of the Italian, Flemish, Dutch, French, Spanish, German and English schools. Notable works by Rembrandt, Claude, Poussin, Watteau and Gainsborough.

262 Greenwich Hospital King Charles block, designed by Webb, finished 1669. Naval Hospital established by Queen Mary end of 17th C, designed by Wren.

263 Goldsmith's Hall Built 1829–35. Magnificent collection of antique plate dating from the 15th C onwards, also foremost collection of modern silver and jewellery in the country.

264 Guildhall Museum Finds from the City of London from Roman times onwards; objects from city churches and guilds, antique clocks and watches.

265 Ham House 17th C brick mansion containing the most sumptous decoration of the Restoration period in existence. Portraits and late 17th C Dutch paintings.

266 Hampton Court Begun by Cardinal Wolsey 1514. Henry VIII added Great Hall 1531–36 (hammer-beam roof) and decorated chapel with fine wooden fan-vaulting. In 1689 William III commissioned Wren to enlarge palace (Fountain Court, Cartoon Gallery built to house Raphael Tapestry cartoons). Orangery houses Mantegna cartoons *Triumphs of Caesar*.

267 Horniman Museum Ethnographical collections from all parts of the world from the prehistoric period onwards.

268 Houses of Parliament Designed by Charles Barrie in late Gothic style, built 1837–60.

269 Swakeleys Brick and stucco house in the Transitional style built by Sir Edmund Wright, in 1638.

270 Imperial War Museum The art gallery houses works by Orpen, Sargent, Nash, Knight, Spencer, Bone, Ardizzone and Epstein.

271 Kensington Palace Fine rooms by Wren, carvings by Gibbons, portraits by Kneller, etc. Contains **London Museum** Stone Age, Bronze Age, Roman, Viking, Medieval and Tudor finds; exhibits from the Stuart period. Armour, paintings, prints, Chelsea and Bow porcelain, Battersea enamels, watches and jewellery, etc.

272 Kenwood 18th C mansion, with some 17th C remains. Adam portico and S front. Adam interiors, notably the library, with wall and ceiling-paintings by Zucchi. 18th C furniture; Iveagh Bequest of paintings of the English, Dutch and other schools.

273 Lambeth Palace London residence for 7 centuries of archbishops of Canterbury, begun 1207. Great Hall rebuilt at Restoration, Guard Chamber contains 5 series of portraits of archbishops by Holbein, Van Dyck, Hogarth, Reynolds, Romney, Lawrence, etc.

274 National Gallery Paintings of the Italian, Flemish, Dutch, German, French, Spanish and British Schools of the 13th to the 19th C. Among the masterpieces exhibited are Duccio *Virgin and Child*, the anonymous *Wilton Diptych*, Uccello *Rout of San Romano*, della Francesca *Baptism* and *Nativity*, Bellini *Doge Leonardo Loredano*, Leonardo *Virgin of the Rocks*, Michelangelo *Entombment*, Titian *Bacchus and Ariadne*, Van Eyck *Marriage of Arnolfini*, Holbein *The Ambassadors*, Rembrandt *Margaretha Trip*, Rubens *Chapeau de Paille*, Van Dyck *Charles I on Horseback*, Velazquez *Rokeby Venus*, Hogarth *Marriage à la Mode*, Constable *Haywain*, Van Gogh *Sunflowers*, and Cézanne *Grandes Baigneuses*.

275 National Maritime Museum Excellent collection of portraits and seascapes.

276 National Portrait Gallery Contemporary portraits of British sovereigns and personalities from 796 to the present in various media.

277 Osterley Park House Palatial mansion built 1577, remodelled by Adam 1761–80. Adam interiors of 1766–77.

278 Percival David Foundation of Chinese Art (University of London) Chinese ceramics of 10th–18th C.

279 Queen's House, Greenwich Commissioned from Jones 1616, completed for Henrietta Maria 1635. Palladian style, brick with Portland stone dressings, colonnades added later.

280 Soane Museum Home of the architect Soane, built to his own designs 1812–14. Egyptian, Roman and medieval sculpture and architectural fragments, etc. Paintings include Hogarth *Rake's Progress* and *Election* series and works by Watteau, Canaletto and Turner. Over 20,000 architectural drawings.

281 Somerset House Palladian building by Chambers 1776–86. E wing added by Smirke 1829–34, W wing by Pennethorne 1852–56.

282 Strawberry Hill Converted by Hugh Walpole in the 18th C from a cottage into a 'Gothic castle'.

283 Syon House Great quadrangular mansion begun 1547 and altered at various periods, notably by Adam from 1762. Magnificent Adam interiors; furniture and Percy portraits.

284 Tate Gallery The national collections of British painting, modern foreign painting, and modern sculpture. The paintings of the British school cover the period from the 16th C to the present and include works by Hogarth, Lely, Reynolds, Gainsborough, Ward, Wilson, Constable, Watts, Whistler, Sickert, Steer, John, Spencer, Pasmore and Bacon, with special collections of the work of Blake, Turner, the Pre-Raphaelites, Stevens and Sargent. The paintings of the foreign schools range from the French Impressionists and Post-Impressionists to contemporary American art with works by Van Gogh, Gauguin, Picasso, Rouault, Braque, Matisse, Chagall, Kandinsky, Ernst, Miró, Mondrian and Pollock. The sculpture collection includes works by Rodin, Epstein, Giacometti, Gabo, Hepworth.

285 Tower of London Fortress, royal residence and state prison. Consists of White Tower (begun c.1078 for William the Conqueror by Gundulf, architect of Rochester Cathedral) and outer fortifications dating from 13th C. Exterior of White Tower restored by Wren, but interior largely unchanged since Norman times. St John's Chapel is oldest church in London and splendid example of pure Norman architecture. Collections of arms and armour; crown jewels.

286 Victoria and Albert Museum Museum of fine and applied art (both European and Eastern) with major collections of furniture, sculpture, ceramics, ivories, bronzes, gold and silverwork, enamels, clocks and watches, textiles, costume, musical instruments, architectural details, arms and armour, etc. Oil paintings by British artists mainly of the 19th C; the Constable gift of paintings, sketches and drawings; 18th C French paintings etc; national collections of British watercolours and miniatures; extensive print collection.

287 Wallace Collection Outstanding collections of paintings (French, Spanish, Italian, Flemish, Dutch and British Schools), French furniture, Sèvres porcelain, arms and armour, sculpture, miniatures, ivories, enamels, snuffboxes, jewellery and maiolica etc. Among the artists represented are Boucher, Watteau, Fragonard, Velazquez, Titian, Hals, Rubens, Reynolds, Gainsborough; busts by Coysevox and Houdon.

288 Wellington Museum Fine paintings from the duke's collection including his great equestrian portrait by Goya; Velazquez *Bearded Man* and *Water-Seller of Seville*, Correggio *Agony in the Garden*, Rubens *Infanta Margarita of the Descalzas Reales*, Canova statue of Napoleon.

289 Westminster Hall Originally built 1097; present form, including hammer-beam roof, dates from 1399.

290 William Morris Gallery Collections of textiles, wallpapers and designs etc by Morris, the Pre-Raphaelites and their contemporaries; also the Frank Brangwyn collection of paintings and sculptures by 19th c and other artists.

LONGLEAT HOUSE, Wiltshire

291 Renaissance mansion built by Sir John Thynne. Great Hall with hammer-beam roof, original chimney-piece, hunting scenes by Wooton. The rest of the interior was almost entirely redecorated by Wyatville (1801-11) and Crace (1870s). Paintings, furniture, tapestries, porcelain and silver.

LONG MELFORD, Suffolk

292 **Holy Trinity** Magnificent Perpendicular church (c.1460 to c.1496) with fine windows, late 15th c stained glass.

LULLINGSTONE, Kent

293 **Castle** Gateway remains from time of Henry VII, castle was largely rebuilt in the 18th c.

294 **Roman Villa** Fine mosaic floors and the earliest known Christian chapel in England (4th c).

LUTON HOO, Bedfordshire

295 Mansion designed by Adam in 1767, enlarged and redecorated in the 18th c French style after 1903. Contains important pictures ranging from the primitive to the Dutch and English schools, tapestries and furniture, English porcelain, medieval ivories, Renaissance bronzes, silver, jewellery.

LYDIARD TREGOZE, Wiltshire

296 **St Mary** Mainly Perpendicular, altered c.1633. Monuments of the 16th to the 18th c.

LYME PARK, Cheshire

297 Present house mainly by the Italian architect Leoni who altered the building in the Palladian style in 1720.

MAES HOWE, Orkney

298 Huge chambered cairn, probably 1500 BC.

MAIDEN CASTLE, Dorset

299 Finest prehistoric hill fort in England. Begun c.2000 BC, given its present size and elaborate defences chiefly between the 1st c BC and AD 43.

MAIDENHEAD, Berkshire

300 **Henry Reitlinger Bequest** Chinese, Persian, Peruvian and European ceramics; European and African paintings, drawings, sculpture and glass.

MALMESBURY, Wiltshire

301 **Abbey** The Norman nave and aisles of c.1160-70 (with an early 14th c lierne vault over the nave) are almost all that remain of the great abbey church. Outstanding s porch.

MANCHESTER, Lancashire

302 **Cathedral** Built in the 15th and 16th c in a conventional Perpendicular style.

303 **City Art Gallery** Paintings mainly representative of development of British school from 16th c to the present. Foreign schools represented include the Italian, Flemish, French, and Dutch. Sculpture by Epstein and Dobson etc, miniatures, fine collection of pottery and porcelain, English glass and silver.

304 **Fletcher Moss Museum** (Didsbury) English watercolours and drawings, 19th c porcelain and furniture.

305 **John Rylands Library** Collection of over 700,000 books and 12,000 MSS including the earliest-known New Testament text of c.100-150 and the earliest-dated piece of European printing in existence-the 'St Christopher' block-print of 1423.

306 **Whitworth Art Gallery** English water-colours of the 18th c to the present; fine old master, Post-Impressionist and 20th c continental drawings; paintings by Gainsborough, Turner, the Pre-Raphaelites, old masters; contemporary paintings and sculpture; textiles etc.

MEREWORTH CASTLE, Kent

307 Palladian villa, built in 1720 by C Campbell, replica of Villa Rotonda, Vicenza. Interior decorated in Palladian manner with stucco-work and ceiling-paintings.

MONASTERBOICE, Louth, Ireland

308 Ruins of 2 churches, a round tower and 3 crosses, the relics of a community founded by St Builthe.

MONKWEARMOUTH, County Durham

309 Church with notable nave, w wall and porch, 9th or 10th c tower, 14th c chancel. Remains of a 7th c standing figure above porch.

MONTACUTE HOUSE, Somerset

310 Elizabethan Mansion built c.1590-c.1600. 3 storeys, surmounted by curved gables and a balustrade, fine oriel windows.

MUCH WENLOCK, Shropshire

311 **Wenlock Priory** Interesting remains of the church (probably c.1200-40), cloisters (possibly c.1150-80), chapter house (Norman), Prior's Lodge (c.1500).

NEW BARNET, Hertfordshire

312 **Abbey Art Centre and Museum** Primitive art from Africa, America and South Seas.

NEWBY HALL, Yorkshire

313 Red-brick house with stone dressings built c.1705, altered by Adam 1767-76. Notable Adam rooms, paintings, tapestries and classical sculpture.

NEWCASTLE UPON TYNE, Northumb.

314 **Central Library** Drawings, blocks and prints by Thomas Bewick.

315 **Greek Museum** (University) Greek and Etruscan art.

316 **Hatton Gallery** (University) Paintings, mainly Italian.

317 **Laing Art Gallery and Museum** British paintings and watercolours of the 17th c onwards, modern and Japanese prints, Egyptian and Greek antiquities, pottery and porcelain, glass, ironwork, costume, textiles.

318 **Museum of Antiquities** (University) Prehistoric, Roman, Anglo-Saxon objects.

NEW GRANGE TUMULUS, County Meath, Ireland

319 Dates from c.2000 BC. Huge cairn of loose stones, unsurpassed among European passage-graves.

NEWPORT, Monmouthshire

320 **Museum and Art Gallery** Archaeological remains from Romano-British town of Caerwent, japan ware, British 20th c paintings.

NEWSTEAD ABBEY, Nottinghamshire

321 13th c Augustinian priory converted into a residence by Sir John Byron 1540. Byron portraits, relics and MSS; Tudor and Stuart furniture.

NORTHAMPTON, Northamptonshire

322 **Central Museum and Art Gallery** Fine archaeological collection (Iron Age antiquities), medieval pottery, English china, old master and modern oil and watercolour paintings, furniture.

NORWICH, Norfolk

323 **Cathedral** Founded 1094. Choir, transepts and nave basically Romanesque, with vaulting of the 14th and 15th c. Tall wooden spire added in the mid 15th c. Contains a medieval retable.

324 **St Peter Hungate Church and Museum** 15th c Parish church, with stained glass windows and fine collection of ecclesiastical art.

325 **Castle Museum** Large collection of art, notably of the Norwich School (Crome, Cotman etc); local antiquities (Snettisham coin hoard) etc, in a massive Norman keep of c.1130.

NOSTELL PRIORY, Yorkshire

326 Palladian mansion designed by J Paine, begun 1733, continued by Adam, 1767-85. Paintings (including Holbein, *Sir Thomas More and his Family*); Chippendale furniture.

NOTTINGHAM, Nottinghamshire

327 **City Museum and Art Gallery** In 17th c castle. Ceramics, glass, medieval alabaster carvings, works of Thomas and Paul Sandby and Bonington.

OLDHAM, Lancashire

328 **Municipal Art Gallery and Museum** Early English watercolours, British paintings of 19th c and 20th c, contemporary sculpture, British glass, oriental objets d'art.

OSBORNE HOUSE, Isle of Wight

329 Built in the Italian style to the designs of Prince Albert (with the assistance of T Cubitt) from 1847. State apartments retain their original decoration, furniture and paintings.

OXBURGH HALL, Norfolk

330 Present house began 1482. Enormous 15th c gatehouse, small chapel built by Pugin, 1835.

OXFORD, Oxfordshire

331 **Cathedral** (See also Christ Church). Basically late 12th c with a late Perpendicular pendant vault. Glass by Morris and Co.

332 **All Souls College** First quad and chapel basically 15th c. A larger quad containing a new hall was added in the 18th c. Gates on Catte St designed by Hawksmoor, 1734.

333 **The Ashmolean Museum of Art and Archaeology** Oldest public museum in Britain with outstanding collections of fine and applied art and antiquities. Paintings of the Italian, Flemish, Dutch, French, German, Spanish and British schools. Fine drawings, watercolours and prints; Renaissance bronzes, busts by Pearce and Rysbrack, applied arts, coins, Egyptian, Cretan, Greek, Hellenistic, Roman, Etruscan and Near Eastern antiquities; European prehistoric, Bronze Age, Iron Age and medieval antiquities; Eastern paintings, pottery, bronzes, sculpture and lacquerwork.

334 **Balliol College** 15th c front quad and library, Victorian chapel with good 17th c glass.

335 **Bodleian Library** Duke Humphrey's Library, 16th c. Contains ancient desks, chained books, valuable MSS and early editions.

336 **Brasenose College** Hall, library and chapel good examples of 17th c architecture. Small modern block by Powell and Moya has been fitted with great ingenuity into older buildings.

337 **Christ Church** Oldest part is the cathedral. Hall and staircase are fine example of 16th c building. Upper part of the entrance tower, 'Tom Tower', is by Wren. Peckwater Quad by Aldrich added in 1705. Fine library, 1772.

338 **Christ Church Art Gallery** Old master paintings and drawings.

339 **Clarenden building** By Hawksmoor. Contains university administration. Wrought-iron gates by Tijou, c.1710.

340 **Divinity School** One of the finest secular Gothic rooms in Europe. Magnificent 15th c fan-vaulting.

341 **Exeter College** One range dates from 15th c, hall from 17th c. Grandiose chapel by George G Scott with a tapestry by Burne-Jones and Morris.

342 **Keble College** Founded 1868, entire college designed by W Butterfield in polychrome brick. The chapel, one of the richest Victorian monuments in Oxford, contains Holman Hunt *Light of the World*.

343 **Law Library** Built in the 1960s by L Martin and St John Wilson; an impressive building low in proportion.

344 **Magdalen College** Chapel completed in 1480; hall and many of the college buildings date from the 16th c. Cloisters and bell tower (1492-1509) form a picturesque group by the river.

345 **Merton College** Chapel was formerly a parish church and contains notable work of the Early English (choir) and Perpendicular periods (tower). Hall and library are also basically medieval, though restored.

346 **Museum of History of Science** Oldest museum in Great Britain, building begun 1679, probably by Thomas Wood.

347 **New College** 14th c chapel, cloister and hall. Chapel has interesting stalls with misericords, stained glass and Epstein *Lazarus*. College owns a number of artistic treasures.

348 **Oriel College** Completely rebuilt 17th c, hall and chapel are interesting.

349 **Pembroke College** Buildings incorporate a range of Tudor almshouses and an 18th c chapel Victorianised in 1885.

350 **The Queen's College** Entirely rebuilt 18th c to designs of Hawksmoor. Fine library.

351 **Radcliffe Camera** Large domed reading-room, designed by Gibbs, 1737. Good example of English Baroque.

352 **Sheldonian Theatre** Built by Wren, 1664-69, for university ceremonies; semicircular plan, with flat pointed ceiling.

353 **St Catherine's College** Built from 1964 onwards by Danish architect Arne Jacobsen who designed exterior, interior and furnishings in an unobtrusive, functional style.

354 St Anne's College New buildings by Howell, Killick, Partridge and Amis.

355 St Edmund's Hall Now includes 12th C church of St Peter's in the East.

356 St John's College Some parts medieval; extensively altered and added to in the 17th C (Canterbury Quad) and later.

357 Somerville College The new wing built in the 1960s by Philip Dawson.

358 Trinity College Founded 1554. Chapel, hall and Garden Quad date from the 16th C. Reredos in chapel by Gibbons.

359 University College Built 1635. Chapel contains fine display of Van Linge glass.

360 University Museum Opened 1860, exterior designed by Deane and Woodward in a Venetian Gothic style owing something to Ruskin. Interior, combination cast-iron and glass. Natural science collection.

361 Wadham College 17th C; particularly fine hall, 1613.

362 Worcester College Includes the oldest university buildings in Oxford, a row of 15th C houses. Provost's lodgings 1770s.

PARHAM, Sussex
363 Elizabethan house begun 1577 with some later alterations of 1710 and 1790. 16th C Great Hall, with original screen; panelled Long Gallery; also rooms of Adam period–all with contemporary furniture.

PEMBROKE, Pembrokeshire
364 Castle Oldest existing part is keep, c.1204. The whole probably completed by late 13th C.

PENRHYN CASTLE, Caern
365 Built in the Norman style in 1827–40 to designs of T Hopper.

PETERBOROUGH, Huntingdonshire
366 Cathedral Present building begun 1117 and finished about 1230. It is almost wholly Norman, with unusual Early English w front of 3 deep porches. New ambulatory to the choir with fan-vaulting was added about 1500.

367 Museum and Maxwell Art Gallery Important Romano-British and Anglo-Saxon finds.

PETWORTH HOUSE, Sussex
368 Built 1688–96, with some later alterations (1869–72). Grinling Gibbons Room, Turner Room, 18th C sculpture gallery. Collections of painting and sculpture.

PLUSCARDEN ABBEY, Morayshire
369 Founded 1230. Church transitional, between Romanesque and Early English.

PLYMOUTH, Devonshire
370 City Museum and Art Gallery Paintings, books, Plymouth and Bristol porcelain, silver, archaeology.

POLESDEN LACEY, Surrey
371 Classical villa built 1824 by Cubitt and remodelled 1906. Paintings of early Flemish and 18th C English schools, portraits by Raeburn, Wren panelling, French marquetry furniture, tapestries, Chinese porcelain, jade and bronzes.

PORCHESTER, Hampshire
372 Castle The great defensive walls still survive from the square fort built by the Romans at the end of the 3rd C. A fine Norman keep was built in N-W corner of enclosure in the 12th C, remains of palace built by Richard II in the 14th C.

PORT SUNLIGHT, Cheshire
373 The Lady Lever Art Gallery Paintings, chiefly British School; English furniture, mainly 18th C; watercolours, engravings and miniatures; antique, Renaissance and British sculpture; Chinese ceramics and Wedgwood vases.

POWDERHAM CASTLE, Devonshire
374 Medieval castle built c.1390 but largely rebuilt and altered 18th and 19th C. Music room by Wyatt, furniture, family portraits.

POWIS CASTLE, Montgomeryshire
375 Imposing medieval castle of red limestone altered and adapted by successive owners. Long Gallery with plasterwork and panelling, Caroline staircase of c.1670 with wall and ceiling-paintings by Lanscroon (1705).

PRESTON, Lancashire
376 Harris Museum and Art Gallery Paintings, drawings and relics of the Devis

family of painters; paintings, drawings and bronzes by 19th and 20th C British artists; prints, pottery and porcelain, glass, archaeology.

RAGLAN CASTLE, Monmouthshire
377 Begun before 1469. Mostly domestic, but has keep, moat, gateway towers and double portcullis grooves. Tudor Great Hall with long windows, grand staircase to state apartments.

READING, Berkshire
378 Museum and Art Gallery Roman antiquities from Silchester and finds of all periods from the Thames; Delftware.

RIEVAULX ABBEY, Yorkshire
379 Founded 1132, the earliest Cistercian house in England. The extensive, mainly Early English ruins include the great 12th C abbey church with choir of 1225–30; unusual apsed chapter house, part of the first abbot's shrine of 1148, and the 13th C refectory.

RIPON, Yorkshire
380 Cathedral Transepts and w front remain from the 13th C. The rest of the church rebuilt between 1480 and 1520.

ROCHESTER, Kent
381 St Andrew's Cathedral Norman detached tower; nave early 12th C, with remains of sculpture on the w front; e end Early English. Restored in the 19th C.
382 Castle Keep and curtain walls remain.

ROTHERHAM, Yorkshire
383 Museum and Art Gallery Roman antiquities; Rockingham porcelain and south Yorkshire pottery, gem-stones, jewellery.

ROUSHAM HOUSE, Oxfordshire
384 Built 1635, transformed by Kent 1738–40. Portraits, paintings, miniatures.

RUFFORD OLD HALL, Lancashire
385 Early Tudor half-timbered house with plaster panels. Great Hall with hammer-beam roof and massive movable screen.

RUTHWELL, Dumfriesshire
386 Cross Carved cross, probably early 8th C. Preserved since 1887 in the church at Ruthwell.

SALFORD, Lancashire
387 Museum and Art Gallery Paintings and drawings by L S Lowry.

SALISBURY, Wiltshire
388 Cathedral Whole building consistently Early English in style and was finished by 1260. Tower and spire by Richard Farleigh added in the mid-14th C. Cloister and Chapter House also 13th C. Drastic alterations were made to the interior but it still contains fine medieval tombs.

SALTRAM HOUSE, Devonshire
389 George II house, with some late Tudor remains, containing fine 18th C decoration and 2 rooms by Adam with their original fittings.

SCARBOROUGH, Yorkshire
390 St Martin 19th C Neo-Gothic style by G F Bodley. Decoration by Bodley and Pre-Raphaelites including glass and murals by Burne-Jones; roof by Webb and Morris.

SELBY, Yorkshire
391 Abbey Begun c.1097 and contains work of the late Norman to Perpendicular period.

SHEFFIELD, Yorkshire
392 City Museum English and foreign cutlery with many rare English and continental pieces (1600–1800); old Sheffield plate; porcelain; silver.
393 Graves Art Gallery Paintings by Verrocchio, Clouet, Rubens, Murillo, Constable, Turner, Cézanne, Corot, Whistler and Nash; sculpture by Epstein, Chinese ivories.

SHERBORNE, Dorsetshire
394 Abbey Abbey church of St Mary with its superb fan-vaulting is an outstanding example of the Perpendicular style.

SHIPLEY, Sussex
395 St Mary Contains much fine Norman carving; the famous Limoges enamel Shipley Reliquary, the Caryll monument.

SHOREHAM-BY-SEA, Sussex
396 St Mary de Haura Mainly Norman parish church with remarkable Early English choir.
397 St Nicholas Norman church with some Saxon remains of c.900 and a few 14th C additions. Heavily restored 1839–40.

SHREWSBURY, Shropshire
398 Abbey Church Founded in 1083 by Roger de Montgomery. Imposing w tower c.1350.

SOMPTING, Sussex
399 St Mary Highly unusual Norman church of c.1180–90 with a remarkable Saxon tower of c.1000 surmounted by unique 'Rhenish helm' or gabled pyramidal cup.

SOUTHAMPTON, Hampshire
400 Art Gallery British paintings; notable collection of works by 20th C artists; continental paintings of the 14th C onwards.

SOUTHWELL, Nottinghamshire
401 Minster Towers, transepts and nave are Norman; e end Early English. Chapter house and vestibule of c;1306 contain fine foliage carving known as the 'Leaves of Southwell'.

ST ALBAN'S, Hertfordshire
402 Cathedral The crossing tower (of Roman bricks) and most of the nave are very plain early Norman; e end was extended in the 13th C and the nave in the 14th; w front and s transept rebuilt disastrously by Lord Grimthorpe 1879–85. The nave retains medieval wallpaintings.
403 Roman Remains Former great Roman city of Verulamium. Most notable remains are the hypocaust (see museum), the surviving sections of the city walls (built 125–50) and the theatre (built 140–206).
404 The Verulamium Museum Important collection of finds from the British (Belgic) and Roman towns including several fine mosaic floors. One of these (AD 150 and 300) is preserved in situ in the Hypocaust Annexe.

ST DAVID'S, Pembrokeshire
405 Cathedral The nave dates from the late Norman period (1180–98) with 16th C coffered wooden roof. Beside the church stands the ruined palace, basically that of Bishop Gower (1328–47) with two large halls.

ST HELEN'S, Lancashire
406 Pilkington Glass Museum Collection illustrating the history of glass.

STALYBRIDGE, Cheshire
407 Astley Cheetham Art Gallery Egyptian, Greek and Roman antiquities; Italian, German, Flemish, and Spanish paintings.

STIRLING CASTLE, Stirling
408 Important castle by 12th C; gatehouse drum-towers 1460–88. James III rebuilt castle, adding the Parliament Hall; James V built a carved palace within outer court c.1540; James VI later rebuilt royal chapel.

STOKE D'ABERNON, Surrey
409 St Mary Dates in part from the Saxon period. Contains the earliest brass in England, that of Sir John d'Abernon (d.1277); there are also monuments, smaller brasses and stained glass.

STOKE-ON-TRENT, Staffordshire
410 City Museum and Art Gallery Staffordshire pottery and porcelain, foreign ceramics, 18th C English watercolours and 20th C paintings, sculpture, textiles, archaeology.
411 Spode-Copeland Museum and Art Gallery Early Spode blue-printed ware, bone china and stone china together with Copeland and Garrett and Copeland wares.
412 Wedgwood Museum Wedgwood vases of the 18th–20th C and experimental pieces by Josiah Wedgwood.

STOKESAY CASTLE, Shropshire
413 Oldest and finest fortified manor-house in England, dates almost entirely from 13th C.

STONEHENGE, Wiltshire
414 Finest Bronze Age sanctuary in Europe. Begun c.1800 BC.

STOURHEAD, Wiltshire
415 Palladian mansion built 1721–24 to designs of C Campbell. Centre gutted by fire in 1902 but carefully restored from photographs. Fine interiors, paintings and furniture (Chippendale the Younger etc). Magnificent garden.

STRATFORD-UPON-AVON, Warks.
416 The Royal Shakespeare Picture Gallery Shakespeare portraits and relics etc.

SUDBURY, Suffolk
417 Gainsborough's House Birthplace of the artist with portraits, landscapes and drawings.

SUDELEY CASTLE, Gloucestershire

418 15th and 16th c castle of Cotswold stone. Chapel (built c.1450), ruins of magnificent Banqueting Hall built by Richard III (15th c). Pictures, furniture, tapestries, stained glass.

SWANSEA, Glamorganshire
419 **Glynn Vivian Art Gallery** Swansea porcelain and pottery, prints and drawings, glass, contemporary art.

SWEETHEART ABBEY, Kirkudbright
420 Early English with decorated alterations. Tracery of main e window fairly intact. Great w window, with some 14th c masonry.

TATTERSHALL CASTLE, Lincolnshire
421 One of the best examples of medieval brick building in Britain. Originally 13th c, greatly enlarged in 15th c. Fine 15th c fireplaces.

TEMPLE NEWSAM HOUSE, Yorkshire
422 Jacobean mansion built 1622, with remains of an earlier Tudor house. Interior partly redecorated in 18th c. Great Hall with 16th and 17th c furniture; series of mid-Georgian rooms. English furniture and silver, Chinese ceramics, paintings.

TEWKESBURY, Gloucestershire
423 **Abbey Church** Begun 1092, choir was completed in 1123, nave and central tower c.1160 Further alterations and additions were made c.1330–50. Church contains a number of exquisite chantries and chapels (Beauchamp Chantry, Founder's Chantry etc), important tombs and monuments, fine vaulting and 14th c stained glass. In the lady chapel is Raphael's *Madonna del Passeggio*.

THORNTON ABBEY, Lincolnshire
424 Founded 1139, only parts of chapter house and fine gatehouse remain.

TINTERN ABBEY, Monmouthshire
425 Cistercian order, founded 1131. Roofless church in transition style from Early English to Decorated. Domestic buildings date from 13th c.

TRUNCH, Norfolk
426 **St Botolph** Perpendicular, with hammer-beam roof decorated with angels. Superb font-canopy; screen with painted saints (1502).

TRURO, Cornwall
427 **County Museum and Art Gallery** Paintings by Rubens, Lely, Kneller, Hogarth, Gainsborough, Romney, Constable, Millais and Opie; Bronze Age objects; English pottery and porcelain; Japanese ivories and lacquer.

TUDELEY, Kent
428 **All Saints** Small brick and stone church containing stained-glass window by Chagall showing Crucifixion etc.

UPPARK, Sussex
429 Red-brick house built c.1690 to designs of W Talman; altered c.1750 and c.1770. Remarkable for the extraordinary survival of its 18th c decoration and furnishings.

UPTON HOUSE, Warwickshire
430 Late 17th c house preserving original main n and s fronts of 1695, but with interior dating almost entirely, apart from staircase, from 20th c. Paintings of Dutch (Bosch *Adoration of the Magi*), English, Flemish, French, German, Italian and Spanish schools; furniture, tapestries, porcelain.

VYNE (THE), Hampshire
431 Diapered red-brick Tudor mansion built by W Sandys, 1500–20. Great classical portico added to the n front in 1654 (architect probably J Webb). Original early Renaissance chapel, with outstanding early 16th c Flemish stained glass; oak Long Gallery, with decorated linen-fold panelling. Palladian staircase and hall built by John Chute c.1765. Other rooms with Rococo and Neo-Gothic features. Furniture, paintings, chimneypieces and Soho tapestries.

WADDESDON MANOR, Bucks.
432 Built 1880–89 in the French château style by Destailleur for Baron Ferdinand de Rothschild. Outstanding collection of French decorative arts of the 17th and 18th c: furniture, Savonnerie carpets, Sèvres porcelain, busts, panelling etc. Paintings of the English, Flemish, French, Dutch and Italian schools.

WAKEFIELD, Yorkshire
433 **City Art Gallery** 20th c paintings and sculpture (works by Sickert, Sutherland, Piper, Hitchens, Hepworth, Butler and Moore), old

masters, 18th c English watercolours and drawings, lithographs.

WALTHAM ABBEY, Essex
434 **Abbey Church of the Holy Cross and St Lawrence** Begun before the conquest, earliest Norman work (nave etc) in the country. Reredos and pulpit of 1876 by Burges, stained glass of 1861 by Burne-Jones; painting of the nave ceiling by E J Poynter.

WARDOUR CASTLE, Wiltshire
435 Palladian mansion built by Paine 1769–76.

WARWICK, Warwickshire
436 **St Mary** Originally Norman (crypt) church largely destroyed by fire in 1694 and rebuilt in the Gothic and Renaissance styles, 1698–1704. Of the earlier church the chancel (1394) and splendid Beauchamp Chapel (1443–64) survive. Fine tombs, notable 15th c English stained glass.

437 **Castle** Built mainly by the Beauchamp Earls of Warwick in the 14th c. 17th and 18th c state rooms with paintings by Van Dyck, Velasquez, Rubens; furniture, tapestries, sculpture, china and armour. In conservatory is the great marble Warwick Vase (4th c).

WELLS, Somerset
438 **Cathedral** Present building begun about 1175 and finished by 1260. First example of Early English uninfluenced by France. Has more 13th c sculpture both inside and out than any other English Cathedral. Strainer-arches were inserted in the crossing when the tower was heightened in the 14th c. Lady chapel and chapter house added c.1290–1320, 2 w towers, one by William Wynford, late 14th and early 15th c.

439 **Archbishop's Palace** Central range basically 13th c, but largely rebuilt mid 19th. Chapel of c. 1290 remains intact.

WEST WYCOMBE PARK, Bucks.
440 Mansion in Palladian style originally built in 1707, but given its present, highly unusual form 1735–65. Interior contains ceiling-paintings by the Italian Borgnis, Brussels tapestries and contemporary pictures and furniture.

WHITBY, Yorkshire
441 **Art Gallery** Early English watercolours and works by Turner, Cox, de Wint etc.

WINDSOR CASTLE, Berkshire
442 Established by William the Conqueror, stone fortifications built 12th and 13th c. Edward III enlarged royal apartments and established Chapel of the Order of the Garter. Further additions made by Charles II, much restoration and embellishment from 17th to 19th c, including that by Wyatville (19th c). Superb state apartments with carvings by Gibbons, ceilings painted by Verrio. Fine collection of paintings, drawings, tapestries and china.

443 **St George's Chapel** Chapel of the Order of the Garter. Begun 1475, rebuilt on grand scale by Edward IV, continued by Henry VII and Henry VIII. The superb fan-vaulting was completed 1528; carving of choir stalls dates from 1480. Much 16th c sculpture; memorial to the Duke of Clarence by Gilbert (completed 1926).

WITHYHAM, Sussex
444 **St Michael and All Angels** Interesting church built 1663–72 (some 14th c remains) containing monuments to the Sackville family in their chapel completed in 1680.

WILTON HOUSE, Wiltshire
445 Present building begun in the Italian style, c. 1630, rebuilt by Inigo Jones and John Webb, and altered by Wyatt in the 19th c. Interior: Jone's famous Single and Double Cube Rooms (outstanding Van Dycks). Other rooms in the Gothic style by Wyatt. Paintings, Kent and Chippendale furniture.

WINCHESTER, Hampshire
446 **Cathedral** Transepts among the earliest Norman work in England (c.1080), crossing tower later, retrochoir and lady chapel added 13th c. From about 1394–1450 the nave was remodelled in Perpendicular style by William Wynford. The choir contains the statue of Ecclesia, one of the masterpieces of 13th c sculpture. In the nave is the best of the 12th c

Tournai fonts.

447 **Castle Hall** Built 1222–36 by Henry III. Hall is aisled, with fine Purbeck marble columns, beautiful 2-light windows and a notable w doorway. Contains the famous 'King Arthur's Round Table', believed to date from the 13th c.

448 **Pilgrim's Hall** Mid-14th c hall, with a roof incorporating the earliest hammer-beams in England.

449 **Winchester College** Public school founded by William of Wykeham in 1382, with many of the original late 14th c buildings still surviving.

WOLLATON HALL, Nottinghamshire
450 Elizabethan Renaissance mansion built by R Smythson, 1580–88. Quadrangular building with huge windows and 4 tall corner towers, lavishly decorated in the Classical and Flemish styles. Outstanding feature is the pseudo-medieval keep which houses the Great Hall surmounted by a Great Chamber with 'Gothic' windows.

WORCESTER, Worcestershire
451 **Cathedral** Norman chapter house (round) and two bays of the nave. The rest rebuilt in 13th c (choir) and 14th c (nave). Tomb of King John (early 13th c).

WORKSOP, Nottinghamshire
452 **St Cuthbert and St Mary** Priory church begun 1103 with a Norman nave of c.1150–60 and an imposing Norman w front with towers. Lady chapel dates from mid-13th c.

WORTH, Sussex
453 **St Nicholas** Anglo-Saxon (probably 11th c), with an apsed chancel and mighty chancel arch.

WREXHAM, Denbighshire
454 **St Giles** 14th c with 15th and 16th c additions, Decorated interior. Magnificent tower (begun 1506). Many 18th c monuments.

YORK, Yorkshire
455 **Minster** The oldest part of the present building is the transept (with 'Five Sisters' window) of 1225–60. The choir and nave were rebuilt on a very large scale during the 14th c and vaulted in wood. w front has 2 towers. The cathedral is very rich in 14th c stained glass.

456 **Castle Museum** Reconstructed streets and period rooms illustrating social life from Tudor to Victorian times.

457 **City of York Art Gallery** Old master and foreign paintings, British paintings of the early 16th–17th c, special collection of works by Etty. Sculpture, ceramics, prints and watercolours.

458 **Mansion House** Built 1725–26. Superb collection of silver.

459 **Yorkshire Museum** Viking, medieval and other antiquities.

Index

The numbers in Roman type refer to text and captions, the heavy type to illustrations, the italics to the Museums and Monuments index.

Acknowledgements

The publishers gratefully acknowledge the following for permission to reproduce the illustrations indicated: The Board of Trinity College, Dublin 29, 52; The Master and Fellows of Magdalene College, Cambridge 62; The National Trust, Waddesdon Manor 196; The Rector and Fellows of Exeter College, Oxford 210; Lord Sackville 137; The Syndics of the Fitzwilliam Museum, Cambridge 78, 127; The Trustees of the Chatsworth Settlement 112, 113.
Numbers 253 and 254 © ADAGP, Paris 1969.
Numbers 218, 220, 239, 252, 255 © SPADEM, Paris 1969.

Photographs were provided by the following:

Aerofilms Ltd 76; Ashmolean Museum 32, 120, 175, 178, 180, 191; Bruce A Bailey 155; Barnaby's 58, 102; Bath Spa Committee 1; British Museum 2, 3, 4, 8, 12, 24, 25, 27, 28, 31, 34, 40, 53, 54, 75, 80, 107, 134, 143, 156, 187, 192, 206, 251; British Petroleum 231; British Travel Association 46, 172, 173; E. Broadbent 10; John Bulmer 6; J. Allan Cash 9, 74; Commissioners of Public Works in Ireland 11; A. C. Cooper Ltd 129, 223; Henry Cooper & Son 96, 117; Courtauld Institute 112, 113, 135, 177, 214; Courtauld Institute Galleries 179, 218, 219, 220; Crown Copyright–Ministry of Public Building and Works 87, 121, 131, 136; Crown Copyright–National Monuments Record 39, 189; Crown Copyright–Royal Commission on Historical Monuments 15; Stuart Devlin 227; Dulwich College Picture Gallery 147, 168; Elsam, Mann and Cooper Ltd 245; Fitzwilliam Museum 78, 127; Fox Photos Ltd 119; Green Studio Ltd 29, 52; R. Guillemot–Connaissance des Arts 159; Hawkley Studio Associates 97; Michael Holford 26, 47, 64, 65, 66, 79, 81, 92, 93, 109, 125, 128, 137, 140, 144, 146, 162, 163, 174, 195, 196, 203, 205, 208, 212, 230, 232, 248, 253; Imperial War Museum 228; Jarrold and Sons 226; J. S. Kerr 36; A. F. Kersting 23, 33, 35, 41, 45, 55, 56, 57, 60, 63, 67, 68, 69, 70, 71, 73, 83, 84, 88, 90, 91, 101, 103, 104, 105, 108, 114, 115, 123, 130, 139, 142, 153, 157, 170, 197, 201, 243; Martin Koretz 249; Trustees of the Lady Lever Art Gallery, Port Sunlight 183; Edward Leigh 62; Manchester City Art Gallery 236; Mansell Collection 138; Henry Moore 240; Morgan-Wells 222; National Gallery **frontispiece**, 110, 133, 141, 145, 148, 149, 160, 161, 166, 185, 186, 193, 234, 246, 255; National Gallery of Ireland 247; National Gallery of Scotland 164; National Museum of Antiquities of Scotland 16; National Museum of Ireland 30; National Portrait Gallery 213; Photo Precision–St Albans 82; Popperphotos 44; Purnell and Sons 182; R.I.B.A. introduction; Scala 49; Edwin Smith 42, 59; Southern Publishing Company 132; Vic Stacey 37; Tate Gallery 167, 188, 199, 202, 215, 216, 224, 225, 237, 238, 239, 241, 242, 250; Thames and Hudson 7, 50; Thomas Photos 210; P. W. & L. Thompson 229, 244; Towneley Hall Art Gallery and Museum 165; University Museum of Archaeology and Ethnology, Cambridge 5; Bertram Unne 171; Victoria and Albert Museum **contents page**, 43, 61, 77, 86, 95, 98, 99, 100, 126, 169, 176, 198, 200, 204, 233, 235; The Warburg Institute 13, 14, 17, 18, 19, 20, 21, 22, 38, 72; John Webb 48, 51, 85, 94, 111, 151, 152, 158, 181, 184, 190, 194, 207, 211, 217, 252, 254; Josiah Wedgwood and Sons 150; C. H. Wood 221.

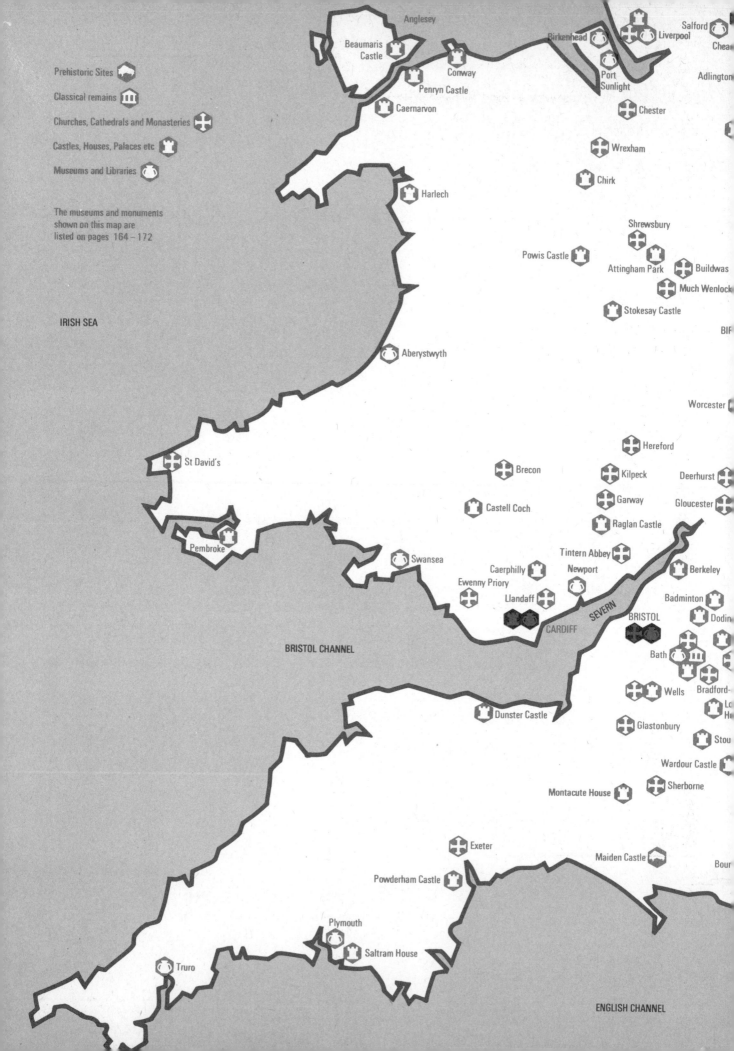

Prehistoric Sites

Classical remains

Churches, Cathedrals and Monasteries

Castles, Houses, Palaces etc

Museums and Libraries

The museums and monuments
shown on this map are
listed on pages 164 – 172

IRISH SEA

Anglesey

Beaumaris
Castle

Conway

Penryn Castle

Caernarvon

Harlech

Powis Castle

Aberystwyth

St David's

Pembroke

Swansea

BRISTOL CHANNEL

Birkenhead

Salford
Liverpool
Chea

Port
Sunlight

Adlington

Chester

Wrexham

Chirk

Shrewsbury

Attingham Park

Buildwas

Much Wenlock

Stokesay Castle

BIF

Worcester

Hereford

Brecon

Kilpeck

Deerhurst

Castell Coch

Garway

Gloucester

Raglan Castle

Tintern Abbey

Caerphilly

Newport

Berkeley

Ewenny Priory

Llandaff

Badminton

CARDIFF

SEVERN

Dodin

BRISTOL

Bath

Wells

Bradford-

Dunster Castle

Glastonbury

Stou

Lo
He

Wardour Castle

Sherborne

Montacute House

Exeter

Maiden Castle

Bour

Powderham Castle

Plymouth

Saltram House

ENGLISH CHANNEL

Truro